always up to date

The law changes, but Nolo is on top of it! We offer several ways to make sure you and your Nolo products are up to date:

Nolo's Legal Updater

We'll send you an email whenever a new edition of this book is published! Sign up at **www.nolo.com/legalupdater**.

Updates @ Nolo.com

Check **www.nolo.com/update** to find recent changes in the law that affect the current edition of your book.

Nolo Customer Service

To make sure that this edition of the book is the most recent one, call us at **800-728-3555** and ask one of our friendly customer service representatives. Or find out at **www.nolo.com**.

please note

We believe accurate, plain-English legal information should help you solve many of your own legal problems. But this text is not a substitute for personalized advice from a knowledgeable lawyer. If you want the help of a trained professional—and we'll always point out situations in which we think that's a good idea—consult an attorney licensed to practice in your state.

NOLO

8th edition

Credit Repair

by Robin Leonard and Attorney John Lamb

EIGHTH EDITION	JUNE 2007
Editor	LISA GUERIN
Cover Photography	TONYA PERME (www.tonyaperme.com)
Book Design	TERRI HEARSH
Production	SARAH HINMAN
CD-ROM Preparation	ELLEN BITTER
Index	MEDEA MINNICH
Proofreading	SUSAN CARLSON GREENE
Printing	DELTA PRINTING SOLUTIONS, INC.

Leonard, Robin.
    Credit repair / by Robin Leonard; updated by John Lamb. -- 8th ed.
    p. cm.
    Includes index.
    ISBN-13: 978-1-4133-0635-4
    ISBN-10: 1-4133-0635-7
    1. Consumer credit--United States--Handbooks, manuals, etc. 2. Finance,
    Personal--United States--Handbooks, manuals, etc. 3. Consumer credit--
    Law and legislation--United States. I. Lamb, John, 1946- II. Title.

    HG3756.U54L46 2007
    332.7'43--dc22

                                        2006039247

Quantity sales: For information on bulk purchases or corporate premium sales, please
contact the Special Sales department. For academic sales or textbook adoptions, ask for
Academic Sales. 800-955-4775, Nolo, 950 Parker Street, Berkeley, CA 94710.

About the Authors

Robin Leonard graduated from Cornell Law School in 1985. She is the author or co-author of numerous Nolo books, including *Solve Your Money Troubles: Get Debt Collectors Off Your Back & Regain Financial Freedom, How to File for Chapter 7 Bankruptcy,* and *Chapter 13 Bankruptcy: Repay Your Debts.*

John Lamb has been a consumer lawyer for most of his career (now measured in decades), emphasizing credit, credit reporting, privacy, automobile, and landlord-tenant issues. John has advocated consumer reforms in court and the Legislature and speaks and writes frequently on consumer issues. He is co-author of the eighth edition of *Credit Repair* and the eleventh edition of *Solve Your Money Troubles,* and has updated several other Nolo publications.

Table of Contents

6 Building and Maintaining Good Credit

Appendixes

1 Resources

2 Federal Credit Reporting and Credit Repair Laws

3 Forms and Letters

4 How to Use the Forms CD-ROM

Index

Introduction to Credit Repair

Whether you've fallen behind on your bills, been sued, or even declared bankruptcy, this book can help you take simple and effective steps to repair your credit. As you read, keep in mind these four important points.

You're not alone. Economic ups and downs have affected many people. Disposable incomes are down and savings are evaporating. Millions of honest, hard-working people—the same ones who receive credit offers almost daily—are having problems paying their bills. And more than two million personal bankruptcy cases were filed in 2005.

You have legal rights. By knowing and asserting your rights, you can do a lot to get bill collectors off your back and give yourself a fresh financial start. Debtors who assert themselves often get more time to pay, have late fees dropped, settle debts for less than the full amount, and get negative marks removed from credit files.

You can do it yourself. The information and forms in this book are good in all 50 states and the District of Columbia. You can follow the instructions on your own, without paying high fees to a lawyer or credit repair clinic. (See Chapter 6 to find out why you should avoid using a credit repair clinic.)

Nobody's credit is too "bad" to repair. If you've been through devastating financial times, you may think you'll never get credit again. That's simply not true. As long as your financial troubles are behind you, you'll probably qualify for limited types of credit relatively quickly. Within about two years, you should be able to repair your credit so that you can obtain a major credit card or loan. Most creditors are willing to extend credit to people who have turned their financial situations around, even if their credit records are less than stellar.

This book contains in-depth information on all aspects of credit repair. Easy-to-use forms in Appendix 3 and on the enclosed CD-ROM help you with the sometimes daunting tasks of assessing your debt situation, planning a budget, contacting your creditors or bill collectors, and dealing with credit bureaus—all necessary steps in repairing your credit. (Instructions on how to use the forms on the CD-ROM are in Appendix 4.)

Credit Repair Fast Facts

Here are some quick answers to many common questions people have about repairing their credit. All of these topics are explored in more detail later in the book.

What's the first step in repairing my credit?

To turn your financial problems around, you must understand your flow of income and expenses. Some people call this making a budget. Others find the term "budget" too restrictive and prefer to use the term "spending plan." Whatever you call it, spend at least two months writing down every cash or cash equivalent (such as check or debit) expenditure you make. At each month's end, compare your total expenses with your income. If you're overspending, you have to cut back or find more income. As best you can, plan how you'll spend your money each month. If you have trouble putting together your own budget, consider getting help from a nonprofit credit or debt counseling agency that provides budgeting help free or at a low cost. (The steps for creating a budget are detailed in Chapter 2; credit and debt counseling agencies are discussed in Appendix 1.)

Okay, I've made my budget. What do I do next?

Now it's time to clean up your credit report. Credit reports are compiled by credit bureaus—private, for-profit companies that gather information about your credit history and sell it to banks, mortgage lenders, credit unions, credit card companies, department stores, insurance companies, landlords, and some employers.

Credit bureaus get most of their data from creditors and collection agencies. They also search court records for lawsuits, judgments, and bankruptcy filings. And they go through county records to find recorded liens (legal claims) against property.

Noncredit data made part of a credit report usually includes your name, names you previously used, past and present addresses, Social Security number, employment history, and current and previous spouses' names. Your credit history includes the names of your creditors, type and number of each account, when each account was opened, your payment history, your credit limit or the original amount of a loan, and your current balance. The report will show whether an account is current, is in default, has been turned over to a collection agency, or is in dispute. Many credit reports also include a credit score: a numerical rating of the likelihood that you will not default on an extension of credit. The report also lists creditors that have requested information about you in the past year or two. (See Chapter 4 for more information on the contents of a credit report.)

How can I get a copy of my credit report?

There are three major credit bureaus: Equifax, Experian, and TransUnion. The federal Fair Credit Reporting Act (FCRA) entitles you to a copy of your credit report, and you can get one free if any of the following are true:

- You've been denied credit because of information in your credit report and you request a copy within 60 days of being denied credit.
- You are unemployed and intend to apply for a job within the 60 days following your request for your credit file.
- You receive public assistance.
- You believe your credit report contains errors due to fraud.
- You have asked a credit bureau to place a "fraud alert" in your file because of fraud or identity theft (see Chapter 4).

The FCRA now also requires that credit bureaus provide consumers with one free copy of their credit reports each year. You can request your credit report by calling 877-322-8228, using the standardized request form in Appendix 3, or going to the credit bureaus' official site for free annual credit reports, www.annualcreditreport.com. (Avoid imposter sites; Chapter 4 explains how.) In some situations, you will have to pay a small fee to obtain your report. (See Chapter 4 for information on obtaining a credit report.)

What should I do if I find mistakes in my report?

As you read through your report, make a list of everything that's out-of-date, such as:

- lawsuits, paid tax liens, accounts sent out for collection, criminal records (but not criminal convictions), late payments, overdue child support payments, and any other adverse information that's more than seven years old, or
- bankruptcies that are more than ten years old.

Next, look for incomplete or inaccurate information, such as:

- incorrect or incomplete name, address, phone number, Social Security number, or employment information
- bankruptcies not identified by their specific chapter number
- accounts that are not yours or lawsuits in which you were not involved
- incorrect account histories—such as late payments when you paid on time
- closed accounts listed as open—it may look as if you have too much open credit
- accounts listed more than once
- any account you closed that doesn't say "closed by consumer," and
- other information that is incomplete or inaccurate.

If you find incomplete or inaccurate information in your report, complete the "request for reinvestigation" form the credit bureau sent you or send a letter listing each item and explaining exactly what is wrong. You can submit this information online, but you should do it by mail if you want to include documents proving your side of the story.

Once the credit bureau receives your request, it must investigate the items you dispute and contact you within 30 days. If you don't hear back within 30 days, send a follow-up letter. If you let them know that you're trying to obtain a mortgage or car loan, they can do a "rush" investigation. (See Chapter 4 for more information on reviewing and correcting your credit report.)

Will the credit bureau automatically remove the incorrect information from my report?

The credit bureau will review your letter or request for reinvestigation form. If the information is incomplete or inaccurate, or if the creditor who provided the information can no longer verify it, the credit bureau must correct the information or remove it from your report. Often credit bureaus will remove an item on request without an investigation if rechecking the item is more bother than it's worth.

If the credit bureau insists that the information is correct, call the bureau to discuss the problem.

If you don't get anywhere with the credit bureau, contact the creditor directly and ask that the information be removed. The FCRA allows you to dispute inaccurate information directly with the creditor, rather than having to go through the credit bureau (federal regulations will identify circumstances in which you can do this). Write to the customer service department (or the deparment specified by the creditor for this purpose), vice president of marketing, and president or CEO. If the information was reported by a collection agency, send the agency a copy of your letter, too.

If a credit bureau continues to include the information in your report, or if you want to explain a particular entry, you have the right to put a brief explanatory statement in your report. (See Chapter 4 for additional information on correcting your credit report.)

What else can I do to repair my credit?

After you've cleaned up your credit report, the key to rebuilding credit is to get positive information into your record. For example:

- If your credit report is missing accounts you pay on time, send the credit bureaus a recent account statement and copies of canceled checks showing your payment history. Ask that these be added to your report. The credit bureau doesn't have to add anything, but often it will.
- Creditors like to see evidence of stability, so if any of the following information is not in your report, send it to the bureaus and ask that it be added: your current employment; your previous employment, especially if you've been at your current job fewer than two years; your current residence; your telephone number, especially if it's unlisted; your date of birth; and your checking account number. Again, the credit bureau doesn't have to add these, but often it will.

(See Chapter 4 for more information on adding positive data to your credit report.)

I've been told that I need to use credit to repair my credit. Is this true?

Yes. The main type of positive information creditors like to see in credit reports is a history of paying credit on time. If you have a credit card, use it every month. Make small purchases and pay them off to avoid interest charges. If you don't have a credit card, apply for one. If your application is rejected, try to find a cosigner. As a last resort, apply for a secured card—a credit card with a line of credit based on an amount of money you deposit into a savings account tied to the card. But don't try to get new credit or use a credit card you already have while you're still steeped in financial trouble. The last thing you want to do is continue down the road you're trying to get off of. (See Chapter 6 for more information about using credit, including cautions about secured credit cards.)

How long will it take to repair my credit?

If you follow the steps outlined in this book, it will usually take about two years to repair your credit so that you won't be turned down for a major credit card or loan. After four years or so, you may be able to qualify for a mortgage.

When to Get Help Beyond This Book

This book can help you assess your financial situation and repair your credit. In some circumstances, however, you may need to take immediate action—or more drastic action—which may be beyond the scope of this book. Nolo publishes several detailed books on debtors' rights and bankruptcy, which may provide the answers you need. In some situations, it may make sense to see a lawyer right away. Use the chart on the following page to fully assess your situation.

When to Get Help Beyond This Book

Seek additional help if...	Explanation	Where to get help
You're behind on your house payments.	Your lender has the option of foreclosing—declaring the entire balance due, selling the house at an auction and kicking you out.	General information on foreclosures is in Chapter 1. You can get more specific help from your lender or a lawyer.
You owe child support or alimony.	If you can't afford to pay your child support or alimony, you need a court order reducing your obligation. Don't hesitate; child support and alimony are virtually never modified retroactively.	Contact your local child support enforcement agency (visit www.acf.dhhs.gov/programs/cse to find your local office). Although these agencies focus on getting support orders enforced, many will also assist with reviewing existing orders. Or visit DivorceNet (www.divorcenet.com) for links to state self-help services. Many states have online legal forms to request child support modification. Or, see a lawyer.
You owe income taxes.	The IRS has the right to seize virtually all of your assets of value and close to 100% of your wages without first suing you. Fortunately, you have several options in dealing with the IRS. You may be able to negotiate an installment agreement for repayment or drastically reduce what you have to pay.	See *Stand Up to the IRS*, by Frederick W. Daily (Nolo). Or, see a tax attorney.
You face eviction.	In some states, an eviction can take place in just three days. Rather than risk being homeless, take steps to get immediate help.	In California, see *California Tenants' Rights*, by Janet Portman and Ralph Warner (Nolo). Or, contact a local tenants' rights group or a tenants' rights lawyer. Outside of California, you can get an overview of eviction and eviction defense issues in *Every Tenant's Legal Guide*, by Janet Portman and Marcia Stewart (Nolo).
You've been sued.	If you just received court papers, you need to file a response with the court within a tight time limit. If the creditor already has a judgment, it can try to attach your wages, take money from bank accounts and place a lien on your real estate (and in some states, personal property). You may be able to prevent certain collection tactics, particularly if you don't own much.	See *Solve Your Money Troubles: Get Debt Collectors Off Your Back & Regain Financial Freedom*, by Robin Leonard and John Lamb (Nolo). Or, see a lawyer.
You are considering filing for bankruptcy.	Many people overwhelmed by their debts conclude that bankruptcy is the best option. There are several types, called "chapters" of bankruptcy. In Chapter 7, you ask that your debts be wiped out. In Chapter 13, you set up a repayment plan whereby your creditors receive some—or all—of what you owe. Chapter 12 bankruptcy is like Chapter 13 bankruptcy, but it's for family farmers. Chapter 11 bankruptcy is for individuals with enormous debts or businesses that want to reorganize.	Forms and instructions for filing a Chapter 7 bankruptcy are in *How to File for Chapter 7 Bankruptcy*, by Stephen Elias, Albin Renauer, Robin Leonard. Forms and instructions for filing a Chapter 13 bankruptcy are in *Chapter 13 Bankruptcy: Repay Your Debts*, by Stephen Elias and Robin Leonard. For information on figuring out if either Chapter 7 or Chapter 13 bankruptcy is right for you, see *The New Bankruptcy: Will It Work for You?*, by Stephen Elias. (All are published by Nolo.)

Assessing Your Debt Situation

efore you jump into rebuilding your credit, take care of any financial emergencies. Then you should tally up your debt burden and assess your options for handling what you owe.

SKIP AHEAD

If your debt problems are behind you and you're only concerned with cleaning up your credit report, skip ahead to Chapter 4, "Cleaning Up Your Credit File." Also read Chapter 2, "Avoiding Overspending."

Take Care of Financial Emergencies

A financial emergency is any situation that may leave you homeless or without some very important property or service. A pending eviction, a letter threatening foreclosure, an IRS seizure of your house, a utility cut-off, and a car repossession are financial emergencies. A nasty letter or threatening phone call from a bill collector, while unpleasant, is not an emergency. (If you are being hassled by a collection agency, see Chapter 3.)

If you face an emergency, act on it at once. Begin by contacting the creditor. You may be able to work out a temporary solution that will keep you off the street or on your wheels. If that doesn't work, you may need to get in touch with a lawyer to help you negotiate with your creditors. One option is to file for bankruptcy, assuming your overall debt burden justifies it. Filing

for bankruptcy immediately stops most of your creditors in their tracks and can buy you some valuable time. However, some evictions may be allowed to proceed under the new bankruptcy rules. (See "File for Chapter 7 Bankruptcy," below, for more information.)

Face Your Debt Problems

Some people with debt problems believe that the less they know, the less it hurts. They think, "I'm having trouble paying a lot of my bills. I can't stand the thought of knowing just how much I can't pay." But you must come to terms with your total debt burden. You cannot take steps to rebuild your credit without knowing exactly where your money goes—or where it needs to go instead.

Figuring out what you owe may result in a pleasant surprise. Most debt counselors find that people tend to overestimate—not underestimate—their debt burden. This may bring little comfort to those of you who find out that you owe more than you thought, but there is always a benefit: Knowing what you really owe will help you make wise choices about how you spend your money.

Use Form F-1, Outstanding Debts (in Appendix 3 and on the CD-ROM) to tally up your total debt burden. Look at the most recent bills you've received. If you've thrown out your bills without opening them, you can probably find out the balance by calling the customer service department of the creditor.

Many creditors' automated telephone systems provide balance and payment information automatically, without having to speak to a person. Some creditors may also provide account information on their websites.

If you must speak with a person and you've long been avoiding your creditors and fear they'll hassle you when you call, ask for balance information only. If the customer service representative turns into a bill collector, explain that you are exploring your options and need to know how much you owe before you proceed. Let the representative know that you will contact the company as soon as possible, but for now you need only to know how much you owe. If the representative still hassles you, hang up and use your best guess as to how much you owe that creditor.

Total up your past due installment bills, such as credit cards and loans, plus any regular monthly obligations that are overdue, such as your utility bill.

Understand Your Options for Dealing With Your Debts

You normally have about a half-dozen options for dealing with your debts— probably more than you imagined. Read this entire section before taking action.

Do Nothing

Surprisingly, the best approach for some people deeply in debt is to take no action at all. If you have very little income and

property and don't expect this to change, you may be what's known as "judgment proof." This means that anyone who sues you and obtains a court judgment won't be able to collect, simply because you don't have anything they can legally take. You can't be thrown in jail for not paying your debts. And state and federal laws prohibit a creditor—even the IRS—from taking away such essentials as basic clothing, ordinary household furnishings, personal effects, food, most Social Security benefits, disability benefits, unemployment, or public assistance.

So, if you don't anticipate having a steady income or property a creditor could grab, sit back. Your creditors may decide not to sue you because they know they can't collect. Many will simply write off your debt and treat it as a deductible business loss on their income tax returns. In several years, the debt will become legally uncollectible under state law. (See Chapter 3 for information on how to stop communications from collection agencies.)

RESOURCE

Keeping exempt property. You can find a complete list of property you get to keep even if your creditors sue you or you file for bankruptcy, called "exempt property," in *Solve Your Money Troubles: Get Debt Collectors Off Your Back & Regain Financial Freedom,* by Robin Leonard and John Lamb (Nolo).

Find Money to Pay Your Debts

If you can come up with a chunk of cash to pay off some of your debts, your financial woes may lessen. But, even if you feel desperate, don't jump at every opportunity to get cash fast. If you make a bad choice, you'll get yourself into deeper debt. This section discusses some of the options you should consider to raise money, as well as the options you should avoid. It's not a complete list. Unfortunately, new scams and bad deals crop up every day. Keep in mind that if an offer or deal seems too good to be true, it probably is. So, proceed cautiously, whatever you are considering.

Sell a Major Asset

One way you can raise cash and keep associated costs to a minimum is to sell a major asset, such as a house or car. This may be a good idea if you can no longer afford your house or car payments. You will almost always do better selling the property yourself rather than waiting to get cash back from a foreclosure or repossession.

With the proceeds of the sale, you'll have to pay off anything still owed on the asset and any secured creditor to whom you pledged the asset as collateral. Then you'll have to pay off any liens placed on the property by your creditors. You can use anything that's left to help pay your other debts. But, before you take this step, be sure you have affordable alternative housing or transportation available. If not, you'll be in worse shape than before—without a roof over your head or a car to get to work.

If you own a house, consider all the pros and cons carefully before you sell it. In today's housing market, your house may be worth more in six months or a year than it is today. Selling it will deprive you of an asset that can make you money over time and may result in your being locked out of the housing market once you are back on your feet. At the very least, consider whether you may get more for your house if you sell it later on, giving you more money to pay your creditors.

Cut Your Expenses

Another excellent way to raise cash is to cut your expenses. This will also help you in negotiating with your creditors, who will want to know why you can't pay your bills and what steps you've taken to live more frugally. Here are some suggestions:

- Shrink food costs by clipping coupons, buying on sale, purchasing generic brands, buying in bulk, and shopping at discount outlets.
- Improve your gas mileage by tuning up your car, checking the air in the tires, and driving less—carpool, work at home (telecommute), ride your bicycle, take the bus or train, and combine trips.
- Conserve gas, water, and electricity.
- Discontinue cable (or at least the premium channels) and subscriptions to magazines and papers. Most cable companies offer a low-rate basic service that they don't advertise. Be sure to ask.

- Instead of buying books and CDs, borrow them from the public library. Read magazines and newspapers there, too.
- Make long distance calls only when necessary and at off-peak hours. Also, compare programs offered by the various long distance carriers to make sure you are getting the best deal.
- Carry your lunch to work; eat dinner at home, not at restaurants.
- Buy secondhand clothing, furniture, and appliances.
- Stop buying gifts and taking vacations until you're back on your feet.
- Stop spending money on luxuries that can add up, such as expensive coffee drinks.
- Don't charge anything that you can't pay off, or that won't exist (like groceries or meals), when the bill comes.

Withdraw or Borrow Money From a Tax-Deferred Account

If you have an IRA, 401(k), or other tax-deferred retirement account, you can get cash to pay off debts by withdrawing money from it before retirement—but in most cases, you'll pay a penalty and taxes. Or, with a 401(k) plan, you may be able to borrow money from it (instead of withdrawing it). There are serious disadvantages to both options—you should only consider doing either to pay off debts if you have other substantial retirement funds or you are truly desperate. And, even then, this should be a last resort. Always

look to raise money from nonretirement resources first.

Different plans have different requirements for borrowing and withdrawing money. Withdrawing money early from a tax-deferred account is expensive. Generally, any money that you take out of your 401(k) plan before you reach age 59½ is treated as an early distribution. The one exception to early distribution penalties and income taxes on early withdrawals from retirement accounts applies to Roth IRAs.

Instead of withdrawing money, you can usually borrow up to half of your vested account balance, but not more than $50,000. Then you pay the money back, with interest, over five years. If you can't pay the money back within five years (or immediately, if you leave your job), your "loan" will be treated like an early withdrawal and you'll pay both an early distribution tax and income tax.

 RESOURCE
If you're seriously considering using the money in your retirement plan or IRA to pay off your debts, get a copy of *IRAs, 401(k)s & Other Retirement Plans: Taking Your Money Out*, by Twila Slesnick and John C. Suttle (Nolo).

Obtain a Home Equity Loan or Credit Line

Many banks, savings and loans, credit unions, and other lenders offer home equity loans (also called "second mortgages") and home equity lines of credit (also called

"HELOCs"). Lenders who make these loans will loan only a percentage of your equity in the market or appraised value of the house—typically between 50% and 80%. For example, if the current value of your house is $200,000 and you owe $100,000 on it, you might qualify for an equity loan of $60,000. A $60,000 loan would increase your total housing debt to $160,000, or 80% of the house's value. The lender will also consider your credit history, income, and other expenses when deciding whether, and how much, to loan to you.

Obtaining a home equity loan has both advantages and disadvantages. If all of your debts are unsecured and your house is exempt from collection, it's almost never a good idea to put your home into jeopardy by getting a second mortgage or home equity line of credit. If you're behind on your house payment, you'll be better off negotiating a mortgage workout with your lender. (For more on mortgage workouts, see *Solve Your Money Troubles: Get Debt Collectors Off Your Back & Regain Financial Freedom*, by Robin Leonard and John Lamb (Nolo).) If you decide that you do want a home equity loan because you aren't able to negotiate a mortgage workout or for some other reason, be sure you understand all the terms before you sign on the dotted line. It is extremely important that you find out how much the loan will cost you each month and determine whether you can afford it. *If you can't afford it, you will likely lose your home.*

Consider the following pros and cons of home equity loans and credit lines.

Advantages of Home Equity Loans and Credit Lines

- You can borrow a fixed amount of money and repay it in equal monthly installments for a set period of time (home equity loan). Or, you can borrow as you need the money, drawing against the amount granted when you opened the account; you'll pay off this type of loan as you would a credit card bill (home equity line of credit or HELOC).
- The interest you pay may be fully deductible on your income tax return.

Disadvantages of Home Equity Loans

- Some home equity loans are sold by predatory lenders at very high rates. Predatory lenders target people in financial trouble or with past credit problems. Often, predatory lenders count on the borrower not being able to make the loan payments and expect to foreclose on the house (force the sale of the house) when the borrower fails to make payments. The Federal Trade Commission (FTC) recommends avoiding any lender who tells you to falsify a loan application, pressures you to apply for a loan, or for more money than you need, or pressures you to take on monthly payments you can't afford. (For more on predatory lenders and mortgages for people with poor credit, see *Solve Your Money Troubles: Get Debt Collectors Off Your Back & Regain Financial Freedom*, by Robin Leonard and John Lamb (Nolo).)

- You are obligating yourself to make another monthly or periodic payment. If you are unable to pay, you may have to sell your house or, even worse, face the possibility of foreclosure (the lender forcing a sale of your house to pay off what you owe). *Before you take out a home equity loan, be sure you can afford the monthly payment.*
- While interest may be deductible, it can be high.
- Some loans are "interest only" loans— your monthly payments pay only the interest on the loan and do not reduce the principal amount that you borrowed. You could make payments for years and still owe the full amount you borrowed.
- You may have to pay an assortment of up-front fees for an appraisal, credit report, title insurance, and points. These fees can run as high as $1,000 or more. In addition, for giving you an equity line of credit, many lenders charge a yearly fee of $25 to $50.
- You must pay off the equity loan, plus what you still owe on your mortgage, when you sell your house.

Use the Equity in Your Home If You Are 62 or Older

A variety of plans help older homeowners make use of the accumulated value (equity) in their homes without requiring them to move, give up title to the property, or make payments on a loan. The most common types of plans are reverse mortgages.

Reverse mortgages are loans against the equity in the home that provide cash advances to a homeowner and require no repayment until the end of the loan term or when the home is sold. The borrower can receive the cash in several ways: a lump sum, regular monthly payments, a line of credit, or a combination. Because the borrower does not make payments, the amount of money owed increases over the life of the loan. While the borrower retains title to the home, he or she must pay the property taxes, insurance, and the costs of keeping up the property.

There are pros and cons to reverse mortgages. In general, a reverse mortgage works best for people who are 62 or older and have a lot of equity in their homes. In most cases, the reverse mortgage lender will look at your age, the amount of equity you have in your home, and current interest rates to determine the amount it will lend you. All reverse mortgages cost money due to closing costs (title insurance, escrow fees, and appraisal fees), loan origination fees, accrued interest, and, in most cases, an additional charge to offset the lender's risk that you won't repay. (A reverse mortgage is usually paid back from the proceeds of selling the house after the owner's death.) Almost every state allows lenders to offer reverse mortgages.

There are some drawbacks to reverse mortgages. Your heirs cannot inherit the house from you unless they pay off the loan after your death. A reverse mortgage may also affect your continued eligibility for need-based government benefits programs like Supplemental Social Security (SSI) and Medicaid.

The most widely available reverse mortgage plans are the FHA's Home Equity Conversion Mortgage Program and Fannie Mae's Home Keeper Mortgage Program.

The lender or another party may suggest that you purchase an annuity in conjunction with a reverse mortgage. An annuity is an insurance product, financed out of the home's equity, that provides monthly payments to the borrower beginning immediately or some years later.

Think carefully about whether an annuity is right for you. Many consumer experts recommend against purchasing an annuity because it ties up the money from the reverse mortgage for an extended period, imposes additional transaction costs, imposes substantial penalties for early withdrawal, and may not benefit elderly homeowners (who may not live to see their first annuity payment, if there is a delay of several years or more). Indeed, California now prohibits lenders from requiring homeowners to purchase an annuity as a condition of obtaining a reverse mortgage.

Additional Resources on Reverse Mortgages

You can get free information on reverse mortgages from the following organizations:

- The federal Department of Housing and Urban Development (HUD). Call them at 800-569-4287 or visit their website, www.hud.gov, for facts about reverse mortgages, referrals to lenders, and lists of HUD-approved housing counselors.
- AARP (formerly the American Association of Retired Persons). Call them at 888-687-2277 or visit their website, www.aarp.org/money/revmort, for tips on evaluating reverse mortgages, eligibility and repayment requirements for federally insured reverse mortgages, and a reverse mortgage calculator.
- Fannie Mae. Call them at 800-732-6643 or visit their website, www.fanniemae.com, for consumer information on reverse mortgages.
- The National Center for Home Equity Conversion. Visit their website, www.reverse.org, for answers to frequently asked questions about reverse mortgages.

Borrow From Family or Friends

In times of financial crisis, some people are lucky enough to have friends or relatives who can and will help out. Before asking your college roommate, mom and dad, uncle Paul, or someone similar, consider the following:

- Can the lender really afford to help you? If the person is on a fixed income and needs the money to get by, you should look elsewhere for a loan.
- Do you want to owe this person money? If the loan comes with emotional strings attached, be sure you can handle the situation before taking the money.
- Will the loan help you out, or will it just delay the inevitable (most likely, filing for bankruptcy)? Don't borrow money to make payments on debts you will eventually discharge in bankruptcy.
- Will you have to repay the loan now, or will the lender let you wait until you're back on your feet? If you have to make payments now, you're just adding another monthly payment to your already unmanageable pile of debts.
- If the loan is from your parents, can you treat it as part of your eventual inheritance? If so, you won't ever have to repay it. If your siblings get angry that you're getting some of Mom and Dad's money, be sure they understand that your inheritance will be reduced accordingly.

Borrow Against Your Life Insurance Policy

If you've had a life insurance policy for some time, you have probably accumulated "cash value" in the policy, which you may be able to borrow. The insurance company will expect you to repay the amount borrowed (typically, in installment payments), and, if you don't repay it before you die, the proceeds received by your beneficiaries will be reduced by the unpaid amount. Your insurance broker or the insurance company can explain more about borrowing against your insurance policy.

Options to Avoid

Borrowing From a Finance Company

A few finance companies lend money to consumers. These companies make secured consolidation loans, requiring that you pledge your house, car, or other personal property as collateral. The loans are just like second mortgages or secured personal loans: You'll usually be charged interest of 10% to 15%, and, if you default on the loan, the finance company can foreclose on your home or take your property.

Finance companies and similar lenders also make unsecured consolidation loans—that is, they may lend you some money without requiring that you pledge any property as a guarantee that you'll pay. But the interest rate on these loans can be astronomical, often reaching 25% or more. Lenders also charge all kinds of fees—many not disclosed—bringing the effective interest rate closer to 50%.

If you want to take out a consolidation loan, you are better off borrowing from a bank or credit union than a finance company. Many finance companies engage in illegal or borderline collection practices if you default and are not as willing as banks and credit unions to negotiate if you have trouble paying. Furthermore, loans from finance companies may be viewed negatively by potential creditors who see them in your credit file. They often imply prior debt problems.

Tax Refund Anticipation Loans

Although getting a tax refund fast is often a good way to get quick cash, you should probably avoid a refund anticipation loan (RAL). An RAL is a loan offered by a private company for the short period between the date when the taxpayer receives it and the date when the IRS repays it by depositing the taxpayer's refund into the lender's account (usually only a week or two). The amount of the loan is the amount of your anticipated refund minus the loan fee (which is often quite high), the fee for electronic filing, and the tax preparation fee. For example, if your refund is $2,150 (the recent average), the loan fee would be about $100 and the filing fee about $30. That results in an effective annual percentage rate (APR) of 235% for the loan! If you also paid the average tax preparation fee of $146, your total loan costs could be as much as $276.

It is usually better to be patient and wait for your refund, rather than pay the high fee for an RAL. In most cases, you can file your return electronically or by fax and get the money quickly (by having the refund deposited directly into your account, for example).

In addition to being extremely expensive, RALs also pose some risks. You must repay the loan even if your refund is denied, is less than expected, or is frozen. If you can't repay the loan, the lender may assign the debt to a collection agency. The unpaid debt will appear on your credit report. And, if you apply for an RAL again next year, the lender may take that refund to pay this year's unpaid RAL debt.

For more information on how to get a refund sooner and for answers to other tax questions, contact the IRS at 800-829-1040 (voice) or 800-829-4059 (TDD), or visit its website at www.irs.gov.

Payday Loans

The payday loan industry is growing fast. In many states, these loans are illegal. In others, lenders may offer a similar type of loan, but call it something else. Either way, think twice before you get one of these loans.

A payday loan works like this: You give the lender a check and get back an amount of money less than the face value of the check. For example, if you give the lender a check for $300, it may give you $250 in cash and keep the remaining $50 as its fee. The lender holds the check for a few weeks (often until your payday). At this time, you must pay the lender the face value of the check ($300), usually by allowing it to cash the check. If you can't make the check good, the lender requires you to pay another fee ($50 in this example). At this point, you owe the lender $300 (the $250 borrowed plus the first $50 fee), plus a new fee of $50. Looking at it another way, you owe $350 on a $250 loan. Many people who can't make the original check good get into a "treadmill of debt" because they must keep writing new checks to cover the fees that have accumulated, in addition to paying off the amount borrowed.

Payday loans have been a particular problem for members of the military in recent years. A new federal law limits to 36% the annual percentage rate that lenders can charge active duty service members or their dependents in extensions of consumer credit, including payday loans. This means, for example, that now a payday lender cannot charge a service member more than $1.38 in interest on a $100 loan for two weeks.

A payday loan is a very expensive way to borrow money. To find out more about the payday loan laws in your state, visit the National Consumer Law Center's website at www.consumerlaw.org.

Pawnshops

Visiting a pawnshop should be one of the last ways you consider raising cash. At a pawnshop, you leave your property, such as jewelry, a television, or a musical instrument. In return, the pawnbroker lends you approximately 50% to 60% of the item's resale value; the average amount of a pawnshop loan is $50 or so.

You are given a few months to repay the loan, and are charged interest, often at an exorbitant rate. If you default on your loan to a pawnshop, the property you left at the shop becomes the property of the pawnbroker.

Auto Title Pawn

In an auto title pawn (a "title loan" in some states), you borrow money against the value of your paid-for motor vehicle. You keep and drive the vehicle after receiving the loan, but the lender keeps the vehicle's title as security for repayment and also keeps a copy of your keys. If you cannot make the loan payments, the lender repossesses the vehicle, sells it, and keeps the proceeds. Some lenders might try to come after you for any deficiency—the difference between what you owe and what the lender was able to get for your car. The lender may repossess the vehicle even if you miss only one payment. The monthly cost of these loans can be as high as $63 to $181 for a one-month, $500 title loan. Monthly finance charges of 25% (300% annual interest) are common. Online title lenders quote annual percentage rates of up to 651%.

Auto title loan businesses often target members of the military. Under a new federal law, creditors cannot take a vehicle's title as security when extending consumer credit to active duty service members or their dependents (other than loans to purchase the vehicle).

Debt Consolidation or Negotiation Companies

Debt consolidating, debt pooling, budget planning, debt adjusting, or debt prorating companies produce poor results. They siphon off your limited resources in debt consolidation charges, pay only a few (if any) creditors, and jeopardize much of your property. Some charge outrageously high interest. Others charge ridiculously high fees. Some promise a quick fix to your financial problems, by which they mean filing for bankruptcy.

Debt consolidating is either regulated or prohibited in most states. These laws usually don't apply to nonprofit organizations, lawyers, and merchant-owned associations claiming to help debtors.

Debt negotiation companies claim that they can negotiate with creditors on your behalf, promising substantially reduced payments and an end to collection calls from creditors. Debt negotiators charge hefty fees for this service, which most consumers can do on their own. Instead of helping you obtain relief and work your way out of debt, the debt negotiator may leave you with even more negative information in your credit report and being sued by collectors. In extreme cases, companies reportedly have used consumers' money to pay the company's operating expenses instead of paying the consumers' creditors. Even if the company provides the services promised, you're better off using the money you would spend on the negotiation fee to make payments to your creditors. If you cannot negotiate with your creditors or make payments on your own, see "Get Outside Help to Design a Repayment Plan," below.

Negotiate With Your Creditors

If you can get some money, consider negotiating with your creditors. Negotiation can buy you time to get your finances in order. You can also negotiate to get your creditors to agree to accept considerably less than you owe as a complete settlement of your debts.

You can find suggestions and forms for negotiating with your creditors in Chapter 3.

> **CAUTION**
>
> **Beware of the IRS if you settle a debt.** A tax law could cost you money if you settle a debt with a creditor or if a creditor writes off money you owe—that is, ceases collection efforts, declares the debt uncollectible, and reports it as a tax loss to the IRS. Debts subject to this law include money owed after a house foreclosure, after a property repossession, or on a credit card bill you don't pay.
>
> Any bank, credit union, savings and loan, finance company, credit card company, other financial institution, or federal government agency that forgives or writes off $600 or more of the principal of a debt (the amount not attributable to fees or interest) must send you and the IRS a Form 1099-C at the end of the tax year. These forms are for reporting income, which means that when you file your tax return for the tax year in which your debt was forgiven or written off, the IRS will consider the amount reported on the Form 1099-C as part of your income.
>
> There are several exceptions to this rule. For example, even if the financial institution issues a Form 1099-C, you do not have to report the income on your tax return if:

- a nonbusiness debt was canceled as a result of Hurricane Katrina (see IRS Publication 525, *Taxable and Nontaxable Income* for details)
- a student loan was canceled because you worked in a profession and for an employer as promised when you took out the loan (see IRS Publication 525, *Taxable and Nontaxable Income,* for details)
- the canceled debt would have been deductible if you had paid it
- the cancellation or write-off of the debt is intended as a gift (this would be unusual)
- you discharged the debt in Chapter 11 bankruptcy, or
- you were insolvent before the creditor agreed to waive or write off the debt.

Insolvency means that your debts exceed the value of your assets. Therefore, to figure out whether or not you are insolvent, you will have to total up your assets and your debts, including the debt that was forgiven or written off. You can avoid reporting the forgiven debt as income only to the extent of your insolvency. For example, if you have debts of $40,000 and assets worth $38,000, you are insolvent by $2,000. If a creditor forgives a debt of $3,000 you must report as income the amount that exceeds your involvency—$1,000 in this example.

If the debt was discharged in bankruptcy or you conclude that you are insolvent, you must complete IRS Form 982, *Reduction of Tax Attributes Due to Discharge of Indebtedness*, and attach it to your tax return. You can download the form and instructions for completing it from the IRS's website at www.irs.gov. Unfortunately, this form is quite complicated; you might need some advice from an accountant to complete it correctly.

Get Outside Help to Design a Repayment Plan

Many people are not well equipped to negotiate with their creditors. They may feel that they are obliged to make full payment. Or, their creditors may be so adamant that the process is too unpleasant to stomach. Some people just haven't honed their negotiation skills.

If you don't want to negotiate with your creditors, there are people and organizations available to help you. Creditors are often more than happy to work with respected organizations that work with debtors who are serious about repaying their debts. Reputable nonprofit credit and debt counseling agencies (see Appendix 1), the United Way, or a church or synagogue are all excellent prospects. These organizations will help you figure out how much you owe, how much you can afford to pay each month, and what your various options are—including bankruptcy. A credit or debt counseling agency will also talk to your creditors for you. Check your phone book's yellow pages under "Counseling." Before signing up with any credit counseling service, talk to others who have used the service and check it out with your local Better Business Bureau.

> **CAUTION**
>
> **Use caution with lawyers, credit repair clinics, and for-profit organizations.** A lawyer can help, but lawyers charge high fees that are rarely justified, especially when you're heavily in debt. Whatever you do, don't use a

credit repair clinic. (For more information on this, see Chapter 6.) As a general rule, you should also avoid for-profit credit and debt counseling agencies. They often charge high fees and may not provide the services they have promised. Avoid debt consolidators and debt negotiators as well.

File for Chapter 7 Bankruptcy

Chapter 7 bankruptcy is the bankruptcy plan most people have heard about. It allows you to wipe out most consumer debts: credit cards, medical bills, and the like. In exchange, however, you might have to surrender some of your property, such as a second car, valuable electronic equipment, or a vacation home. To file for Chapter 7 bankruptcy, you fill out a packet of forms that describe your property, current income and expenses, debts, and any recent purchases and gifts. Then you file the forms with the federal bankruptcy court in your area.

Filing for bankruptcy puts into effect an "automatic stay" that immediately stops most of your creditors from trying to collect what you owe them. So, at least temporarily, creditors cannot legally "garnish" (take) your wages; empty your bank account; go after your car, house, or other property; or cut off your utility service.

CAUTION

The automatic stay may not protect you from eviction. Under the old bankruptcy law, filing for bankruptcy prohibited landlords from proceeding with an eviction, unless they got a court order allowing them to move forward. The new law is different: If the landlord already has a judgment for possession, he or she can evict you despite the automatic stay. Even if the landlord doesn't yet have a judgment, you can be evicted—despite your bankruptcy filing—for endangering the property or illegal use of controlled substances on the premises.

Until your bankruptcy case ends, your past financial problems are in the hands of the bankruptcy court. Nothing can be sold or paid without the court's consent. You keep control, however, of virtually all property and income you acquire after you file for bankruptcy.

At the end of the bankruptcy process, most of your debts are "discharged" (wiped out) by the court. You no longer legally owe the debts you owed when you filed for bankruptcy. If you incur debts after filing, however, you are still obligated to pay them. And you can't file for Chapter 7 bankruptcy again for another eight years from the date of your filing.

Before the bankruptcy process ends, a creditor might try to convince you to "reaffirm" (commit to paying off) a debt after the bankruptcy court has discharged your other debts. Think twice before you reaffirm a debt. You do not have to reaffirm any debt; if you do, you must pay it off even though your other debts have been discharged. Any agreement to reaffirm a debt must be written and filed with the bankruptcy court. You can cancel a reaffirmation agreement before your debts are discharged or within 60 days after the agreement is filed with the court.

If an attorney did not help you negotiate the reaffirmation agreement, it must be approved by the court.

Of course, bankruptcy isn't for everyone. One reason is that many types of debts *cannot* be erased in Chapter 7 bankruptcy, including:

- child support or alimony obligations
- student loans, unless repaying would cause you undue hardship (which is very tough to prove)
- court-ordered restitution—payments you're ordered to make after a criminal conviction
- most federal, state, and local income taxes less than three years past due, and any money borrowed or charged to pay those tax debts
- debts arising from intoxicated driving
- debts from a marital settlement agreement or divorce decree, unless the bankruptcy judge rules it would be impossible for you to pay or that the benefit you'd get from discharging this debt outweighs any harm to your ex-spouse, and
- debts that a bankruptcy judge rules were incurred as a result of a wrongful act on your part—for example, debts incurred from fraud (such as lying on a credit application or writing a bad check); intentional injury (such as assault, battery, false imprisonment, libel, or slander); larceny (theft); or breach of trust or embezzlement.

Not everyone can use Chapter 7 bankruptcy. You won't be eligible if:

- You received a previous discharge of your debts in a Chapter 7 case within the last eight years, or a Chapter 13 case within the last six years.
- You defrauded your creditors.
- A previous bankruptcy case you filed was dismissed within the previous 180 days because you violated a court order, the court found that your filing was fraudulent or constituted an abuse of the bankruptcy system, or you requested a dismissal after a creditor asked the court to lift the automatic stay.
- Your average income in the six months before you file is higher than the median income in your state for a family of your size, and you would have sufficient money left—after subtracting certain allowed expenses—to pay certain debts over a five-year period. This requirement is referred to as "the means test," and those who flunk it can be required to use Chapter 13 rather than Chapter 7.

RESOURCE

For more information on Chapter 7 bankruptcy, see *How to File for Chapter 7 Bankruptcy,* by Stephen R. Elias, Albin Renauer, and Robin Leonard, or *The New Bankruptcy: Will It Work for You?,* by Stephen Elias, both published by Nolo.

Pay Over Time With Chapter 13 Bankruptcy

If you have steady income and think you could squeeze out regular monthly payments, Chapter 13 bankruptcy may be a good option. Chapter 13 allows you to keep your property and use your disposable income (net income less reasonable expenses) to pay all or a portion of your debts over three to five years. You can use wages, benefits, investment income, business earnings, or any other income to make your payments.

> **CAUTION**
>
> **Your "income" may be higher than you think.** The new bankruptcy law requires filers to use some odd (and possibly inaccurate) figures when calculating how much they will have left over each month to repay their debts. For example, your "income" is not the actual amount you bring home each month; it is your average gross income during the six months before you filed for bankruptcy, which could well be higher than your current income. And, filers who earn more than the median income for their state cannot deduct their actual expenses when figuring out their disposable income. Instead, they must use expense figures set by the IRS, which might be lower than actual expenses, especially in metropolitan areas. For more information, see *Chapter 13 Bankruptcy: Repay Your Debts*, by Stephen Elias and Robin Leonard (Nolo).

Most people file for Chapter 13 bankruptcy to make up missed mortgage or car payments and get back on track with their original loan, or to pay off a tax debt or student loan. These are not the only reasons people file for Chapter 13 bankruptcy, however.

If you cannot complete a Chapter 13 repayment plan—for example, you lose your job six months into the plan and can't make the payments—the bankruptcy court has the authority to change your plan. If the problem looks temporary, you may be given a grace period, an extended repayment period, or a reduction of the total owed. If it's clear that you can't possibly complete the plan because of circumstances beyond your control, the bankruptcy court might even let you discharge (cancel) your debts on the basis of hardship.

If the bankruptcy court won't let you modify your plan or give you a hardship discharge, you have the right to:

- convert to a Chapter 7 bankruptcy, or
- dismiss your Chapter 13 case. A dismissal of your case would leave you in the same position as you were in before you filed, except that you'll owe less because of the payments you made. Your creditors will add to the debt the interest that was suspended from the time you filed your Chapter 13 petition until it was dismissed.

> **RESOURCE**
>
> **For more information on Chapter 13 bankruptcy,** see *Chapter 13 Bankruptcy: Repay Your Debts*, by Stephen Elias and Robin Leonard, or *The New Bankruptcy: Will It Work for You?*, by Stephen Elias, both published by Nolo. ∎

Avoiding Overspending

SKIP AHEAD

If you skip this section, come back later. If you'd rather clean up your credit report or pay off your debts before doing a budget, skip ahead, but be sure to return to this chapter later. If you don't make a budget, you'll have a very tough time repairing and maintaining your credit.

An essential step in repairing your credit is to understand where your money goes. With that information in hand, you can make intelligent choices about how to spend your money. If you'd rather not create a budget yourself, you can contact a nonprofit credit or debt counseling organization. Information on credit and debt counseling agencies is located in Appendix 1.

RESOURCES

Budgeting help. Several excellent computer programs, such as Quicken, can help you keep track of your expenses, particularly those paid by check or credit card. Many of these programs have budget features as well. Be sure you have an opportunity to record your cash outlays, however, before relying on these budgeting features: Many commercial budgeting programs analyze expenses you pay by check but overlook the most obvious source of payment—cash.

Keep Track of Your Daily Expenditures

Your goal in this chapter is to create a monthly budget comparing your average monthly expenses to your total monthly income. This section introduces Form F-2, Daily Expenditures (copies are below, in Appendix 3, and on the CD-ROM), on which you have space to record everything you spend over the course of a week. Here's how to use the form:

1. Make eight copies of the form so you can record your expenditures for two months. (To create your monthly budget, record expenses for two months. By doing this, you avoid creating a budget based on a week or a month of unusually high or low expenses.) If you are married or live with someone with whom you share expenses, make 16 copies so you each can record your expenditures.

2. Select a Sunday to begin recording your expenses.

3. Record that Sunday's date in the blank at the top of one copy of the form.

4. Carry that week's form with you at all times.

5. Record every expense you pay for by cash or cash equivalent. "Cash equivalent" means check, ATM or debit card, or automatic bank withdrawal. Be sure to include bank fees. Also, don't forget savings and investments, such as deposits into savings accounts, certificates of deposit, or money market accounts,

Daily Expenditures for Week of _____

Sunday's Expenditures	Cost	Monday's Expenditures	Cost	Tuesday's Expenditures	Cost	Wednesday's Expenditures	Cost
Daily Total:		**Daily Total:**		**Daily Total:**		**Daily Total:**	

Thursday's Expenditures	Cost	Friday's Expenditures	Cost	Saturday's Expenditures	Cost	Other Expenditures	Cost
Daily Total:		**Daily Total:**		**Daily Total:**		**Weekly Total:**	

F-2

or purchases of investments such as stocks or bonds.

Do not record credit card charges, as your goal is to get a picture of where your cash goes. When you make a payment on a credit card bill, however, list the items your payment paid for. If you don't pay the entire bill each month, list older items you charged that total a little less than the amount of your payment, and attribute the rest of your payment to interest.

EXAMPLE: On Sunday night, you pay your bills for the week and make a $450 payment toward your $1,000 credit card bill. The $1,000 includes a $500 balance from the previous month, a $350 airline ticket, a few restaurant meals, and accrued interest. On your Daily Expenditures form for Sunday, you list $450 in the second column. In the first column, you identify corresponding expenses—for example, the plane ticket and one restaurant meal—and attribute some of it to interest. In this example, you have to look at your credit card statement from the previous month.

6. At the end of the week, put away the form and take out another copy. Go back to Step 3.

7. At the end of the eight weeks, list on any form under the category "Other Expenditures" seasonal, annual, semiannual, or quarterly expenses you incur but did not pay during your two-month recording period. The most common are property taxes, car registration, magazine subscriptions, tax preparation fees, and insurance payments. But there are others. For example, if you do your recording in the winter months, don't forget summer expenses such as camp fees for your children or pool maintenance. Similarly, in the summer or spring you probably won't account for your annual holiday gift expenses. Think broadly and be thorough.

Total Up Your Income

Your expenditures account for only half of the picture. You also need to add up your monthly income. Use Form F-3, Monthly Income From All Sources (copies are below, in Appendix 3, and on the CD-ROM).

If you are married or live with someone with whom you share expenses, include income information for both partners.

Column 1: Source of income. In Part A, list the jobs for which you receive a salary or wages. In Part B, list all self-employment for which you receive income, including farm income and sales commissions. In Part C, list any other sources of income. Here are some examples of other kinds of income:

- **Bonus pay.** List all regular bonuses you receive, such as an annual $1,000 end-of-year bonus.
- **Dividends and interest.** List all sources of dividends or interest—for example, bank accounts, security deposits, or stocks.

Monthly Income From All Sources

1 Source of income	2 Amount of each payment	3 Period covered by each payment	4 Amount per month
A. Wages or Salary			
Job 1: _____ _____	Gross pay, including overtime:: $ _____	_____	
	Subtract: _____		
	Federal taxes _____		
	State taxes _____		
	Social Security (FICA) _____		
	Union dues _____		
	Insurance payments _____		
	Child support wage withholding _____		
	Other mandatory deductions (specify): _____ _____ _____		
	Subtotal: $ _____	_____	_____
Job 2: _____ _____	Gross pay, including overtime:: $ _____	_____	
	Subtract: _____		
	Federal taxes _____		
	State taxes _____		
	Social Security (FICA) _____		
	Union dues _____		
	Insurance payments _____		
	Child support wage withholding _____		
	Other mandatory deductions (specify): _____ _____ _____		
	Subtotal: $ _____	_____	_____
Job 3: _____ _____	Gross pay, including overtime:: $ _____	_____	
	Subtract: _____		
	Federal taxes _____		
	State taxes _____		
	Social Security (FICA) _____		
	Union dues _____		
	Insurance payments _____		
	Child support wage withholding _____		
	Other mandatory deductions (specify): _____ _____ _____		
	Subtotal: $ _____	_____	_____

Monthly Income From All Sources (cont'd)

1 Source of income		2 Amount of each payment	3 Period covered by each payment	4 Amount per month
B. Self-Employment Income				
Job 1: _____	Gross pay, including overtime::	$ _____	_____	
_____	Subtract:			
	Federal taxes	_____		
	State taxes	_____		
	Self-employment taxes	_____		
	Other mandatory deductions (specify): _____			
	_____	_____		
	Subtotal:	$ _____	_____	_____
Job 2: _____	Gross pay, including overtime::	$ _____	_____	
_____	Subtract:			
	Federal taxes	_____		
	State taxes	_____		
	Self-employment taxes	_____		
	Other mandatory deductions (specify): _____			
	_____	_____		
	Subtotal:	$ _____	_____	_____
C. Other Sources				
Bonuses _____		_____		_____
Commissions _____		_____		_____
Dividends and interest _____		_____		_____
Rent, lease, or license income _____		_____		_____
Royalties _____		_____		_____
Note or trust income _____		_____		_____
Alimony or child support you receive _____		_____		_____
Pension or retirement income _____		_____		_____
Social Security _____		_____		_____
Other public assistance _____		_____		_____
Other (specify): _____		_____		_____
_____		_____		_____
_____		_____		_____
_____		_____		_____
_____		_____		_____
_____		_____		_____
_____		_____		_____
	Total monthly income			$ _____

F-3

- **Alimony or child support.** Enter the type of support you receive for yourself (alimony, spousal support, or maintenance) or on behalf of your children (child support).
- **Pension or retirement income.** List the source of any pension, annuity, IRA, Keogh, or other retirement payments you receive.
- **Other public assistance.** Enter the types of any public benefits, such as SSI, public assistance, disability payments, veterans benefits, unemployment compensation, workers' compensation, or other government benefits you receive.
- **Other.** Identify any other sources of income, such as a tax refund you received within the past year or expect to receive within the next year, or payments you receive from friends or relatives. If, within the past 12 months, you received any one-time lump sum payment (such as the proceeds from an insurance policy or from the sale of a valuable asset), do not list it as income.

Column 2: Amount of each payment. For each source of income you listed in Parts A and B of Column 1, enter the amount you receive each pay period. If you don't receive the same amount each period, average the last 12. Then enter your deductions for each pay period. Again, if these amounts vary, enter an average of the last 12 months. For the income you listed in Part A, you probably need to get out a pay stub to see how much is deducted from your paycheck.

Subtract the deductions and enter your net income in the "Subtotal" blank in Column 2.

In Part C, enter the amount of each payment for each source of income. If these amounts vary, enter an average of the last 12 months.

Column 3: Period covered by each payment. For each source of income, enter the period covered by each payment—such as weekly, twice monthly (24 times a year), every other week (26 times a year), monthly, quarterly (common for royalties), or annually (common for farm income).

Column 4: Amount per month. Multiply or divide the subtotals (or amounts in Part C) in Column 2 to determine the monthly amount. For example, if you are paid twice a month, multiply the Column 2 amount by two. If you are paid every other week, multiply the amount by 26 (for the annual amount) and divide by 12. (The shortcut is to multiply by 2.167.)

When you are done, total up Column 4. This is your total monthly income.

Make a Budget or Spending Plan

Once you've tracked your expenses and income for a couple of months, you're ready to create a budget or spending plan. Use Form F-4, Monthly Budget (copies are below, in Appendix 3, and on the CD-ROM).

You have two goals in making a budget: to control any impulse you may have to overspend and to help you start saving money (an essential part of repairing your credit). The figures you entered on Forms F-2 and F-3 will form the basis for your budget.

To make and use a monthly budget, follow these steps:

1. Make several copies of Form F-4. Making a budget you can live with is a process of trial and error, and you may have to draft a few plans before you get it right.

2. Get out Forms F-2 and F-3, which include your income and expense figures.

3. Review the expenses listed on Form F-4. As you'll see, they are divided into common categories, such as home expenses, food, and transportation. If you don't have any expenses in a particular category, you can cross it out, delete it on your computer, or simply leave it blank. If you have a type of expense that isn't listed on the form, add that category to a blank line.

4. In the first column (labeled "Projected"), list your average actual monthly expenses in each category. Calculate these amounts by adding together your actual expenses for the two months you tracked, then dividing the total by two. If you have seasonal, annual, or quarterly expenses, include a monthly amount for those as well. For example, if you pay $3,600 in property taxes each year, you should list a projected expense of $300 a month ($3,600 divided by 12) in this category.

5. Add up all of your projected monthly expenses and enter the total on the line marked "Total Expenses" at the bottom of the "Projected" column.

6. Enter your projected monthly income (from Form F-3) below your projected total expenses.

7. Compare your projected income to your projected expenses. If you are spending more than you earn, you'll either have to earn more or spend less to make ends meet. Unless you're anticipating a big raise, planning to take on a second job, or selling valuable assets, you'll probably have to lower your expenses. Review each category to look for ways to cut costs. Rather than trying to cut out an entire expense, look for expenses you can reduce slightly without depriving yourself of items or services you really need. For example, you might be willing to forego one trip to a restaurant per month, subscribe to a less expensive cable package, or spend less on clothing.

8. Return to your budget and enter the adjustments you came up with. When you're finished, add up these new figures and come up with a new total expense amount. If it's less than your income, your budget is complete. If not, go back and try to find other places to cut back.

9. Label the remaining columns with the months of the year. Unless you wrote your budget on the first of the month, start with next month. During the course of the month, use a pencil (or computer) to write down and update your expenses in each category.

10. At the end of the month, total up how much you spent. How did you do? Are

Monthly Budget

Expense Category	Projected											
Home												
Rent/mortgage												
Property tax												
Insurance												
Homeowners assn. dues												
Telephone												
Gas/electric												
Water/sewer												
Cable												
Garbage/recycling												
Household supplies												
Housewares												
Furniture/appliances												
Cleaning												
Yard/pool care												
Repairs/maintenance												
Food												
Groceries												
Breakfast out												
Lunch out												
Dinner out												
Coffee/tea												
Snacks												
Clothing												
Clothes, shoes/ accessories												
Laundry, dry cleaning												
Mending												

Monthly Budget (continued)

Self Care													
Toiletries/cosmetics													
Haircuts													
Massage													
Gym membership													
Donations													
Health Care													
Insurance													
Medications													
Vitamins													
Doctor													
Dentist													
Eye care													
Therapy													
Transportation													
Car payments (buy or lease)													
Insurance													
Registration													
Gas													
Maintenance/repairs													
Parking													
Tolls													
Public transit													
Parking tickets													
Road service (such as AAA)													
Entertainment													
Music													
Movies/rentals													
Concerts, theater, ballet, etc.													
Museums													

Monthly Budget (continued)

Sporting events													
Hobbies /lessons													
Club dues or membership													
Film/developing costs													
Books, magazines/ newspapers													
Software/games													
Dependent Care													
Child care													
Clothing													
Allowance													
School expenses													
Toys /entertainment													
Pets													
Food /supplies													
Veterinarian													
Grooming													
Education													
Tuition													
Loan payments													
Books/supplies													
Travel													
Gifts/Cards													
Personal Business													
Supplies													
Copying													
Postage													
Bank/credit card fees													
Legal fees													
Accountant													

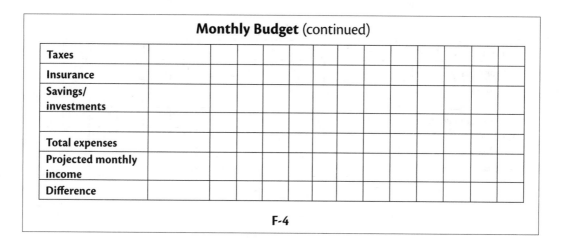

Monthly Budget (continued)

Taxes														
Insurance														
Savings/ investments														
Total expenses														
Projected monthly income														
Difference														

F-4

you close to your projected figures? If not, go back and try to make some changes to keep the numbers in balance.

Check your figures periodically to help you keep track of how you're doing. Don't think of your budget as etched in stone. If you do, and you spend more on an item than you've budgeted, you'll only find yourself frustrated. Use your budget as a guide. If you constantly overspend in one area, don't berate yourself: Instead, change the projected amount for that category and find another place to cut. Keep in mind that a budget is just a tool to help you recognize what you can afford and where your money is going.

Prevent Future Financial Problems

There are no magic rules that will solve everyone's financial troubles. But the following suggestions should help you stay out of trouble. If you have a family, everyone will have to participate—one person cannot do all the work alone. So make sure your spouse or partner, and the kids, understand that the family is having financial difficulties and agree together to take the steps that will lead to financial recovery.

1. **Create a realistic budget and stick to it.** This means periodically checking it and readjusting your figures and spending habits.

2. **Don't impulse buy.** When you see something you hadn't planned to buy, don't purchase it on the spot. Go home and think it over. It's unlikely you'll return to the store and buy it.

3. **Avoid sales.** Buying a $500 item on sale for $400 isn't a $100 savings if you didn't need the item to begin with. It's spending $400 unnecessarily.

4. **Get medical insurance if at all possible.** Even a stopgap policy with a large

deductible can help if a medical crisis comes up. You can't avoid medical emergencies, but living without medical insurance is an invitation to financial ruin.

5. **Charge items only if you can afford to pay for them now.** If you don't currently have the cash, don't charge based on future income—sometimes future income doesn't materialize. An alternative is to toss all of your credit cards in a drawer and commit to living without credit for a while. Or, even better, cancel the cards that you really don't need. (To learn the correct way to cancel a credit card, see Chapter 6.) If you must charge, here's a good rule of thumb: Don't charge anything that won't exist when the statement arrives (such as meals, groceries, or movie tickets).

6. **Avoid large rent or house payments.** Obligate yourself only to what you can now afford and increase your mortgage or rent payments only as your income increases. Consider refinancing your house if your payments are unwieldy.

7. **Avoid cosigning or guaranteeing a loan for someone.** Your signature obligates you as if you were the primary borrower. You can't be sure that the other person will pay.

8. **Avoid joint obligations with people who have questionable spending habits—even a spouse or significant other.** If you incur a joint debt, you're probably liable for all of it if the other person defaults.

9. **Don't make high-risk investments.** Invest conservatively, opting for certificates of deposit, money market funds, and government bonds over riskier investments such as speculative real estate, penny stocks, and junk bonds.

10. **Use common sense.** People today use credit and debit cards for everything—dry cleaning, sandwiches, frappuccinos, groceries, movies, cocktails, postage, gum, and so on—and feel that their finances are in good shape because they have cash in their wallets or purses. These little expenses are hard to keep track of and add up quickly by the end of the month, often becoming budget busters. If you're in tough financial times, leave the credit and debit cards at home and pay cash for these things (or forgo them). If you find that you really love expensive coffee drinks, pay cash for them or, better yet, enjoy one as a treat when your finances are back on track. ■

Handling Existing Debts

To repair your credit, you must pay attention to two different kinds of debts: debts that aren't overdue (such as current charges on your utility bill) and your past due accounts (such as an unpaid phone bill from last month or a doctor's bill from last year). You cannot repair your credit if you ignore your past due debts—those default notations will stand out in your credit report. In addition, if you repair your credit and later default on debts that are now current, you will have wasted the hard work you did to repair your credit in the first place.

Stabilize your financial situation before you worry about repairing your credit. Focus your energy on finding a job or other income source and paying accounts in order to keep your home, car, and other necessities. There are some things you can do to improve your credit even when your financial situation is still shaky (see Chapter 4 on how to clean up your credit report), but for the most part, your credit record will improve only after you demonstrate to creditors that you are back on your feet financially.

RESOURCES

More on past due bills. For more detail on paying your past due bills and contacting your creditors about accounts on which you are current, see *Solve Your Money Troubles: Get Debt Collectors Off Your Back & Regain Financial Freedom,* by Robin Leonard and John Lamb (Nolo).

Tips For Sending Letters

Throughout this chapter, we advise you to send various letters to your creditors, depending on your situation. When you send a letter, follow these guidelines:

- Type your letters or neatly fill in the blanks of the letters in Appendix 3 or on the CD-ROM.
- Keep a copy of all correspondence for yourself.
- *Never* send originals of documents that support your claim (such as a note marked "paid" or a canceled check); send only copies and keep the originals.
- Send by certified mail, with a return receipt requested.
- If you are enclosing money, use a cashier's check or money order if you have any debts in collection—not a check. Otherwise, the recipient of the check could pass your checking account number on to any debt collector, which will make it easier for the collector to grab your assets to collect the debt.
- Follow up telephone calls with a letter confirming the details of the discussion and any promises made by you or the other party.
- If you communicate with a creditor or debt collector by email, print and keep copies of all your emails and email discussion chains. Always keep copies of all communications—and don't handle important discussions by phone or some other medium that won't give you a written record of the conversation.

Secured and Unsecured Debts

To successfully negotiate with your creditors, you must understand your options, which often depend on whether your debts are secured or unsecured. Understanding this distinction will also help you decide which debts to pay first.

A **secured debt** is one for which a specific item of property (called "collateral") guarantees payment of the debt. One way for a debt to be secured is for you to sign an agreement to create a secured debt and specify the collateral. If you don't pay, the creditor has the legal right to take the collateral. Because of this, these debts will usually be your highest priority (unless you don't care if you lose the collateral). The other way a debt becomes secured is for a creditor to record a lien (a notice that you owe the creditor money) against the property.

Common examples of secured debts include:

- mortgages and home equity loans (also called "second mortgages")—loans to buy, refinance, or fix up a house or other real estate
- loans for cars, boats, tractors, motorcycles, planes, or RVs
- personal loans from finance companies for which you pledge real estate or personal property, such as a paid-off motor vehicle
- charges on a department store charge account when the store requires you to sign a security agreement stating that the item purchased is collateral for your repayment (most store charges are not secured), and

- tax liens, judgment liens, mechanics liens, and child support liens.

Unsecured debts have no collateral. For example, when you charge a television set on your Visa card, the creditor can't take the television back if you don't pay your Visa bill. If the credit card company wants to be paid, it must sue you, get a judgment for the money you owe, and try to collect. A creditor who wins a lawsuit typically can go after your wages, bank accounts, and valuable property.

The majority of debts are unsecured. Some common unsecured debts include:

- credit and charge card purchases and cash advances (such as Visa, MasterCard, American Express, or Discover Card)
- gasoline charges
- most department store charges
- student loans
- bills from doctors, dentists, hospitals, accountants, and lawyers
- alimony and child support
- loans from friends or relatives, unless you gave the person a note secured by some property you own
- rent, and
- utility bills.

Usually, paying unsecured debts should be a lower priority than paying secured debts. However, because collectors of some unsecured debts—such as student loans and unpaid child support—are allowed to use more aggressive collection tactics than the typical unsecured creditor, those debts deserve more attention.

Deal With Current (or Not Seriously Overdue) Debts

SKIP AHEAD

If you've already fallen behind on all your debts, jump ahead. Go to "Deal With Creditors on Past Due Accounts," below.

One important step in repairing and maintaining your credit is to stay current—or to not get too far behind—on your existing debts. If it looks like you can't pay, your best bet is to contact your creditors before you miss a payment.

Negotiating with your creditors to get more time to pay or to change the terms of your agreement isn't particularly difficult. Creditors generally like to hear from people who anticipate having problems paying their bills. If you simply skip your payment, the creditor assumes the worst—that you're a deadbeat trying to get away with not paying. If you call or write in advance, however, your creditor will often help you through your difficulties. Merchants, lenders, and other creditors are aware of unemployment rates, underemployment trends, income reductions, corporate mergers and downsizing, and other sour economic realities. And, when times turn good again, they're going to want—and need—your business. So they may be accommodating now.

As soon as you realize that you're going to have trouble paying your bills, contact your creditors. Your goals are twofold: You want time to pay and you don't want the creditor to report your bill as past due to credit bureaus. Calling your creditors is faster than writing, but if you find it easier to express yourself on paper than over the phone, go ahead and write. If you call, follow up your call with a confirming letter so that you and the creditor have some evidence of what you agreed to. If you write, make sure your letter will get there before your payment is due.

Your success with your creditors will depend on the type of debt, the creditor's policies, and your ability to negotiate. Follow these key points when dealing with your creditors:

- **Explain the problem clearly.** Creditors can easily grasp accidents, job layoffs, emergency expenses for your child's health, costs of caring for an aged family member, or a large back tax assessment.

- **Mention any development that points to an improving financial condition.** Creditors like to hear about disability or unemployment benefits beginning, job prospects, an expense about to end (such as a child finishing school), the end of a strike, a job recall, or a small inheritance on the way.

- **If you can afford it, send a token payment.** This tells the creditor that you are serious about paying but just can't pay the full amount now. Of course, the creditor might also take your money and continue to refuse to negotiate with you.

Negotiation is often a good strategy, but it doesn't always work. Increasing numbers of creditors simply will not negotiate with debtors. Despite the fact that creditors get at least something when they negotiate settlements with debtors, many ignore debtors' pleas for help, continue to call demanding payment, and leave debtors with few options other than filing for bankruptcy. In fact, nearly one-third of the people who filed for bankruptcy during the mid-1990s stated that the final straw that sent them into bankruptcy was the unreasonableness of their creditors or the collection agencies hired by their creditors. However, even if some creditors are unwilling to negotiate, you'll never know until you try.

SKIP AHEAD

Skip ahead if you don't have a particular kind of debt discussed below. Below is advice for dealing with specific types of debts: rent and mortgage payments, utility and telephone bills, car payments, secured loans, student loans, insurance policies, bills from professionals, and credit card payments. Read only the sections that apply to you.

Rent Payments

Many landlords will let their tenants pay rent late for a month or two, especially if the tenant has been reliable in the past. You will have the best chance of working out a payment plan if you contact the landlord promptly.

If your rent is too steep for your budget, you could try asking for a reduction. Many landlords won't agree, but in areas where property values have declined or the vacancy rate has increased (there are many empty units on the market), it might work. The landlord may agree to accept a partial payment now and the rest later. The landlord may even temporarily lower your rent, rather than have to evict you or rerent the place if you move out.

If your landlord agrees to a rent reduction or late payments, send by certified mail, or hand deliver, a letter confirming the arrangement. (See the sample, below.) Be sure to keep a copy for yourself. If you hand deliver the letter, ask the landlord or manager to initial and date your copy of the letter to confirm that it was received. Once the understanding is written down, the landlord will have a hard time evicting you as long as you live up to your new agreement.

Sample Letter to Landlord

May 5, 2007

Frank O'Neill
1556 North Lakefront
Minneapolis, MN 67890

Dear Frank:

Thanks for being so understanding. This letter is to confirm the telephone conversation we had yesterday.

My lease requires that I pay rent of $1,000 per month. You agreed to reduce my rent to $850 per month, beginning June 1, 2007, and lasting until I find another job, but not to exceed six months. That is, even if I haven't found a new job, my rent will go back to $1,000 per month on December 1, 2007.

You also agreed that I can pay my rent this month on the 15th, and on the 5th of each month after that until December 2007, when my rent will once again be due on the 1st.

Thank you again for your understanding and help. As I mentioned on the phone, I am following all leads in order to secure another job shortly.

Sincerely,

Abigail Landsberg
Abigail Landsberg

If your landlord refuses to help out, your options are limited. If you don't pay the amount of rent you obligated yourself to pay, your landlord can—and no doubt will—evict you. You are usually better off trying to get a roommate (with the landlord's permission, if it's required) or moving out before any eviction takes place.

If you have a month-to-month lease, you merely have to give your landlord the amount of notice required under your rental agreement before you move out (often 30 days). Of course, if moving out means living on the streets, you might as well stay and see what action the landlord takes. This is especially true in areas where evictions can take several weeks.

If you have a written lease, you will violate it by moving out before the lease term expires. If you know of someone who can take over your lease, recommend that person to your landlord. The landlord should accept the person unless the landlord has another tenant in mind, the person's rental history is poor, or the person's credit is bad and the landlord is convinced that he or she couldn't pay the rent. Even if you don't find someone to take over the lease, in most states the landlord has a duty to "mitigate" damages, which means that the landlord must use reasonable efforts to rerent the place in order to collect the rent lost by your moving. If the landlord rerents the property, you'll have to pay only for the period during which the property is vacant, plus the landlord's reasonable costs to find a new tenant (advertising expenses, for example). If you advanced one or two months' rent or paid a security deposit when you moved in, the landlord should put that money toward any amount you owe.

If you end up owing your landlord some money and don't pay it, your landlord might report the amount due to the credit bureaus or to tenant-screening services (which are similar to credit bureaus but gather information for property owners and managers). Not all landlords report this information. But any time the landlord takes court action—files an eviction lawsuit or sues you for a balance owed—you can be sure it will appear in your credit file and tenant history.

RESOURCES

Tenant information. You can find complete information on your rights as a tenant in *Every Tenant's Legal Guide,* by Janet Portman and Marcia Stewart (Nolo).

Mortgage Payments

You have a number of options for dealing with house payments:

- If you anticipate having trouble making payments for a few months, contact the lender. Lenders may be willing to defer or waive late charges, accept interest-only payments, apply prior prepayments to the current debt, or temporarily reduce or suspend payments. (For more on these options, see *Solve Your Money Troubles: Get Debt Collectors Off Your Back & Regain Financial Freedom,* by Robin Leonard and John Lamb (Nolo).)
- If your problem looks long term, the lender may let you refinance the loan to reduce the amount of your monthly payments. Because you're looking to refinance with your original lender,

the lender may waive many of the costs. Be realistic when considering this option. If you can't afford your new payments, refinancing won't help your financial situation—and may even make it worse.

- If you can't refinance your loan with the original lender, you may be able to find another lender who will loan you money to pay off all or some of your first loan. Again, be aware of the potential costs involved. And read everything carefully before you sign on the dotted line. Many unscrupulous lenders try to take advantage of people with financial problems.

If you can't pay your mortgage and can't work out a deal with your original or a new lender, you have three options:

- **Sell the house.** This is usually the best option. Many investors and savvy buyers look to buy "distressed" houses—houses in or near foreclosure. You won't get top dollar, but you should be able to at least save some of the equity you have built up and avoid doing serious damage to your credit. But do not get taken by an unscrupulous "equity skimmer" or "foreclosure consultant." Equity skimmers try to buy houses for a small fraction of their market value, often through misrepresentation, deceit, or intimidation. Foreclosure consultants promise to help homeowners in foreclosure, charge high fees for little or no service, and then purchase the home at a fraction of its value.

Types of Foreclosure Scams

A recent national study found that foreclosure scams fall into three general categories. These scams rely on the homeowner's desperation and ignorance for their success. They also often rely on the homeowner's faith in humanity ("no one would kick me when I'm down") or shared heritage or national origin ("someone of my culture wouldn't trick me"). The more you know about these scams, the less likely you are to fall victim to one of them, so here are brief summaries of the three types:

- **Phantom rescue:** The scammer charges excessive fees for a few phone calls or a little paperwork that the homeowner could have done and for a promise of representation that never happens. The scammer abandons the homeowner when the time for reinstatement—which should have been used to get current on the loan, negotiate with the lender, or find effective assistance—runs out. The foreclosure then proceeds.

- **Bailout:** The scammer tells the homeowner to surrender title to the house, with the promise that he or she can rent it and buy it back from the scammer later. The homeowner may be told that surrender of the title is necessary so that someone with better credit can get new financing to save the house. The terms of the buyback are so onerous that the homeowner can't buy the house back, and the rescuer pockets the equity.

- **Bait and switch:** Here, the homeowner doesn't realize that he or she is surrendering title to the house in exchange for the promised rescue. The scammer may trick the homeowner into surrendering title (perhaps when signing new loan documents), or may simply forge the homeowner's signature on the deed. The scammer then keeps the house or sells it and keeps the profit.

- **Walk away from your house.** Especially if you owe more than your house is worth, you may be best off moving out and giving the keys to the lender. To do this, you transfer your ownership interest in your home to the lender—called a "deed in lieu of foreclosure." Lenders don't have to accept your deed in lieu, but many will. Keep in mind that with a deed in lieu, you won't get any cash back, even if you have lots of equity in your home. And it may have negative tax consequences. The deed in lieu will also appear on your credit report as a negative mark. If you opt for a deed in lieu, try to get concessions from the lender—after all, you are saving it the expense and hassle of foreclosing on your home. For example, ask the lender to eliminate negative references on your credit report or give you more time to stay in the house. (*Solve Your Money Troubles: Get Debt Collectors Off Your*

Back & Regain Financial Freedom, by Robin Leonardand John Lamb (Nolo), discusses steps to take if you plan to walk away from your home.)

- **Let the lender foreclose.** If the lender forces a sale of your house, you may still owe money. In most states, if the sale price doesn't cover what you owe, the lender is entitled to a "deficiency balance"—the difference between the amount you owe the foreclosing lender and the amount for which the foreclosing lender sells the house.

RESOURCES

Want more information on foreclosure and mortgages? The U.S. Department of Housing and Urban Development (HUD) can give you the name of a reputable local housing counseling agency. If you'd like a referral, or if you are at risk of default on your mortgage or foreclosure, call 800-569-4287. For more information on predatory lenders, check out the "Financing Homes" area of AARP's website at www.aarp.org/money/wise_consumer/financinghomes and the HUD website at www.hud.gov.

How a Foreclosure Works

If you haven't been able to sell your house and you don't just walk away, your lender will probably foreclose. Here's a general description of what to expect (the exact process and timelines vary from state to state). After you miss a few payments, the lender will send you a letter reminding you that your payments are late and imposing a late fee. If you don't respond, the lender will wait another 60 days or so and then send you a notice telling you that your loan is in default and that it will begin foreclosure proceedings unless it receives payment.

After getting this notice, you have about 90 days to "cure" the default and reinstate the loan— pay all your missed payments, late fees, and other charges. If you can't bring the loan current, the only way to avoid foreclosure is to sell the house during this period. If you were being picky before, now is the time to accept any offer.

If you don't cure the default, the lender applies to a court for an order allowing it to sell your house at an auction. (Obtaining court approval is not necessary when the lender issues a deed of trust instead of a mortgage. The two documents are virtually the same, except that the holder of a deed of trust can forgo court involvement.) Then the lender publishes a notice of the sale in a newspaper. Between the dates when the notice is published and the sale takes place, most lenders let you reinstate the loan by making up the back payments and penalties.

If you don't reinstate the loan or sell the house, the lender will "accelerate" the loan. This means you no longer can reinstate the loan. The only way you can keep your house is by paying the entire mortgage balance immediately.

If you don't pay the balance, your house will be sold at a foreclosure sale. Anyone with a financial interest in your house will attend. The house is sold to the highest bidder.

Even if your problem looks long term, the lender may try to work with you to avoid foreclosure. In the past, lenders were quick to start foreclosure proceedings. In recent years, however, they have looked at new ways to work out mortgage delinquencies short of foreclosure.

If you want to try to work something out with your lender, begin negotiating as early as possible. Also, it's often a good idea to get help from a nonprofit debt counselor or lawyer with experience in mortgage workouts. For information on HUD-approved mortgage counseling agencies in your area, call 800-569-4287.

When the Federal Government Owns Your Loan

Millions of American homeowners' loans are owned by Fannie Mae or Freddie Mac. These are private corporations created by the United States government.

Both companies' default programs emphasize foreclosure prevention whenever feasible. They offer rate reductions, term extensions, and other changes for people in financial distress, especially for people experiencing involuntary money problems due to things such as an illness, death of a spouse, or job loss. One possible option would allow you to make partially reduced payments for up to 18 months.

If you can't get help from your loan servicer, contact Fannie Mae or Freddie Mac directly at:

- Fannie Mae, 800-732-6643, www.fanniemae.com
- Freddie Mac, 800-373-3343, www.freddiemac.com

Utility and Telephone Bills

Most electric, gas, water, and telephone companies will let you get two or three months behind before turning off your service or taking other steps to collect what you owe. Some utility companies have programs that allow delinquent customers to pay the overdue amount in installments over several months. Call the company's billing department to see if it offers this type of program.

Many utility companies offer reduced rates to elderly and low-income people and have emergency funds to help pay the bills of low-income people. If you face high heating bills in the winter or air conditioning bills in the summer, you may want to see if your utility company offers "level payments." This means that the annual bill is averaged and paid in equal payments over 12 months. During a designated month of the year, the actual bills are calculated against your level payments and you are either billed for the balance owed or given a refund for any overpayment.

To find out if you qualify for reduced rates, level payments, "lifeline" programs," or other assistance offered by the utility company, call and ask. In addition, in many areas, charitable groups—especially religious organizations—offer assistance to low-income people who need help with their utility bills. Take advantage of any assistance available to you. It can be a real hassle, and expensive, to get your utility service back after it's been shut off for nonpayment of your bill.

Keep in mind that most northern states prohibit termination of heat-related utilities during the winter months. Other states also have a limited prohibition against shutoffs for households with elderly or disabled residents and occasionally for households with infants. Usually, you must show financial hardship to qualify. But, even if you qualify for a prohibition against utility shutoff, you'll still owe the bill.

Car Payments

Handling car payments depends on whether you buy or lease your vehicle.

Purchase Payments

If you suspect you'll have trouble making your car payments for several months, your best bet is to sell the car, pay off the lender, and use whatever is left to pay your other debts, or to buy a more affordable used car that will get you where you need to go.

Selling the car is not a good strategy if you're "upside down" (that is, you owe more on the car than you can sell it for). If you can pay the difference between the loan amount and the car's market value, then selling the car at least will free up the amount of your car payment each month. Don't even consider transferring the car to someone who promises to make the monthly payments for you. Such a transfer almost certainly will violate your purchase contract and probably is illegal. Also, the business or person who takes the car may not make the payments. Then you'll be responsible for the default on the loan, which will become part of your credit record.

If you want to hold onto your car and you miss a payment, call the lender *immediately* and speak to someone in the customer service or collections department. Don't delay. Cars can be, and often are, repossessed within hours of the time payment was due. There are several reasons for this: The creditor doesn't have to get a court judgment before seizing the car; cars lose value fast, so a creditor who has to auction it off will want to do so quickly to get the largest possible return; and cars are mobile and have been know to disappear before they can be repossessed.

If you present a convincing argument that your situation is temporary, the lender will probably grant you an extension, meaning that you can make the delinquent payment at the end of your loan period. However, the lender probably won't grant an extension unless you've made at least six payments on time. Also, most lenders charge a fee for granting an extension and don't grant more than one a year.

Instead of granting an extension, the lender may rewrite the loan to reduce the monthly payments. This means, however, that you'll make payments for a longer period of time and pay more total interest.

In deciding whether to hold onto the car, don't forget to consider your monthly insurance payment. You will have to maintain your insurance coverage if you decide to keep the car. Lenders usually consider failure to maintain insurance to be a default, which can lead to repossession. Also, the lender can obtain insurance to protect its interest in the car, which usually is very expensive, and hold you responsible for the premiums.

Lease Payments

More than 30% of new cars are leased, rather than purchased. The reasons are many, but most people who lease like the lower monthly payments that accompany vehicle lease contracts.

If you can't afford your lease payments, your first step is to review your lease agreement. If your total obligation under the lease is less than $25,000 and the lease term exceeds four months (many leases meet these two requirements), the federal Consumer Leasing Act (15 U.S.C. §§ 1667-1667e) requires that your lease include disclosures regarding the cost and terms of ending your lease agreement early.

If you want to cancel your lease, look carefully at the provisions of your lease agreement describing what happens if you default and how you can terminate the lease early. You can count on incurring an early termination penalty.

If you can't figure out how much you'll owe, inform the dealer in writing that you want to end the lease early and ask how much you'll owe. The dealer will contact you with the amount. If the dealer has already assigned (sold) the lease, then contact the leasing company—for example, Ford Motor Credit.

Some consumers have successfully challenged the amount owed or persuaded the leasing company to drop large penalties for early termination where the formula used to calculate the amount owed was not defined in a clear manner or not included in the lease agreement. If you want to pursue this option, you'll need to contact a lawyer. Not all courts agree about what "confusing" means in this context—the best way to find out how your local court has dealt with the issue is to speak to a lawyer who is experienced with auto leasing issues.

Loans for Which You Pledged Collateral Other Than a Motor Vehicle

If a personal loan or store agreement is secured—for example, you pledged a refrigerator or couch as collateral for your repayment on that item—the lender probably won't reduce what you owe. Instead, it may threaten to send a truck over and take the property. Rarely do lenders repossess personal property other than motor vehicles, however, because appliances and furniture bring in little money at auctions. Thus, if you simply stop paying, the lender will probably sue you before grabbing your new couch.

If you propose something reasonable, the lender may extend your loan or rewrite it to reduce the monthly payments. This will keep the property from being repossessed and keep you from being sued.

Student Loans

Under certain circumstances, you may be able to cancel your obligation to repay your federally guaranteed student loans, defer your payments, or enter into a payment schedule that better fits your income. If you're in default, you may be able to get out of default and avoid a lawsuit, wage garnishment, or loss of your tax refund.

The student loan scheme is quite complex, depending on the type of loan you have and when you obtained it. Before taking action on your loan, you must understand what kind of loan it is. Your ability to negotiate with your lender, defer your payments, or possibly cancel your loan may depend on the type of loan you have.

There are three primary kinds of federally guaranteed student loans: campus-based loans, bank loans, and Department of Education-issued loans. Campus-based loans are called Perkins Loans or the older National Direct/Defense Student Loans (NDSLs). Bank loans are called Federal Family Education Loan Program (FFELP) loans and include Stafford Loans (previously called Guaranteed Student Loans (GSLs) or Federal Insured Student Loans (FISLs)), PLUS Loans (loans for parents), SLS Loans, and consolidation loans. Loans issued directly by the Department of Education are called Direct Loans and include Stafford, PLUS, and consolidation loans.

How to Get More Information About Your Student Loans

You can find information about your student loans through the National Student Loan Data System at www.nslds.ed.gov. (or call 800-4-FED-AID). It will provide you with loan and grant amounts, outstanding balances, loan status, and disbursements.

If you've tried the above and still have trouble getting information, call the Student Loan Ombudsman toll-free at 877-557-2575.

RESOURCES

Student loan information. You can find further information on student loans in *The Student Guide*, published by the U.S. Department of Education. You can obtain a copy from the Department of Education's Federal Student Aid Information Center (800-433-3243), the Department of Education's Debt Collection Services Office (800-621-3115), or the Department of Education's website (www.ed.gov).

Canceling a Student Loan

Depending on the type of loan you have and when you obtained it, you may be able to cancel all or a portion of your loan under one of the following circumstances:

- The former student for whom the loan was taken has died.
- You become totally and permanently disabled.
- Your school closed before you could complete your program of study.

- Your school falsely certified that you were eligible for a student loan.
- You left school and were entitled to a refund but never received the money.
- You teach in a Department of Education-approved school serving low-income students or in a designated teacher shortage area (other types of teacher cancellations are available for Perkins loans).
- You serve in the U.S. military in an area of hostility or imminent danger (partial cancellation for Perkins loans only).
- You're a full-time employee of a public or nonprofit agency providing services to low-income, high-risk children and their families (Perkins loans only).
- You're a full-time nurse or medical technician (Perkins loans only).
- You're a full-time law enforcement or corrections officer (Perkins loans only).
- You're a full-time staff member in a Head Start program (Perkins loans only).
- You're a Peace Corps or VISTA volunteer (Perkins loans only).

To cancel a student loan—or to determine whether you qualify for cancellation—call the holder of your loan or the Department of Education's Debt Collection Services Office at 800-621-3115. Be aware that your loan holder may not inform you of all the options available to you. For this reason, it pays to first learn about your options by reading *The Student Guide* (see above).

Obtaining a Deferment of Your Student Loan Payments

You may be able to defer (postpone) repayment of a federal student loan if you are not in default—that is, you have made your payments on time, are in the grace period after graduation, or have been granted other deferments.

This section lists deferments only for loans disbursed after July 1, 1993. If you have loans disbursed at an earlier date, you can get more information from the Department of Education's website at www.ed.gov or by calling your loan holder.

You can request a deferment on any federal loan disbursed after July 1, 1993, if any of the following are true:

- You are enrolled in school at least half-time.
- You are enrolled in an approved graduate fellowship program or a rehabilitation program for the disabled.
- You are unable to find full-time employment.
- You are suffering from economic hardship.

In addition, you can defer a Perkins loan for most of the reasons listed in "Canceling a Student Loan," above.

To obtain a deferment of a federal student loan, contact the current holder of your loan. If you don't know who currently holds your loan, contact the financial or educational institution you initially borrowed from. If that institution has sold your loan or sent it elsewhere, it will tell you.

Ask the holder of your loan to send you a deferment application form. The holder of your loan may require that you submit supporting documentation, such as periodic verifications of your job search if you obtain an unemployment deferment. Be sure to comply. Deferment forms are available on the Department of Education's website at www.ed.gov.

Obtaining a Forbearance of Your Student Loan Payments

If you don't qualify for a deferment but are facing hard times financially, your lender may still allow you to postpone payments or temporarily reduce them. An arrangement of this sort is called a "forbearance." Although forbearances are easier to obtain than deferments—you may be able to obtain a forbearance even if your loan is in default—they are less attractive because interest continues to accrue while you are not making payments, no matter what type of loan you have.

Lenders typically have the authority to grant forbearances in six-month increments for up to two years. There is no stated condition for qualifying—it's usually just up to the lender. Call your lender and ask.

Consolidating Your Student Loans

If you want to repay your loans but can't afford the payments and don't qualify for cancellation, deferment, or forbearance, you may be able to consolidate your loans.

When you consolidate, you lower your monthly payments by combining multiple loans into one packaged loan and extending your current repayment period. You may also be able to refinance several loans, or just one loan, at a lower interest rate. But be aware that if you extend your repayment period, you will increase the amount of money you pay in interest over the life of your loan—sometimes dramatically. Even so, consolidation is one way to keep your head above water and avoid default. And if you've already defaulted, consolidation can help you get back on track.

Requesting a Flexible Payment Option

If you have a Direct or FFELP Stafford loan, you can pay it back in any of the four ways listed below. If you have a Direct PLUS loan, you can pay it back in the first three ways listed below:

- the standard ten-year repayment schedule
- an extended repayment schedule— the length of your payback period depends on the amount of your loan, from 12 years for loans under $10,000 to 30 years for loans over $60,000
- a graduated repayment schedule—you can pay off your loan in as many as 30 years by making lower payments in the early years of the loan and higher payments later, and
- an income-contingent repayment plan (for Direct loans) or an income-sensitive repayment plan (for FFELP loans)—your payments change each year based on the amount of your income, the amount of your student loan, and your family size.

Financial institutions are not obligated to offer extended, graduated, or income-contingent repayment plans, but many do so in order to remain competitive with the government direct lending program. While these payment options can offer much relief, using them can cost you a lot. For example, if you stretch your payments out for 20 or 30 years, you will wind up paying thousands—possibly tens of thousands—of dollars more in interest than you would have if you paid your loans off in ten years.

Many websites have calculators to help you figure out your monthly payments under different payment plans. Check out the calculators on the Department of Education's website at www.ed.gov. Many loan servicers also have online payment calculators.

Getting Out of Default

You can get out of default on any government loan if you make a certain number of payments under a "reasonable and affordable" payment plan and then rehabilitate the loan. This is how it works: You have the right to a payment plan that is reasonable and affordable based on your financial circumstances. If you make six consecutive timely payments under this plan, you will become eligible for new student loans and grants. Only enter into this payment arrangement if you can truly afford it. If you default, you won't get another chance to get out of default this way.

If you make nine payments on time within ten consecutive months, you will be able to "rehabilitate" your loan—meaning you'll no longer be in default.

Once you're out of default, you will have to repay the loan within ten years (unless you qualify for deferment or roll the loan into a consolidation loan). So, if you've been paying very small amounts under the reasonable and affordable payment plan, when you get out of default, your monthly payment amount may rise dramatically. If you can't afford the new amount, you should request one of the flexible repayment options described above.

Insurance Policies

Most insurance policies have 30-day grace periods—that is, if your payment is due on the tenth of the month and you don't pay until the ninth of the following month, you won't lose your coverage. A few companies won't terminate your policy as long as you pay your premium within 60 days after it's due. If you don't pay within 60 days, your policy will surely be canceled.

If you want to keep your insurance coverage, contact your insurance agent. You can reduce the amount of your coverage or increase your deductible, thereby reducing your premiums. This can usually be done easily for auto, medical, dental, renters', life, and disability insurance. It will be harder for homeowners' insurance, because you'll probably have to get authorization from your mortgage lender, who won't want your house to be underinsured.

If you have a life insurance policy with a cash value—an amount of money building up that you'll receive if you cancel the policy before it pays out—you can usually apply the cash value toward your premiums. The company will treat the use of the cash value as a loan. Your policy's cash value won't decrease, but you are theoretically required to repay the money. (If you don't repay it, the proceeds your beneficiaries receive when you die will be reduced by what you borrowed.) Or, you can simply ask that the cash reserves be used to pay the premiums. This will reduce your cash value, but you won't have to repay anything.

Perhaps the best way to keep life insurance coverage while reducing the payments is to convert a whole or universal policy (with relatively high premiums and a cash value build-up) into a term policy (with low premiums and no cash value.) You may lose a little of the existing cash value as a conversion fee, but it may be worthwhile if you get a policy that costs far less to maintain.

Doctor, Dentist, Lawyer, and Accountant Bills

Many doctors, dentists, lawyers, and accountants are accommodating if you communicate how difficult your financial problems are and try to get their sympathy. They may accept partial payments, reduce the total bill, drop interest or late fees, and delay sending bills to collection agencies.

Credit Card Bills

If you can't pay your credit card bill (including a department store or gasoline card bill), contact the credit card company. Most will insist that you make the minimum monthly payment, usually 5% of the outstanding bill, but in no event less than $20. If you convince the company that your financial situation is bleak, it may reduce your payments to between 2% and 2.5% of the outstanding balance. And, if you have an excellent payment history, the company may let you skip a month or two altogether.

> **CAUTION**
>
> **It's important to pay your credit card bills on time.** Paying late can result in a hefty late fee (sometimes $39 or more), an increase in the interest rate on your account (the new rate can be as high as 32% or more), and a negative entry on your credit report. All of these actions can cause other creditors to increase their interest rates as well. If you pay less than the full amount owed, you incur more interest charges. This is a strategy you should employ only temporarily. Otherwise, your balance will increase faster than you will be able to pay it off.

While you are paying off your balance, some credit card companies will help by waiving late fees. It's almost impossible to get a credit card company to reduce interest that has already accumulated. Some will stop adding future interest charges, however, if you get assistance from a reputable credit or debt counseling agency. (See Appendix 1.) The company also will probably freeze your credit line—that is, not let you incur any more charges—if you pay less than the minimum.

Ask the company to report your payments to a credit bureau as on time while you pay off your balance. If you keep to the new schedule, the credit card company shouldn't report the debt as past due.

If you can't pay a charge card bill—such as an American Express Green Card—you must approach the creditor differently. Charge cards are much less common than credit cards. Normally, you are required to pay off your entire charge card balance when your bill arrives. If you don't, you'll get one month in which no interest is charged. After that, you'll be charged interest in the neighborhood of 20%. Call the charge card company and ask that you be given a monthly repayment plan for paying off the bill. Offer to pay only what you can afford. But remember, if you pay only a very small amount, interest will accumulate and your balance will go up faster than you can pay it off. The company usually doesn't report this arrangement to credit bureaus if you pay the monthly amount you agreed to.

If You Dispute a Credit Card Bill

If you buy a defective item or service and pay for it with your credit card, you can often withhold payment if the seller refuses to replace, repair, or otherwise correct the problem. (15 U.S.C. §1666i.) You can withhold only the balance on the disputed item or service that is unpaid when you first notify the seller or card issuer of the problem.

However, there are conditions you must meet in order to use this law. First, you must make a good-faith effort to resolve the dispute with the seller. Second, you are required to explain to the credit card company in writing why you are withholding payment. Third, if you used a Visa, MasterCard, or other card not issued by the seller, you can refuse to pay only if: (1) the purchase was for more than $50, and (2) you made the purchase in the state where you reside or within 100 miles of your home. These limitations do not apply if the credit card was issued by the seller, (such as a department store card issued by the store), if the seller controls the card issuer or vice versa, or if the seller obtained your order by mailing you an advertisement in which the card issuer participated and urged you to use the card for the purchase.

If you conclude that you are entitled to withhold payment, write a letter to the credit card company and explain why you aren't going to pay. Detail how you tried to resolve the problem with the merchant. Before you mail the letter, look at the fine print on the back of your bill or call the credit card company and find out where to send it. Credit card companies have special addresses for mailing these types of letters. If you don't send it to the correct address, the company can disregard your letter. Use Form F-5, Dispute Credit Card Bill in Appendix 3 or on the CD-ROM. Keep a copy for your own records.

If Your Bill Contains an Error

If you find an error in your credit card statement, immediately write a letter to the company that issued the card; don't just scribble a note on the bill. The credit card company must receive your letter within 60 days after it mailed the bill to you. You can use Form F-6, Error on Credit Card Bill in Appendix 3 or on the CD-ROM. Give your name, your account number, an explanation of the error, and the amount involved. Also enclose copies of supporting documents, such as receipts showing the correct amount of the charge. Send the letter to the particular address designated by the creditor for this purpose. Check the back of your statement for this address or call the company to get it. You can withhold the portion of the required payment that you dispute, including finance charges, but you must pay the portion that you do not dispute.

What Is a Billing Error?

Most people think the definition of "billing error" includes only a mistake in the amount you owe. In fact, for purposes of the remedies described in this section, it also includes:

- an extension of credit to someone who was not authorized to use your card
- an extension of credit for property or services that were never delivered to you
- the company's failure to credit your account properly, and
- an extension of credit for items that you returned because they were defective or different from what you ordered.

The credit card company must acknowledge receipt of your letter within 30 days, unless it corrects the error within that time. The card issuer must, within two billing cycles (but in no event more than 90 days after it receives your letter), correct the error or explain why it believes the amount to be correct. If your bank issued the card and you have authorized automatic payments from your deposit account, the bank cannot deduct the disputed amount or related finance charges from your account while the dispute is pending if it receives your billing error notice at least three business days before the automatic payment date.

During the two-billing-cycle/90-day period, the card issuer cannot report to a credit bureau or other creditors that the disputed amount is delinquent. Likewise, the card issuer cannot threaten or actually take any collection action against you for the disputed amount. But it can include the disputed amount on your monthly billing statements. And it can apply the amount in dispute to your credit limit, thereby lowering the total credit available to you. Furthermore, the card issuer can add interest to your bill on the amount you dispute, but if the issuer later agrees you were correct, it must drop the interest accrued.

If the card issuer sends you an explanation but doesn't correct the error and you are not satisfied with its reason, you have ten days to respond. Send a second letter explaining why you still refuse to pay. If the card company then reports your account as delinquent to a credit bureau or anyone else, it must also state that you dispute that you owe the money. At the same time, the issuer must send you the name and address of each credit bureau and anyone else to whom it reports the delinquency. When the dispute is resolved, the issuer must send a notice to everyone to whom it has reported the delinquency. If the card issuer doesn't comply with any of these error resolution procedures, it must credit you $50 of the disputed balance, even if you are wrong.

> ! **CAUTION**
>
> **Check your credit file following a billing dispute or error.** Despite laws designed to protect consumers, a credit card issuer may negligently report an outstanding balance it removed from your card, fail to report that you dispute a charge, or fail to report that the dispute is resolved. Be sure to check your credit file. (See Chapter 4.)

If Someone Uses Your Credit Card Without Your Permission

Unauthorized credit card use—when someone steals your credit card number or otherwise uses it without your permission—is a growing problem, due in part to the huge volume of credit card business transacted over the phone and Internet. Fortunately, federal law offers some protection if this happens to you.

Your liability for unauthorized use of your credit card is limited to $50. So, if someone steals your card and uses it, your credit card lender cannot require you to pay more than $50 of those charges. Some credit card issuers waive the $50, especially for Internet transactions.

It is very important to report unauthorized credit card use as soon as you know about it. If you call before any charges are incurred, you are not liable for anything—not even $50. If there is an unauthorized charge on your bill, you can dispute the charge the same way you dispute a billing error.

! CAUTION

Be careful using debit cards. The protections discussed above don't apply to charges made with debit cards. You may be liable for $500 in unauthorized transfers if you don't notify the card issuer within two business days after you realize your card is missing. You may be liable for unlimited loss if (1) you gave your debit card and PIN to someone who drains your account (unless you instructed the card issuer not to honor that person's transactions) or (2) you didn't notify the card issuer that an unauthorized transfer appears on your statement within 60 days after it was mailed, and providing proper notice could have prevented the loss. Some card issuers, and some states, cap your potential loss at $50.

Debts You May Not Owe

This chapter focuses on handling debts that you do owe, not on ones you think you don't owe. If you've been cheated by dishonest creditors or the product you bought was defective, there may be consumer laws that will help you eliminate the underlying debt. For more information on what to do with debts you dispute, see *Solve Your Money Troubles: Get Debt Collectors Off Your Back & Regain Financial Freedom*, by Robin Leonard and John Lamb (Nolo).

Use the Form Negotiation Letters Provided in This Book

Negotiating with your creditors to request a reduction, extension, or other repayment program can be somewhat intimidating. Fortunately, sending a short letter can simplify the process considerably. Appendix 3 and the CD-ROM include several form letters you can send to creditors. Use these to confirm telephone conversations or to start the negotiation process. You can fill in the blanks and send the forms or, if you prefer, retype the letters. Be sure to keep a copy of whatever you send.

At the top of the form you're using, above the "Attn: Collections Department" line, type or write the creditor's name and address. Most items on the forms are self-explanatory. At the bottom, be sure to sign your name and provide the address that appears on your bill. If you are asking the creditor to get in touch with you, include your home phone number.

If you use Forms F-8, F-9, F-10, F-11, or F-12 (see Appendix 3 and "Forms for Negotiating With Creditors," below), you will need to state reasons why you can't make full payment. Here are the kinds of things creditors and lenders look for:

- a job layoff, reduction in hours, sporadic employment, or pay cut, coupled with a good-faith effort to find work or increase your income
- a large and unexpected tax assessment
- a divorce or separation resulting in more bills you have to pay or your ex-spouse's failure to pay bills the court ordered him or her to pay

- a permanent or temporary disability— temporary disabilities may include a heart attack, stroke, or cancer, or something less drastic like repetitive motion syndrome, or
- inadequate medical insurance coverage following a major illness or accident.

Deal With Creditors on Past Due Accounts

It's important to know whether the person trying to collect your past due debt works for the business or person who first extended you credit (the creditor) or for a company or lawyer hired by a creditor to collect the creditor's debt (a collection agency). A creditor who sets up a separate office (operated under a different name) to collect its own debts also qualifies as a collection agency. Depending on who is trying to collect, you have different legal rights and may want to employ different strategies. If any of your debts are being pursued by a collection agency, read "Deal With Collection Agencies," below, too.

CAUTION

Don't assume you must deal with a collector. If you have no money, plan to file for bankruptcy, or just don't feel like paying right now, you can opt to not speak with the collector at all. Or you may want to seek outside help. Depending on the complexity of your situation and your negotiating skills, negotiating with your creditors on your own may not always be wise. A savvy lender who refuses to rewrite your car loan may think twice if he hears from a credit or debt counselor or lawyer. (See Appendix 1.)

If you have past due accounts, you may be able to take care of the debts and start repairing your credit. Here are two requests you can make to a creditor using Form F-7, Make Payment If Negative Information Removed or Account Re-Aged, in Appendix 3 or on the CD-ROM:

- Ask that an unpaid debt and negative information in your credit file associated with the debt be removed from your credit file in exchange for full or partial payment. Creditors rarely withdraw reporting, but you may be able to convince a debt collector to do so. If so, be sure to get written confirmation from the creditor or collector that it will acknowledge the debt as paid in full when you pay the agreed amount, and that it will submit a Universal Data Form to the three major credit bureaus deleting the account/trade line (see Form F-7 in Appendix 3).
- If the creditor puts you on a new schedule for repaying the debt, consider asking the creditor to "re-age" your account, meaning it makes the current month the first repayment month and shows no late payments. Sometimes, the creditor won't re-age the account until you make two or three monthly payments first.

Think carefully before asking a creditor to re-age the account, especially if it's been reported as delinquent for some time.

Re-aging means that the account will appear on your credit report for seven years after the repayment date, rather than seven years after the earlier delinquency date. Some consumer advocates argue that re-aging an account is a bad idea for this reason. On the other hand, some debt management plans favor re-aging because the account appears as current on the credit report.

Most creditors will not remove negative marks or re-age accounts, but it never hurts to ask. Contact the creditor's collections or customer service department and make an offer. Tell whomever you speak to that you cannot afford to pay more, but that you'd really like to pay a good portion of the bill. Explain your financial problems—be bleak, but never lie. Get the creditor's agreement in writing (send your own confirming letter if need be) before sending any money.

When negotiating, it's helpful to know where you are in the collection process. Collection efforts almost always begin with past due invoices or letters. One day, you open your mail box and find a polite letter from a creditor reminding you that you seemed to have overlooked the company's most recent bill. "Perhaps it's already in the mail. If so, please accept our thanks. If not, we'd appreciate prompt payment," the letter or invoice states.

This "past due" form letter is the kind that almost every creditor sends to a customer with an overdue account. If you ignore it, you'll get a second one, also automatically sent. In this letter, most creditors remain friendly but want to know what the problem is. "If you have some special reason for withholding payment,

please let us know. We are here to help." Some creditors also suspend your credit at this point; the only way to get it back is to send a payment.

If you don't answer the second letter, you'll probably receive three to five more form letters. Each will get slightly firmer. By the last letter, expect a threat: "If we do not receive payment within ten days, your credit privileges will be canceled. Your account will be sent to a collection agency and your delinquency will be reported to a credit reporting agency. You could face a lawsuit, wage attachment, or lien on your property."

After you've received a series of collection letters, you may conclude that you no longer have leverage to negotiate. This is not so: You always have leverage, because you have what they want—money.

Appendix 3 and the CD-ROM include several form letters you can use to send to creditors for your past due accounts. The forms are described in the chart on the previous page. Find the form that fits your situation and send it off.

If the creditor rejects your proposal or wants more evidence that you are genuinely unable to pay, consider contacting a nonprofit credit or debt counseling agency. (See Appendix 1.)

If the debt is quite large or one of many, consider hiring a lawyer to write a second letter asking for additional time. The lawyer won't say anything different from what you would, but a lawyer's stationery carries clout. And it may be especially worth the few hundred dollars it will cost if you have many outstanding debts and need substantial help. When a creditor learns that

Tips on Negotiating With Creditors

You are most vulnerable at this time. Be sure you truly understand any new loan terms and can afford to make the payments required by a new agreement.

Here are some tips that will help you in your negotiations:

- Get outside help negotiating if you need or want it.
- If you're told "no" in response to any request, ask to speak to a supervisor.
- Adopt a plan and stick with it. If you owe $1,100 but can't afford to pay more than $600, don't agree to pay more.
- Try to identify the creditor's bottom line. For example, if a bank offers to waive two months' interest if you pay the principal due on your loan, perhaps the bank will actually waive three or four months of interest. If you need to, push it.
- Don't split the difference. If you offer a low amount to settle a debt and the creditor proposes that you split the difference between a higher demand and your offer, don't agree to it. Treat the split-the-difference number as a new top and propose an amount between that and your original offer.
- Don't be intimidated by your creditors. If they think you can pay $100, they will insist that $100 is the lowest amount they can accept. Don't believe them. It's fine to hang up and call back a day later. Some of the best negotiations take weeks.
- Try to settle with a lump sum. Many creditors will settle for less than the total debt if you pay in a lump sum, but will insist on 100% if you pay over time.
- Get a signed release. If you settle for less than the full amount owed, make sure the creditor signs a release stating that your partial payment excuses you from the remaining balance.
- Be careful not to give up more than you get. A creditor may waive interest, reduce your payments, or let you skip a payment and tack it on at the end. But tread cautiously. The creditor is likely to ask for something in exchange, such as getting a cosigner (who will be liable for the debt if you don't pay, even if you erase the debt in bankruptcy), waiving the statute of limitations (the number of years the lender has to sue you if you stop making payments), paying higher interest, paying for a longer period, or giving a security interest in your house or car.

Forms for Negotiating With Creditors

No.	Form Name	Use if ...
F-8	Request Short-Term Small Payments	You need a few months to make reduced payments but then intend to resume full payments.
F-9	Request Long-Term Small Payments	You need to make reduced payments indefinitely.
F-10	Request Short-Term Pay Nothing	You can't make any payment for a few months but intend to resume full payments shortly.
F-11	Request Long-Term Pay Nothing	You've concluded that your situation is bleak and you cannot make any payment for an indefinite period.
F-12	Request Rewrite of Loan Terms	You would like the lender to rewrite the loan to permanently reduce the amount of each payment.
F-13	Offer to Give Secured Property Back	You want the lender to take the collateral back, making sure you won't owe any balance on the debt after the property is taken back.
F-14	Cashing Check Constitutes Payment in Full (Outside of California)	You live outside of California and plan to send the creditor part of what you owe with a notation on the check, "Cashing this check constitutes payment in full."
F-15 & F-16	Cashing Check Constitutes Payment in Full (California)	You live in California and want to send the creditor part of what you owe with a notation on the check, "Cashing this check constitutes payment in full." You must send two letters. The first (Form F-15) is to let the creditor know that you intend to send a check for a lesser amount in full satisfaction of the claim. To do this, the amount of the claim must be uncertain, you must dispute the amount of the claim in good faith, and you must offer the check in good faith as full satisfaction of the claim. State all of this in the first letter. Then, send a second letter (Form F-16) along with the check within a reasonable amount of time after the first—two weeks is probably reasonable, but more or less time may be reasonable in your particular situation. When you send the check, state on the front of it and in your cover letter that the check is offered as full satisfaction of the claim. Be sure to send the letters to the person, office, or place the creditor has designated for communications regarding disputed debts (often indicated in a billing statement)—or to the proper collection agent working for the creditor, if you are no longer dealing with the creditor company itself. If the creditor cashes the check and all other conditions have been met, the claim against you is discharged, *unless* the creditor proves that you did not send the check to the

No.	Form Name	Use if ...
Forms for Negotiating With Creditors (Continued)		
F-15 & F-16	Cashing Check Constitutes Payment in Full (California) (con't.)	correct person, office, or place as specified by the creditor, or *unless* the creditor repays you the amount of the check within 90 days after cashing it. (However, if the creditor did specify a person, office, or place to which you sent your communication correctly, it cannot avoid the discharge by repaying the amount of the check it cashed.)
F-17	Inform Creditor of Judgment Proof Status	You have no property that can be taken by your creditors to pay what you owe them, even if you file for bankruptcy or they sue you. (This is called being judgment proof.) You are judgment proof if your only source of income is exempt government benefits or disability, you have little or no equity in a house or car, and you have limited personal property.
F-18	Inform Creditor of Plan to File for Bankruptcy	You plan to file for bankruptcy. Incur no more charges on the account after sending the letter. If you do, you will not be able to erase those debts in bankruptcy, because the creditor will argue that you knew you were going to file and incurred debts anyway, never intending to pay.

a lawyer is in the picture, the creditor may be willing to compromise, assuming that you'll file for bankruptcy otherwise.

Unless you're judgment proof or plan to file for bankruptcy, the best overall advice is not to ignore the debt or try to hide from the creditor. Usually, the longer you put off resolving the issue, the worse the situation and consequences will become. Whether you negotiate directly with the creditor or obtain a lawyer's assistance, the best strategy almost always is to engage with the creditor.

> **CAUTION**
>
> **Be specific with the lawyer about what you want done.** If you're not clear with the lawyer that you want him or her only to write a letter to your creditors on your behalf, the lawyer may do much more and send you a bill for work you didn't authorize and can't afford, giving you one more debt to add to your pile.

Deal With Collection Agencies

If you ignored (or didn't receive) the creditor's letters and phone calls, or you failed to make payments as promised on a new repayment schedule, your bill was probably turned over to a collection agency.

In dealing with collection agencies, remember this: A person who works at a collection agency is not your friend and does not have your best interest at heart. *A collection agent wants your money.* To get it, the agent may ask you to confide in him or her regarding your personal problems. The agent may claim to be trying to save you from ruining your credit or pose as your friend and counselor. Don't believe it: A collection agent doesn't really care about your problems or your credit rating. His or her only goal is to get you to send money.

By taking some time to understand how collection agencies operate, you'll know how to respond when they contact you. Consider the following facts about collection agencies.

A collection agency takes its cues from the creditor that hired it. The collection agency can't sue you without the creditor's authorization, although that authorization is routinely granted. Similarly, if the creditor insists that the agency collect 100% of the debt, the agency cannot accept less from you, although it can agree to accept install-ment payments. To reduce the total amount you pay, the collection agency must get the creditor's okay, or you'll have to contact the creditor yourself.

Contacting the creditor directly can often be to your benefit, because the creditor has broader discretion in negotiating than the collection agency does. Unfortunately, however, some creditors won't deal with you after your debt has been sent to a collection agency, unless you raise a legitimate dispute with the creditor or make three consecutive monthly payments to the collection agency first. Even if you don't have a dispute, try negotiating with the creditor before negotiating with a collection agency. Send Form F-19, Request Direct Negotiation With Creditor, in Appendix 3 or on the CD-ROM, to the collection agency and send a copy to the creditor.

A collection agent will try to contact you very soon after the creditor hires the agency. Professional debt collectors know that the earlier they strike, the higher the chance of collecting. For example, if an account is three months overdue, bill collectors typically have a 75% chance of collecting it. If it's six months late, the chances of collecting drop to 50%. And, if the bill's been owed for more than a year, collectors have only a one in four chance of recovering the debt.

A collection agency usually keeps between 25% and 60% of what it collects. The older the account, the higher the agency's fee. Sometimes, the agency charges per letter it writes or phone call it places—usually about 50¢ per letter or $1 per call. Thus, some collection agencies are very aggressive about contacting debtors.

If you're contacted by a collection agency, you can delay collection efforts if you raise legitimate questions about the debt. For example, if you question the accuracy of the balance owed or the quality of the goods you received, the agency will have to verify the information with the creditor. If you raise a legitimate concern, the collection agency will send the debt back to the creditor—collection agencies don't pursue debtors who have a legitimate beef with creditors. Getting the debt sent back to the creditor should remove any "sent to collection agency" notation in your credit file; ask the creditor to instruct the credit bureaus to remove this notation.

Use Form F-20, Dispute Amount of Bill or Quality of Goods or Services Received, in Appendix 3 and on the CD-ROM, to raise a legitimate concern about the amount of a bill or the quality of goods or services received.

Getting a Collection Agency Off Your Back

You have the legal right to tell a collection agency to leave you alone. Simply write to the collection agency and tell it to cease all communications with you. Use Form F-21, Collection Agency: Cease All Contact, in Appendix 3 and on the CD-ROM. By law, the agency must then stop contacting you, except to tell you that:

- collection efforts against you have ended, or
- the collection agency or creditor will invoke a specific remedy against you, such as suing you.

If a collection agency contacts you to tell you that it intends to invoke a specific remedy, it must truly plan to do so. The agent cannot simply write to you several times saying "We're going to sue you" and then drop the matter.

You also can buy some time by requesting information from the collection agency. The collection agency must send you a so-called "validation notice" when it first contacts you. The validation notice tells you the amount of the debt and the name of the original creditor. It also says that you may dispute the validity of the debt or part of it within 30 days after receiving the notice; that if you don't, the agency will assume the debt is valid; that if you do dispute the debt or part of it, the agency will send you a verification of the debt; and that the agency will send you the name and address of the original creditor if you request it.

You can buy some time by sending the agency a written request for any of the following information within 30 days after you receive the validation notice:

- The name and address of the original creditor. Your request can say, "Please send me the name and address of the original creditor who claims that I owe this debt."
- Verification of the existence and amount of the debt. Your request can say, "I dispute the debt," or "I dispute this portion of the debt: _____ ."
- Verification of the existence and amount of the judgment on which the claim is based. Your request can say, "I dispute the debt represented by the judgment and request verification of the debt's existence and amount."

If you request any of this information, the agency must stop efforts to collect the debt, or any part that you dispute, until it mails you the information.

Negotiating With a Collection Agency

Although most creditors initially insist that collection agencies collect 100% of a debt, if you make a sweet enough offer, the collection agency may convince the creditor to accept less. Often, the creditor has all but given up on you and will be thrilled if the collection agency can collect anything. Knowing that, keep in mind the following:

- The collection agency didn't lay out the money initially. It doesn't care if you owe $250 or $2,500. It just wants to maximize its return, which is usually a percentage of what it collects.
- Time is money. Every time the collection agency writes or calls you, it spends money. The agency has a strong interest in getting you to pay as much as you can as fast as possible. It has less interest in collecting 100% of what you owe over five years.

Offering a Lump Sum Settlement

A collection agency has more incentive to settle with you if you can pay all at once. If you owe $500 and offer $300 on the spot to settle the matter, the agency can take its fee, pass the rest on to the creditor (who writes off the difference on its tax return as a business loss), and close its books.

If you decide to offer a lump sum, understand that no two collection agencies accept the same amount to settle a debt. Some want 75%-80%. Others—especially if they are the second or third agency to try to collect your debt—will take 50¢ on the dollar. But be careful. Once the agency sees you are willing to pay something, it will assume it can talk you into paying more. Of course, this is a good reason to start by offering less than you know you can pay.

Although you don't want to agree to pay more than what you initially decided was your top amount, if you can get the debt removed from your credit file in exchange for paying a little more, it may be worth it. But never agree to more than you can truly pay. And don't let the collection agency know where that money is coming from. If you mention a parent, friend, or distant relative who "may be able to help you out," the collection agent will sit back and wait for the entire amount.

Whatever you agree to over the phone, be sure to send a confirming letter and keep a copy for your records. The letter should state that the creditor is accepting the lump sum payment in settlement of the entire amount that you owe. You could use Form F-14, Cashing Check Constitutes Payment in Full, and describe your agreement in the blank space above "Sincerely." For example, "This check is being sent per our agreement of October 2, 2005, in which you agreed to accept $565 as payment in full for my outstanding bill." If your agreement includes getting the debt removed from your credit file, use Form F-7, Make Payment If Negative

Information Removed or Account Re-Aged, in Appendix 3 or on the CD-ROM.

Payments should be made by cashier's check or money order. Payment by personal check is less desirable, because the agency will know your account number. If you pay in cash, get a signed receipt and keep it for at least four years. Don't pay the *original creditor* unless the agency instructs you to do so in writing.

Offering to Make Payments

If you offer to make monthly payments, the agency has little incentive to compromise for less than the full amount. It still must chase you for payment, and statistics show that many debtors stop paying after a month or two. If you succeed in convincing the creditor (through the collection agency) to remove the "past due" notation in your credit file in exchange for paying off the debt or to re-age your account in agreement for paying under a new schedule (see "Deal With Creditors on Past Due Accounts," above), remember that the past due notation goes back into your file as soon as you miss a payment under your new agreement.

But if you have no choice—you simply can't afford a lump sum—offer installments. If the creditor (through the collection agency) won't remove the negative credit file notation right away, get back in touch after you've made six months of payments and again ask them to remove the notation. State that the negative marks are keeping you from getting good credit, a place to live, a good job, or anything else you've been denied, and that with better credit/place to live/job, you will be more secure and better able to pay off the debt. Be sure to keep a copy of the letter for your records.

> **CAUTION**
> **Don't offer more than you can afford.** Make sure you can afford any lump sum payment or installment arrangement that you offer. And be sure that making these payments won't keep you from paying higher-priority debts (like your mortgage).

When the Collection Agency Gives Up

If collection efforts by the collection agency fail, the creditor and agency will put their heads together and decide whether or not to pass your debt on to an attorney for collection. They will consider the following:

- the likelihood of winning
- the likelihood of collecting—whether you are currently employed or apt to become employed or have other assets from which the creditor could collect (such as a bank account or a house on which the creditor could record a lien)
- whether the contract calls for the collection of the lawyer's fees (most loan agreements and credit contracts do)—which means the collection agency can tack its lawyer's fee onto the judgment against you, and
- whether or not you recently filed for bankruptcy (you may have to wait eight years to file again).

Illegal Debt Collection Practices

The federal Fair Debt Collections Practices Act (FDCPA) prohibits a collection agency from engaging in many kinds of activities. (15 U.S.C. §§ 1692 and following.) If a collection agency violates the law, you have the right to sue both the agency and the creditor that hired the agency. If the behavior is truly outrageous, the creditor may waive the debt and remove the negative marks from your credit file in exchange for your agreement not to sue.

Under the FDCPA, a collection agency cannot legally engage in any of the following activities.

Communications with third parties. With a few exceptions, a collection agent cannot contact other people except to locate you. When contacting other people, the agent must state his or her name and that he or she is confirming or correcting location information about you. The agent cannot:

- give the collection agency's name, unless asked
- state that you owe a debt, or
- contact the person more than once unless the person requests it or the agent believes the person's first response was wrong or incomplete.

There are a few exceptions to this general rule. Collectors are allowed to contact:

- your attorney. If the collector knows you are represented by an attorney, it must only talk to the attorney, not you, unless you give it permission to contact you or you attorney doesn't respond to the collector's communications.
- a credit reporting agency, and

- the original creditor.

Collectors are also allowed to contact your spouse, your parents (only if you are a minor), and your codebtors. But collectors cannot contact these people if you have already told them (in writing) to stop contacting you.

Communications with you. A collection agent cannot contact you:

- at an unusual or inconvenient time or place—the debt collector must assume that calls before 8 a.m. and after 9 p.m. are inconvenient unless the collector knows otherwise, or
- at work, if the collector knows that your employer prohibits you from receiving collections calls at work—if you are contacted at work, tell the collector that your boss prohibits such calls.

Harassment or abuse. A collection agent cannot engage in conduct meant to harass, oppress, or abuse you. The agent cannot:

- use or threaten to use violence or harm you, another person, or your or another person's reputation or property
- use obscene or profane language
- publish your name as a person who doesn't pay bills, such as in a "deadbeats" list
- list your debt for sale to the public
- call you repeatedly, or
- place telephone calls to you or any other person without identifying him- or herself.

False or misleading representations. A collection agent cannot:

- claim to be a law enforcement officer, suggest that he or she is connected with the government, or send you a document that looks like it's from a court or government agency
- falsely represent the amount you owe, the character or legal status of the debt, or the amount of compensation the agent will receive
- falsely claim to be an attorney or send you a document that looks like it's from a lawyer
- communicate false credit information, including failing to tell someone you dispute a debt
- use a false business name
- claim to be employed by a credit bureau, unless the collection agency and the credit bureau are the same company, or
- threaten to take action that he or she does not intend to take or cannot take. For example, one creditor recently got in trouble for threatening to refer an overdue account to an attorney and file a lawsuit when it apparently never intended to do either. In that case, the creditor sent a collection letter to a debtor stating that she must make payment arrangements in five days or the matter *could* result in referral to an attorney and a lawsuit being filed. Applying the "least sophisticated debtor" test, the U.S. Court of Appeals found that it would be deceptive for the creditor to assert that it could take action it had no intention of taking and had rarely taken before. *(Brown v.*

Card Service Center, 464 F.3d 450 (3rd. Cir. 2006).)

Unfair practices. A collection agent cannot engage in any unfair or outrageous method to collect a debt. Specifically, the agent cannot:

- add interest, fees, or charges not authorized in the original agreement or by state law
- solicit a postdated check for the purpose of threatening you with criminal prosecution
- accept a check postdated by more than five days unless the agent notifies you between three and ten days in advance of when it will be deposited
- deposit a postdated check prior to the date on the check, or
- call you collect or otherwise cause you to incur communications charges.

If a Collection Agency Violates the Law

More than a few collection agencies engage in illegal practices when attempting to collect debts. Low-income and non-English speaking debtors are especially vulnerable. Some collectors send fake legal papers and visit debtors pretending to be sheriffs. The collectors tell debtors to pay immediately or threaten to take the debtors' personal possessions. Other collectors use vulgarity and profanity to threaten debtors. Another favorite tactic is to harass the debtor's parents or adult children.

If a collection agent violates the law—be it a large or small violation—complain loud and clear. If you're loud enough about the abuse you suffered—and you've got a witness backing you up—you have a chance to get the whole debt canceled in exchange for dropping the matter. Use Form F-22, Complaint About Collection Agency Harassment, in Appendix 3 and on the CD-ROM, to complain about a collection agency.

Here are some suggestions of where to send your complaint letter:

- **The creditor.** The creditor may be disturbed by the collection agency's tactics and concerned about its own reputation.
- **The Federal Trade Commission.** See Chapter 4 for addresses and phone numbers.
- **Your state consumer protection office.** See Appendix 1.

You also have the right to sue a collection agency for harassment and for violation of the FDCPA. You can represent yourself in small claims court or hire an attorney; you can recover attorney's fees and court costs if you win. You're entitled to any actual damages (including pain and suffering) and, even if you didn't suffer damages, up to $1,000 for any FDCPA violation. You might also get punitive damages if the collector's conduct was particularly horrible. To win, you'll probably need to have a witness and to produce documentation of repeated abusive behavior. If the collector calls five times in one day and then you never hear from him again, you probably don't have a case.

Some attorneys specialize in debt collection abuse cases. For a list of consumer-oriented lawyers, see the National Association of Consumer Advocates website, www.naca.net.

 RESOURCES

State debt collection laws. For more information on debt collectors—including state laws that govern collection agencies and creditors collecting their own debts—see *Solve Your Money Troubles: Get Debt Collectors Off Your Back & Regain Financial Freedom*, by Robin Leonard and John Lamb (Nolo). ∎

Cleaning Up Your Credit File

Credit bureaus are for-profit companies that gather and sell information about a person's credit history. They sell credit information on consumers to banks, mortgage lenders, credit unions, credit card companies, department stores, insurance companies, landlords, and employers. These companies and individuals use the credit information to supplement applications for credit, insurance, housing, and employment.

Credit bureaus may also provide identifying information concerning a consumer—name, address, former address, place of employment, and former place of employment—to government agencies. If a government agency is considering extending credit, reviewing the status of an account, or attempting to collect a debt, the agency is entitled to the complete credit report.

There are three major credit bureaus: Equifax (www.equifax.com), Experian (www.experian.com), and TransUnion (www.transunion.com). Recently a fourth, Innovis, has joined the scene (www.innovis .com). There are also thousands of smaller credit bureaus, known as "affiliates." Open up your yellow pages and look under "Credit Reporting Agencies." You may see none, one, two, or all three of the major credit bureaus. You will probably also see dozens of affiliates. The affiliated companies get their information from Equifax, Experian, and TransUnion, so this chapter focuses on the reports issued by those companies.

What Is in a Credit Report?

Information in your credit report can be broken down into five main categories:

- personal information about you
- accounts reported monthly
- accounts reported when in default
- public records, and
- inquiries.

Most credit reports also contain a credit score. (See Chapter 5.) Finally, some special credit reports, called investigative reports, contain even more information.

Credit reports do not contain information about race, religious preference, medical history, personal lifestyle, political preference, friends, criminal record, or other information not related to credit.

Personal Information

A credit file usually includes your name and any former names, past and present addresses, Social Security number, and employment history (including salary). Credit bureaus get this information from creditors, who get it from you every time you fill out a credit application. For this reason, it is very important that your credit applications be accurate, complete, and legible.

Whether you are married, separated, divorced, or single, your credit file should contain information about you only. Information about your spouse should appear in your file only if you are both permitted to use or obligated to pay an account. For example, information about joint accounts should appear on both spouses' credit reports.

Expanding Credit Checks

We expect credit card issuers and other lenders to conduct a credit check before approving an application. But employers? Insurance companies? What could your credit history have to do with job performance or insurability? A lot, say the companies that do preemployment and preissuance (of insurance policies) screening. In fact, tens of thousands of employers review credit reports as part of evaluating job candidates. Employers use this information to judge financial honesty and integrity, as well as the risk of bribery of people with a lot of debt. And, once you're hired, employers can use the report for just about anything related to the job, including promotion and reassignment decisions.

Federal law requires that an employer obtain your written approval before conducting a credit check. Deciding whether to authorize an employer to get your credit report leaves many employees and job applicants in a bind. If you say no, you may look like you're hiding something and be turned down for the job. If you say yes, and the employer doesn't like what it sees, you have the right to see your report and dispute any inaccuracies before being rejected for the job. (In some states, you can get a copy of your credit report at the same time the employer does.)

But what if the contents are accurate? The best you can do is claim that your problems are behind you and have little or no bearing on job performance.

Insurance companies, too, routinely check on applicants before issuing a policy. Most health and life insurers request information on your medical history—mostly about major illnesses—from the Medical Information Bureau (MIB) in Boston (www.mib.com). Other insurers are permitted to check reports, although their use is infrequent and questionable. An insurance company cannot obtain a consumer report that contains medical information without your consent.

Other specialized bureaus provide information to creditors, employers, landlords, or insurance companies. U.D. Registry and other similar companies provide information to landlords about evictions (also called unlawful detainer actions). A few companies provide check account histories (check bouncing, ATM use, debit card payment) to banks reviewing checking account applications. All of these companies are governed by the federal and state laws regulating credit bureaus.

Accounts Reported Monthly

The bulk of information in your credit file is your credit history. Certain creditors (see below) provide monthly reports to credit bureaus showing the status of your account with them. Your credit report will contain the following information on these accounts:

- name of the creditor
- type of account
- account number
- when the account was opened
- maximum credit allowed
- your payment history—that is, whether you take 30, 60, 90, or 120 days to pay; whether the account has been turned over to a collection agency; whether the account has been discharged in bankruptcy; or whether you are disputing any charges
- your credit limit or the original amount of a loan, and
- your current balance.

Creditors who provide monthly reports generally include:

- banks, savings and loans, credit unions, finance companies, and other commercial lenders that issue credit cards and make mortgage, personal, car, and student loans
- nonbank credit and charge card issuers (such as American Express, Discover, and Diner's Club)
- large department stores
- oil and gas companies, and
- other creditors receiving regular monthly installment payments.

Accounts Reported When in Default

Many businesses provide information to credit bureaus only when an account is past due or the creditor has taken collection action against you, including turning the account over to a collection agency. In these situations, your credit report will generally include the following:

- name of the creditor
- type of account
- account number, and
- your delinquency status—whether you're 60, 90, or 120 days late; whether the account has been turned over to a collection agency or you've been sued; or whether the account has been discharged in bankruptcy.

If a creditor has placed an account for collection or charged it off, the creditor must report the month and year of the delinquency—the last payment you missed—that caused the action. The creditor must report the delinquency date within 90 days of reporting the account as charged off or placed for collection. Credit bureaus use the delinquency date as the start of the seven years for which the information can remain in your file.

Creditors who generally report accounts only when they are past due or in collection include:

- landlords and property managers
- utility companies
- local retailers
- insurance companies
- magazines and newspapers
- doctors and hospitals, and
- lawyers and other professionals.

While creditors tend to report these accounts only when they are past due, credit bureaus increasingly gather monthly information from utility companies, phone companies, and local retailers to add to credit reports. The goal is to increase the data contained in files of people who don't have much traditional credit history, such as young people and immigrants.

Public Records

Public records are maintained by government agencies and are accessible to anyone. Local, state, and federal court filings are public records. So is the data kept at land records offices. Credit bureaus use private companies to search public records for information such as:

- lawsuits (including divorces and evictions)
- court judgments and judgment liens
- foreclosures
- bankruptcies
- tax liens
- mechanic's liens, and
- wage garnishments.

In addition, federal law requires child support enforcement agencies to report child support delinquencies to credit bureaus.

Inquiries

The final items in your credit report are called "inquiries." These are the names of creditors and others (such as a potential employer) who requested a copy of your report during the previous year or two.

Credit inquiries usually fall into two categories. The first category contains inquiries that show up only on the report that you see, not on the report that creditors get. There are several types of inquiries in this category, including creditors that request your credit report for promotional purposes (think of all those preapproved credit card applications you get in the mail), current creditors that review your report periodically to check up on you, and notations when you've requested a copy of your own credit report. These are often called "soft" inquiries

The second category of inquiries appears on the report sent to prospective creditors and employers (they also appear on the report you get). These inquiries—often called "hard" inquiries— consist of creditors that have requested your report after you have applied for credit with them.

Creditors don't like to see a credit report with lots of hard inquiries. It makes you look like you're desperately applying for new credit. This is why it's important to be careful when shopping for new credit. Used car dealers, in particular, often try to get you to sign a form allowing them to look at your credit report, even if you're just window-shopping. Don't agree to this until you are serious about entering into a deal. (For more on how this can affect your credit score, see "Tips for Raising Your Credit Score," in Chapter 5.)

Investigative Reports

Some special credit reports, called investigative reports, have even more information than regular credit reports.

The big difference is that they include information on your character, general reputation, personal characteristics, or mode of living, gathered from interviews with third parties such as your neighbors or friends. Because this information is personal and invasive, there are additional rules that apply to these reports.

Creditors do not usually request these investigative reports. Insurers and employers are the most likely to ask for them, but they must tell you when they request a report, and must disclose the nature and scope of the investigation upon your request. They also must have a legitimate reason to request the report. Businesses that procure employees for prospective employers (such as "headhunters") must get the consumer's consent before conducting the investigation and again before telling the employer the results.

Get a Copy of Your Credit Report

The major step in repairing your credit is cleaning up your credit report. You can't do that unless you know exactly what's in it. You start by getting a copy. Then you review it and dispute the incorrect items.

You can get your credit report by asking Equifax, Experian, TransUnion, or all three companies to send you one. (Contact information appears at the end of this section.)

Develop Good Habits

Now is the time to develop good habits. Even after you have cleaned up your credit report, you should still get a copy of your reports each year. Look for old or inaccurate information. Also check for anything that looks fishy—if someone has stolen your identity, you want to know as soon as possible. (See "Avoid Identity Theft," below, for more information.)

Getting Free Reports

The federal Fair Credit Reporting Act (FCRA) now requires each major credit bureau—Equifax, Experian, and TransUnion—to give you a free copy of your credit report once every 12 months.

You can request your free report by one of these means:

- telephone (toll-free) at 877-322-8228
- Internet at www.annualcreditreport .com, or
- mail at Annual Credit Report Service, P.O. Box 105281, Atlanta, GA 30348-5281.

You must provide your name, address, Social Security number, and date of birth when you order a report. If you have moved in the last two years, you may have to give your previous address. You also may be required to provide information that only you would know, such as the amount of your monthly mortgage payment.

Tips for Sending Letters

Throughout this chapter, we advise you to send various letters to your creditors, depending on your situation. When you send a letter, follow these guidelines:

- Type your letters or fill in the blanks of the letters in Appendix 3 or on the CD-ROM.
- Keep a copy of all correspondence for yourself.
- *Never* send originals of documents that support your claim (such as a note marked "paid" or a canceled check); send only copies and keep the originals.
- Send by certified mail, with a return receipt requested.
- If you are enclosing money, use a cashier's check or money order—not a personal check—if you have any debts in collection. Otherwise, the recipient of the check could pass your checking account number on to a debt collector, which will make it easier for the collector to grab your assets to collect the debt.
- Follow up telephone calls with a letter confirming the details of the discussion and any promises made by you or the other party.
- If you communicate with a creditor or debt collector by email, print and keep copies of all your messages and discussion chains.

You are also entitled to a free copy of your credit report if any one of the following is true:

- **You've been denied credit because of information in your credit file.** You are entitled to a free copy of your file from the bureau that reported the information. (A creditor that denies you credit in this situation will tell you the name and address of the credit bureau reporting the information that led to the denial.) You must request your copy within 60 days of being denied credit.
- **You are unemployed and planning to apply for a job within 60 days** following your request for your credit report. You must enclose a statement swearing that this is true. It might also help to include a copy of a recent unemployment check, layoff notice, or similar document verifying your unemployment. You are entitled to one free report in any 12-month period.
- **You receive public assistance.** Enclose a statement swearing that this is true and a copy of your most recent public assistance check as verification. You are entitled to one free report in any 12-month period.
- **You reasonably believe your credit file contains errors due to someone's fraud,** such as using your credit cards, Social Security number, name, or something similar. Here, too, you will need to enclose a statement swearing that this

is true. You are entitled to one free report in any 12-month period.

- **You are a victim of identity theft or fraud or think that you may be.** The FCRA gives consumers the right to request free credit reports in connection with fraud alerts.

  - If you suspect in good faith that you are, or may be, a victim of identity theft or another fraud, you can instruct the major bureaus to add a "fraud alert" to your file. You can request a free copy of your report from each bureau once it places the fraud alert in your file.

  - If you are a victim of identity theft, you can send the major bureaus an identity theft report and instruct them to add an extended fraud alert to your file. You can request two free copies of your credit report from each bureau during the next 12 months once it places the extended fraud alert in your file.

  See "Avoid Identity Theft," below, for more on identity theft and fraud alerts.

For additional copies—or if you don't qualify for a free copy—you'll have to pay a fee of up to $10. Many websites offer a free copy with a 30-day trial membership for one of their services, such as credit monitoring. If you don't want the service, be sure to cancel it within the 30 days to avoid a monthly fee. You should receive your credit report in a week to ten days.

Beware of Imposter Sites

The three major credit bureaus have set up one central website, toll-free number, and mailing address for ordering free credit reports (listed above). The only authorized website is www.annualcreditreport.com.

Other websites have similar names and advertise that they offer free credit reports, but beware. The free report often comes with strings attached, such as a service that you have to pay for when the introductory period ends, and some sites collect personal information. Don't respond to an email or click on a pop-up ad claiming it's from annualcreditreport.com: The official annualcreditreport.com website will never send you an email solicitation for your free report, use pop-up ads, or call you to ask for personal information.

Some imposter sites have names confusingly similar to annualcreditreport.com. The best way to get to the authorized website is through the Federal Trade Commission's website, www.ftc.gov.

Once you have provided the required information to annualcreditreport.com, you will be directed to the three major credit bureaus' individual websites. They may offer to sell you additional services (credit monitoring products, for example) but you are not required to purchase them to receive your free report.

Which Credit Bureaus to Use

You can request your credit report from just one or two bureaus, but it's best to get a report from all three. (You can order a three-in-one report from a bureau website for about $35.) If you've been denied credit, get a copy of your credit report from the bureau that reported the information leading to the denial. (In this era of rampant identity theft, it's very important that you check your report to be sure that it contains only information about you.) If you haven't been denied credit, request a copy from the bureau closest to where you live. If you find errors in the first credit file, obtain copies of your file from the other two bureaus.

Use Form F-23, Request Credit File, in Appendix 3 or on the CD-ROM, to request your credit file. You may have to provide the following information:

Full name. A credit bureau cannot process your request without your name. It's important that you provide your full name, including generations (Jr., Sr., III) and any other versions of your name that you use, such as "Trevor J. (aka T.J.) Williams."

Date of birth. A credit bureau may provide your report without your date (or at least year) of birth. But this information helps distinguish you from anyone else with a similar name, so you should include it.

Social Security number. Most credit bureaus require this. They use it to distinguish between people with the same or similar last names. You can instruct the bureau not to include the first five digits of your Social Security number (that is, to truncate your

Social Security number) on the report it sends you.

Spouse's name. It's not absolutely necessary, but, again, it helps distinguish you from anyone else with a similar name.

Telephone number. You may not get your report if you don't include your telephone number. You may hesitate to include it, knowing that bill collectors can get it by getting a copy of your credit file. But, unless it's unlisted, they can also get it from directory assistance, a reverse directory, or an Internet "people finder" service. If you're trying to repair your credit, you will want to make sure your phone number is in your file. It is one sign of stability your future creditors look for.

Current address. You won't get a copy of your credit report if you don't include your address.

Previous addresses. Credit bureaus ask for this if you've been at your current address fewer than two to five years. Again, it helps distinguish you from other people with similar names. If you don't want the bureau to have this information, you can leave it off, but your request may be rejected.

Your signature. You must sign the letter.

Credit bureaus are trying to move away from paper requests for credit reports by encouraging people to order through their websites. If you prefer not to order over the Internet, the bureau may have a toll-free number (Experian, for example) or may accept written requests (Equifax, for example). Check each bureau's requirements on its website.

Credit Bureau Contact Information

Equifax
P.O. Box 740241
Atlanta, GA 30374
800-685-1111
www.equifax.com

Experian
888-397-3742
www.experian.com

TransUnion
877-322-8228
www.transunion.com

Review Your Credit Report

Review your report carefully. One of the biggest problems with credit files is that they contain incorrect or out-of-date information. In a recent investigation by the U.S. Public Interest Research Group, more than 70% of the credit reports contained an error.

Sometimes credit bureaus confuse names, addresses, Social Security numbers, or employers. If you have a common name—say, John Brown—your file may contain information on other John Browns, John Brownes, or Jon Browns. Your file may erroneously contain information on family members with similar names.

Ironically, concern over identity theft (see "Avoid Identity Theft," below) contributes to mistakes in credit reports. Businesses now ask consumers for minimal identifying information when they open accounts, to avoid inadvertently making that information available to thieves. The unintended consequence of not including a full Social Security number or a date of birth in a reported consumer transaction or delinquency is that it's easier than ever for a credit bureau to confuse one consumer for another. It's also common for bureaus to fail to note accounts in which delinquencies have been remedied.

Review Sample Credit Reports

Before you order your credit reports from Experian, TransUnion, and Equifax, you may want to review each bureau's sample credit report to familiarize yourself with its layout and contents. The presentation of information varies considerably among the bureaus' reports.

To find each bureau's sample report, use the following instructions:

- **Experian.** Go to www.experian.com. Select "Personal Services," then select "Credit Education" at the bottom of the page. Choose "Credit Report Basics," then "Your Credit Report." Scroll down to the bottom of the page and click "View a sample Experian credit report."
- **TransUnion.** Go towww.transunion. com. Under the heading "Learning Center," select "True Credit Learning Center." Choose "How to read your credit report" on the right side of the page.
- **Equifax.** Go to the website www .equifax.com. Under the "Products" tab at the top of the page, click on

"Equifax Credit Report." Looking at the middle of the page, scroll down until you see the link "Sample Credit Report," and click on it.

The sample reports provide explanations of their contents and are supplemented by educational materials. However, their descriptions of the dispute resolution process are lacking. Here's what else you should know.

Under the FCRA, you have the right to dispute the accuracy or *completeness* of *any* item in your file, not just inaccurate information. This distinction can be important. For example, your credit report might state accurately that a creditor sued you. Yet this information might be incomplete because you later paid the debt or are not actually liable for it. You can dispute the information about the lawsuit because it is incomplete.

Each bureau's materials encourage consumers to submit their disputes online. However, you may have documents that support your position (for example, a canceled check, a note marked "paid," a statement with a zero balance, or a letter abandoning a claim). When you dispute an item, the bureau must review and consider all relevant information that you provide in a timely manner and must forward this information to the creditor that provided the information. Submitting your dispute online may work for some kinds of disputes, but, as a general rule, disputes that involve documentation should be handled by mail.

If the investigation shows that the disputed information is inaccurate, *incomplete,* or *cannot be verified*, the bureau must delete the information from your file or modify it so that it is correct. The bureau also must notify the creditor of the action taken. Under the FCRA, the entire investigation process must be free for consumers. (15 U.S.C. § 1681i.) (Disputing information and adding a statement to your file if the dispute isn't resolved to your satisfaction are both covered below.)

Also, the sample reports and supplemental materials don't mention what to do if you find inaccurate information in your report that is due to fraud. See "Avoid Identity Theft," below, for help.

Combined Reports

Experian, TransUnion, and Equifax offer "combined" or "3-in-1" credit reports. As the name suggests, these reports combine information from all three bureaus into one report. Because your creditors report to different credit bureaus, each bureau's report on you will vary. A combined report can show you the differences in the information each bureau has on you.

If you're planning to make a major purchase (like a house or a car) or a major financial commitment (like an equity line on your home), you may consider buying a combined report. But the $35 (or so) it costs may not be worth it because you can get a free copy of your credit report from each of the major credit bureaus. While a combined report may make it easier to spot differences in the bureaus' information on you, you can accomplish the same thing using free reports and a little study.

Whatever approach you choose, you should definitely check your credit information at all three bureaus as far in advance as possible. This gives you the opportunity to try to add missing information (covered below), and dispute incomplete or inaccurate information. That way, no matter which bureau your lender uses, your credit file looks as good as possible. Or, if your lender purchases a combined report from a reseller, the information provided by the three major bureaus is as consistent and favorable as possible. (A reseller is a credit bureau that assembles and merges information from other bureaus into a single report for use by a third party, often a mortgage lender.)

How Long Items Can Stay in a Credit Report

Once a credit bureau gathers information about you, it can report that information (that is, include it in a credit report) as follows:

- Bankruptcies may be reported for no more than ten years after the date of the last activity. The date of the last activity for most bankruptcies is the date you receive your discharge or the date your case is dismissed.
- Lawsuits and judgments may be reported from the date of the entry of judgment against you for up to seven years or until the governing statute of limitations has expired, whichever is longer.
- Paid tax liens may be reported from the date of payment for up to seven years.

- Most criminal records, such as information about indictments or arrests, may be reported for only seven years. But records of criminal convictions may be reported indefinitely. (Experian's website states that it does not collect or report criminal record information. The same appears to be true for Equifax and TransUnion, although their websites are not explicit on this point.)
- Accounts sent to collection (within the creditor company or to a collection agency), accounts charged off, or any other similar action may be reported for up to seven years. The seven-year period begins 180 days after the delinquency (the last missed payment) that led to the collection activity or charge-off. A creditor has 90 days to notify the credit bureau of the date of the delinquency once it has reported that an account has been placed for collection or charged off. The clock does not start ticking again if the account is sold to another collection agency, you make a payment on it, or you file a dispute with the credit bureau.
- Overdue child support may be reported for seven years.
- Some adverse information regarding student loans guaranteed or insured by the U.S. government, or national direct student loans, may be reported for more than seven years.
- Bankruptcies, lawsuits, paid tax liens, accounts sent out for collection, criminal records, overdue child

support, and any other adverse information may be reported beyond the usual time limits if you apply for $150,000 or more of credit or life insurance, or if you apply for a job with an annual income of at least $75,000. As a practical matter, however, credit bureaus usually delete all items after seven or ten years.

Laws Regulating Credit Bureaus

Credit bureaus are regulated by the Federal Trade Commission under the provisions of the Federal Fair Credit Reporting Act (FCRA). (15 U.S.C. §§ 1681 and following.) The FCRA is designed to bar inaccurate or obsolete information from appearing in credit reports. Recent amendments to the FCRA have addressed the accuracy of information in credit transactions and identity theft. The Act requires credit bureaus to adopt reasonable procedures for gathering, maintaining, and distributing information and sets accuracy standards for creditors that provide information to bureaus. The FCRA also regulates who can access credit reports. Most states have passed similar laws.

Appendix 2 contains the text of the FCRA. To get a copy of your state law governing credit bureaus, contact your state consumer protection agency (listed in Appendix 1).

Review Your Report

As you read through your credit report, make a list of everything that is inaccurate, incomplete, or not authorized to be in your file. In particular, look for the following:

- incorrect or incomplete name, address, or phone number
- incorrect Social Security number or birthdate
- incorrect, missing, or outdated employment information
- incorrect marital status—such as a former spouse listed as your current spouse
- bankruptcies that are more than ten years old or not identified by the specific chapter of the bankruptcy code
- lawsuits or judgments reported beyond seven years or beyond the expiration of the statute of limitations
- paid tax liens or criminal records more than seven years old, or delinquent accounts that are more than seven years old or that do not include the date of the delinquency
- overdue child support that is more than seven years old
- other adverse information that is more than seven years old
- credit inquiries by automobile dealers from times you simply test drove a car or from other businesses when you were only comparison shopping (such creditors cannot lawfully pull your credit report without your permission until you indicate a desire to enter into a sale or lease)

- commingled accounts—credit histories for someone with a similar or the same name
- duplicate accounts—for example, a debt is listed twice, once under the creditor and a second time under a collection agency
- premarital debts of your current spouse attributed to you
- lawsuits you were not involved in
- incorrect account histories—such as a late payment notation when you've paid on time or a debt shown as past due when it's been discharged in bankruptcy
- voluntary surrender of your vehicle listed as a repossession
- paid tax, judgment, mechanic's, or other liens listed as unpaid
- paid accounts listed as unpaid
- a missing notation when you disputed a charge on a credit card bill
- accounts that incorrectly list you as a cosigner
- closed accounts incorrectly listed as open—it may look as if you have too much open credit, and
- accounts you closed that don't indicate "closed by consumer"—it looks like your creditors closed the accounts.

Dispute Incomplete and Inaccurate Information

Under the Fair Credit Reporting Act, you have the right to dispute all incomplete or inaccurate information in your credit file. Once the credit bureau receives your letter, it must reinvestigate the items you dispute and record the current status of the disputed information or delete it within 30 days. (45 days if you send the bureau additional relevant information during the 30-day period).

These requirements are not hard for a credit bureau to meet. Credit bureaus and more than 6,000 of the nation's creditors are linked by computer, which speeds up the verification process. Furthermore, if you let a credit bureau know that you're trying to obtain a mortgage or car loan, it can often do a "rush" verification.

If the credit bureau cannot verify the information in dispute, it must remove it. Credit bureaus might remove an item on request without an investigation if rechecking the item is more bother than it's worth. If the bureau finds that the information is inaccurate or incomplete, it must remove the information or modify it based on the results of the investigation. Requesting an investigation won't cost you anything.

Once you've compiled a list of all incomplete and inaccurate information you want corrected or removed, complete the "request for reinvestigation" form which was enclosed with your credit report. If the bureau did not enclose such a form, use Form F-24, Request Reinvestigation, in Appendix 3 or on the CD-ROM or use the bureau's own dispute form (check its website). Don't simply handwrite a letter. Handwritten letters on plain paper often are given minimal attention.

Incorrect information does not have to be negative to be challenged. It is enough that the information is incomplete or inaccurate.

Below are some examples of the types of responses you might include on Form F-24.

☒ The following personal information about me is incorrect:

Erroneous Information	Correct Information
Spouse: Morton Lyle	I divorced Morton Lyle on
	8/23/00. I'm now married to
	Brian Jones.

☒ The following accounts are not mine:

Creditor's Name	Account Number	Explanation
Dept. of Education	123456789	Premarital debt
		of my husband
		Brian Jones.
Strong's Dept. Store	0987654321	I've never had a
		Strong's account.

☒ The account status is incorrect for the following accounts:

Creditor's Name	Account Number	Correct Status
Big Bank	1234 5678 9012	Discharged in
MasterCard		bankruptcy;
		balance owed
		is $0.

☒ The following inquiries were not authorized:

Creditor's Name	Date of Inquiry	Explanation
Wowza Bank Visa	2/14/01	I did not apply
		for credit
		with Wowza Bank
		nor authorize them
		to conduct a credit
		check of me.

☒ Other incorrect information:

Explanation

(1) My credit report states that I filed a Chapter 13 bankruptcy on July 23, 200x. That is not correct. In fact, I filed a Chapter 7 case and received a discharge of my debts on October 19, 200x.

(2) American Express account is listed twice—one listing indicates the account was discharged in bankruptcy (this is correct); the other listing shows the account with Tenacious Collection Services (incorrect). Furthermore this account is missing the date of delinquency.

Send your letter to the address provided by the credit bureau for disputing information (keep a copy for your records). Also, enclose copies of any documents you have that support your claim. It may help to include a copy of your credit report with the disputed items highlighted. Keep your original documents.

Soon, rather than asking the credit bureau to investigate inaccurate information, you will be able to ask the creditor that furnished the information to investigate it. The Federal Trade Commission is developing regulations to define when a consumer can dispute inaccurate information directly with the furnishing creditor. The creditor will have 30 days to complete its investigation and send the consumer the results (45 days if the consumer sent it additional information). When information is found to be inaccurate, the creditor will have to provide corrected information to each bureau that received the incorrect information.

In any event, it's always a good idea to send a copy of your letter to the creditor who furnished the incorrect or incomplete information to the credit bureau. These "furnishing" creditors have a duty to correct and update information they send to credit bureaus that they determine is inaccurate or incomplete.

If you don't hear from the credit bureau within 30 (or 45) days, send a follow-up letter using Form F-25, Request Follow-Up After Reinvestigation, in Appendix 3 or on the CD-ROM. Send a copy of your letter to the Federal Trade Commission (addresses are listed below), the agency that oversees credit bureaus. Again, keep a copy for your records.

Once the credit bureau receives your request for reinvestigation, it must:

- complete its investigation within 30 days of receiving your complaint (45 days if the bureau receives relevant information from you during the 30-day period)
- contact the creditor reporting the information you dispute within five business days of receiving your dispute

- review and consider all relevant information submitted by you, and
- provide you with the results of its reinvestigation within five business days of completion, including a revised credit report if any changes were made.

The bureau is not required to investigate any dispute that it determines is frivolous or irrelevant because, for example, you don't provide enough information to investigate the dispute. Once the bureau makes a determination, it has five business days to notify you of what it decided and why.

If the credit bureau cannot verify the information in the report or agrees that the information is inaccurate or incomplete, the bureau must modify the information or remove it from your file. The bureau also must inform the furnishing creditor that the information has been modified or deleted.

You can ask the bureau to notify past users that inaccurate or unverifiable information has been deleted from the report. But, the credit bureau will only do this if you ask. And, even then, it is only required to send notice to anyone who requested your report within the previous six months, or two years if requested for employment purposes.

Even if the credit bureau agrees that the information is incorrect and fixes it, don't assume that the negative information will be permanently eliminated from your report. The bureaus are required to have procedures to keep incorrect information from reappearing, but, unfortunately, those procedures often fail. To make sure the errors stay out of your report, you should do all of the following:

- Obtain another copy of your credit report three to six months later to confirm that the corrections still appear.
- Check to see whether your credit reports at the other major credit bureaus contain the same error, and, if so, send the results of your successful investigation from the first credit bureau to the others.
- After three to six months, get another copy of your report from the first credit bureau and check to see whether the information has reappeared.

If the credit bureau responds that the creditor reporting the information verified its accuracy and completeness, and that, therefore, the information will remain in your file, you will need to take more aggressive action to clean up your credit report. This may be frustrating and time-consuming.

Here are some ideas to help you in your efforts to fix your credit file.

Contact the creditor associated with the incorrect information and demand that it tell the credit bureau to remove the information. Write to the customer service department, vice president of marketing, and president or CEO. If the information was reported by a collection agency, send the agency a copy of your letter, too. Use Form F-26, Request Removal of Incorrect Information by Creditor, in Appendix 3 or on the CD-ROM, to make your request. Be sure to keep a copy of your letter and your original documentation. If the creditor is local, pay a visit. Sit down in the office of the customer service department, vice president of marketing, or president or CEO. Do not leave until someone agrees to meet with you and hear your problem. *Remember: You have the right to demand attention; this creditor has verified incorrect information and it should be removed from your credit report.*

Under the Fair Credit Reporting Act, creditors who report information to credit bureaus must do the following:

- not report incorrect information when they learn that the information is, in fact, incorrect
- provide credit bureaus with correct information when they learn that the information they have been reporting is incorrect
- notify credit bureaus when you dispute information
- note when accounts are "closed by the consumer"
- provide credit bureaus with the month and year of the delinquency of all accounts placed for collection, charged off, or similarly treated, and
- finish their investigation of your dispute within the 30- or 45-day periods the credit bureau must complete its investigation.

(The full text of the FCRA is included in Appendix 2.)

If you get a letter from the creditor agreeing that the information is incorrect and should be removed from your credit file, send a copy of the creditor's letter to the credit bureau that reported the information. Use Form F-27, Creditor Verification, in Appendix 3 or on the CD-ROM.

If a creditor cannot or will not assist you in removing the incorrect information, call the credit bureau directly. Credit bureaus have toll-free numbers to handle consumer disputes about incorrect items in their credit files that are not removed via the normal reinvestigation process. Use the credit bureau's toll-free number (see "Credit Bureau Contact Information," above).

You may be able to sue if you were seriously harmed by the credit bureau—for example, it continued to give out incomplete or inaccurate information after you requested corrections. The FCRA lets you sue a credit bureau for negligent or willful noncompliance with the law within two years after the bureau's harmful behavior first occurred. In some very limited circumstances, you may have more than two years to sue. You can sue for "actual damages," including court costs, attorney's fees, lost wages, and, if applicable, defamation and intentional infliction of emotional distress. In the case of truly outrageous behavior, you can recover "punitive damages" meant to punish malicious or willful conduct. Under the FCRA, the court decides the amount of the punitive damages.

You may also be able to sue the creditor that supplied the inaccurate information. However, these types of lawsuits are complicated, and the FCRA provides creditors with many ways to avoid liability. You will need to consult a lawyer if you want to pursue this type of lawsuit.

If all else fails, consider calling your congressional representative or senator. He or she can call the FTC and demand some action.

RESOURCES

To complain about a credit bureau. You can file a complaint against a credit bureau with the Federal Trade Commission using its online form. Go to www.ftc.gov/ftc/bcppriv.htm and select "File a Complaint." You can also contact the FTC by phone (877-382-4357) or mail:

FTC Consumer Response Center
CRC-240
600 Pennsylvania Ave., NW
Washington, DC 20580

Add Information to Your Report

In addition to disputing incorrect information, you can also add information to your report that makes you look more creditworthy. There are three types of information you may want to add:

- positive account histories that are missing from your report
- information demonstrating your stability, and
- explanations of any incomplete or disputed information in your report.

<table>
<tr><td>

Sample Statements

Here are a few examples of statements describing disputes:

- A credit report includes a lawsuit filed by a roofing company for failure to pay for its work. The information is accurate, but the consumer didn't pay because the work was done incorrectly. The consumer might add a statement to the file reading, "Defective workmanship, refuse to pay until fixed."

- A credit report indicates that a consumer is unemployed, but the consumer has in fact worked as an independent contractor during that time. The consumer might send a statement reading, "I work as a freelance technical writer, averaging $50,000 annually."

- A credit report states that the consumer owes a debt to an electronics store. The consumer bought a CD player that doesn't work, and the store refused to take it back or provide a refund. The consumer might submit this statement, "Merchandise is defective, and the store refuses to provide a refund or replacement."

</td></tr>
</table>

Positive Account Histories

Often, credit reports don't include accounts that you might expect to find. Some major commercial lenders don't report mortgages or car loans. Local banks or credit unions often don't provide information to credit bureaus.

If your credit file is missing credit histories for accounts you pay on time, send the credit bureaus a copy of a recent account statement and copies of canceled checks (never originals) showing your payment history. Ask the credit bureaus to add the information to your file. While the bureaus aren't required to add account histories, they often do—but may charge you a fee for doing so. Use Form F-28, Request Addition of Account Histories, in Appendix 3 or on the CD-ROM, to make your request.

It may be that credit histories for accounts you pay on time are missing from only one or two credit reports—the third report may have included all accounts when you received it, or you may have focused on cleaning up that report first. In this situation, try sending the bureaus that aren't reporting the information a copy of your credit report that includes all your accounts, with a cover letter asking that the missing information be included in your file. You can modify Form F-28 in Appendix 3 for this purpose.

Information Showing Stability

Creditors like to see evidence of stability in your file. If any of the items listed below are missing from your file, consider sending a letter to the credit bureaus asking that the information be added. Use form F-29, Request Addition of Information Showing Stability, in Appendix 3 or on the CD-ROM, to make your request.

You may want to add:

- **Your current employment,** including your current employer's name and address and your job title. You may wisely decide not to add this if you think a creditor may sue you or a creditor has a judgment against you. Current employment information may be a green light for a wage garnishment.
- **Your previous employment,** especially if you've had your current job fewer than two years. Include your former employer's name and address and your job title.
- **Your current residence,** and, if you own it, say so. (Not all mortgage lenders report their accounts to credit bureaus.) Again, don't do this if you've been sued or you think a creditor may sue you. Real estate is an excellent collection source.
- **Your previous residence,** especially if you've lived at your current address fewer than two years.
- **Your telephone number,** especially if it's unlisted. If you haven't yet given the credit bureaus your phone number, consider doing so now. A creditor who cannot verify a telephone number is often reluctant to grant credit.
- **Your date of birth.** A creditor will probably not grant you credit if it does not know your age. However, creditors also cannot discriminate against you based on your age. (See Chapter 6.)
- **Your Social Security number.**

Credit bureaus aren't required to add any of this information, but they often do. They are most likely to add information on jobs and residences, as that information is used by creditors in evaluating applications for credit. They will also add your telephone number, date of birth, and Social Security number, because those items help identify you and lessen the chances of "mixed" credit files—that is, getting other people's credit histories in your file. (Expect to pay a small fee when a credit bureau adds information to your file.)

Enclose any documentation that verifies information you're providing, such as copies (never originals) of your driver's license, a canceled check, a bill addressed to you, or a pay stub showing your employer's name and address. Remember to keep photocopies of all correspondence.

Explanatory Statements

If the credit bureau's investigation doesn't resolve the dispute to your satisfaction, you have the right to file a brief statement about the dispute. The bureau must include your statement, or a summary or codification of it, in any report that includes the disputed information. If the reporting agency helps you write the summary, the statement will be limited to one hundred words. Otherwise, there is no word limit, but it is a good idea to keep the statement very brief.

The credit bureau is required to provide only a summary or codification of your statement (not your actual statement) to anyone who requests your file. If your statement is short, the credit bureau is more likely to pass on your statement, unedited. If your statement is long, the credit bureau will probably condense your explanation to just a few sentences or codes. To avoid this problem, keep your statement clear and concise.

If you request it, the bureau must also give the statement or summary to anyone who received a copy of your file within the past six months—or two years if your file was given out for employment purposes. This service is free if you request it within 30 days after the bureau gave you notice of the results of the investigation. Otherwise, you will have to pay the same amount as the bureau would normally charge for a credit report (up to $10).

Credit bureaus are only required to include a statement in your file if you are disputing the completeness or accuracy of a particular item. The bureau does not have to include a statement if you are only explaining extenuating circumstances or other reasons why you haven't been able to pay your debts. If the bureau does allow you to add such a statement, it can charge you a fee.

Don't assume that adding a brief statement is the best approach. It's often wiser to simply explain the negative mark to subsequent creditors in person than to try to explain it in such a short statement. Many statements or summaries are simply ineffective. Few creditors who receive credit files read them, and credit scoring programs ignore these statements. In any David (consumer) vs. Goliath (credit bureau) dispute, creditors tend to believe Goliath.

Avoid Identity Theft

Identity theft is a growing national epidemic. The Federal Trade Commission has said that identity theft has nearly 10 million victims each year, costs to businesses of $52 billion, and costs to consumers of nearly $5 billion. The sad truth is that the Internet and its vast collections of easily accessible personal data make identity theft a simple and tantalizing endeavor for the criminally inclined. Contributing to the problem are businesses without stringent privacy policies and corporate and government mistakes in handling sensitive customer information. Incidents of computers and storage devices loaded with personal information being stolen, sensitive databases being compromised, information-rich files being left unsecured in garbage bins, and credit slips left unshredded are common—and even unsavvy thieves know it.

Unfortunately, local police agencies are ill-equipped to handle these sophisticated crimes, which often cross state borders. From a police perspective, identity theft is a silent crime. It just doesn't merit the priority of crimes like murder, robbery, and other violent crimes more easily reported and televised. District attorneys are in a similar bind. Reelection is secured by winning big verdicts in publicity-generating cases.

But times are changing. Federal and state law enforcement agencies are taking the problem more seriously, especially now that the FBI has declared identity theft as the fastest-growing white collar crime in the country.

What's in a Stolen Name?

A lot. A thief can obtain a loan, open credit accounts and max them out, rent an apartment, buy a car, purchase a cell phone, talk to someone in China all day, and, worse—commit a serious crime—all using your name.

Financially, if a credit card in your name is used in a credit scam, you'll likely be responsible for only $50, or possibly nothing, because of federal laws capping your liability for unauthorized use of your card. (See Chapter 3.) But the financial burdens may be the least of your worries. You may spend months hassling with credit agencies, financial institutions, and police departments trying to clear your name and repair the lingering damage. You may have to take time off from work to write letters, make calls, collect evidence, and demand action.

And who knows what it will take to repair the anxiety and mental suffering you'll endure. Typically, victims of identity theft report that police agencies are often dismissive or even abusive, credit reporting agencies unresponsive,

collection agencies hostile, and creditors disbelieving. Psychological scarring can be severe. Some victims liken the experience to feeling physically assaulted; continued sleep disturbances, paranoia, and other post-traumatic stress symptoms are not uncommon.

How Can an Identity Be Stolen?

In a word—easily. Here are some typical ways in which thieves gather information about you:

- stealing wallets or mail
- filling out a change of address form using your name and collecting your mail
- snatching preapproved credit offers from the trash, recycling bin, or mailbox
- ordering unauthorized credit reports on you by posing as a potential employer, landlord, or even you
- illegal computer tapping by a dishonest employee at a business where you have provided information or been granted credit
- looking over your shoulder at phones and ATMs to gather PIN numbers, sometimes with binoculars, listening devices, cell phones, or mini-cameras
- breaking into computer systems and searching for people with good credit
- using phony telemarketing schemes to con you into giving them your personal data
- using personal information you shared on the Internet

- a former friend, lover, roommate, or coworker with a grudge gathering sensitive information and using it in an attempt to extract revenge (a more common occurrence than most people realize), and

- a family member who steals another family member's identity to get access to credit or to try to avoid arrest or debt.

Perhaps the most frightening—and most thorough—way to steal your identity is by purchasing your Social Security number, mother's maiden name, home and employment address, previous addresses, credit history, and more for just a few dollars from one of the identity search companies on the Internet.

It's also unsettling to learn that supposedly secure electronic repositories of personal information can be easily compromised. The media have reported that computers and storage devices belonging to the federal government and containing personal information on millions of people have been stolen. In the private sector, data brokers' huge databases, with billions of files, have been compromised by criminals, according to published reports. Because of a California law that requires notification of security breaches, many thousands of Californians and others have received notices that these databases were breached. (Since these breaches, several other states have enacted security breach notification laws.)

If you think that your identity has been compromised by an event like this, consider taking the steps described in "If Your Identity Is Stolen," below.

How to Protect Yourself

You must guard your personal information assiduously. Here are some tips for keeping your private information secure:

- Do not routinely carry your Social Security card, birth certificate, or passport.

- Don't leave outgoing bill payments in your mailbox for the postman to pick up.

- Keep changing your passwords and PIN numbers. Don't use obvious codes such as birthdays or spouse's, children's, or pet's names. Memorize passwords and shred any piece of paper where they are written.

- Diligently review credit card statements and phone and utility bills. Get a copy of all of your credit reports at least once a year. Promptly challenge any inaccurate information.

- Always take your credit card, debit card, and ATM receipts, and don't throw them away in public.

- Tear up or shred any item with personal information on it, as well as any offers of preapproved credit cards you don't intend to use. Also, beware of offers from companies you don't recognize. It's easy to create an official-looking and completely phony credit application offering you preapproved credit if you provide your Social Security number, mother's maiden name, and a signature.

- Buy a shredder and use it religiously.
- Don't give personal information over the phone unless absolutely necessary, and never give it unless you initiated the phone call.
- Beware of anyone asking for your Social Security number. If a company refuses to complete a transaction without it, consider taking your business elsewhere.
- Beware of requests to obtain or update personal information that appear to come from a research firm or a company or financial institution that you do business with. Legitimate businesses hardly ever contact customers for this purpose. Any such request, whether by phone or over the Internet, most likely is from a scammer who wants to steal your personal information. If you feel you must respond, first call the firm's toll-free number (printed on a statement or receipt), or go to its correct Web address, to verify that the request is legitimate. A current Internet scam called "phishing" uses spam email or pop-up messages to trick you into disclosing personal or financial information. The message appears to be from a firm that you do business with and directs you to a phony website that looks legitimate. The FTC advises not to respond to these messages by clicking on the reply button or link provided. Instead, call the firm using a number you know to be legitimate, or begin a new Internet browser session and go to the firm's correct Web address. Do not cut and paste the link in the message.
- The FTC advises never to send personal or financial information by email. Email is not a secure method of transmitting this kind of information.
- Be alert to signs that your identity has been compromised, such as bills that do not arrive as expected, unexpected credit cards or account statements, denials of credit for no apparent reason, or calls or letters about purchases you did not make.
- Pick up your new checks from the bank instead of having them sent to your home. Do not have your Social Security or driver's license number printed on your checks.
- Don't put your personal information on any computer home page or personal computer profile. Provide as little personal and credit information as possible in Internet transactions. Never provide personal or financial information unless the site is secure (for example, look for a security symbol such as an unbroken padlock in the corner of the screen, a Web browser that includes an "s," such as "https://," or the words "Secure Sockets Layer (SSL)" in the browser or firm's privacy statement).
- If you find your personal information somewhere on the Internet, demand that it be removed.

It is also important to learn more about what happens to the personal information you provide to companies, marketers, and government agencies. These organizations may use your personal information to promote their own products and services, or they may share it with others.

Many companies and organizations allow you to "opt out" of having your information shared with others or used for promotional purposes. Opting out will help keep some of your information private and less vulnerable to identity theft. You can find out more about your opt out choices from the Federal Trade Commission, www.ftc.gov. The national credit bureaus have a toll-free number (888-567-8688) and a website (www.optoutprescreen .com) through which you can opt out of receiving offers of credit and insurance that you did not request (so-called prescreened offers that are based on information in your credit report).

Privacy-conscious consumers pay attention to the "privacy notices" that businesses send them when they open accounts. These consumers opt out of every use of their personal information possible under the business's privacy policy. Doing this reduces the distribution of the consumer's personal information somewhat and also cuts down the number of offers and solicitations that the consumer receives.

In some states, you can instruct the credit bureau to place a "security freeze" or "file freeze" in your credit file. A security freeze is a notice in your file that prohibits the credit bureau from releasing your credit report or information in it without your consent. You can "unfreeze" your file for a period of time or to allow a specific creditor to access your file.

Security freezes currently are available in California, Colorado, Connecticut, Delaware, Florida, Hawaii, Illinois, Kansas, Kentucky, Louisiana, Maine, Minnesota, Nevada, New Hampshire, New Jersey, New York, North Carolina, Oklahoma, Rhode Island, South Dakota, Texas, Utah, Vermont, Washington, and Wisconsin. Security freezes are different than the initial, extended, and military alerts that the Fair Credit Reporting Act now makes available (see "If Your Identity Is Stolen," below).

You should carefully consider the pros and cons of a security freeze. Consumer advocates favor them if you are worried about identity theft, while the credit bureaus favor their own credit monitoring services. As a practical matter, having a security freeze can delay your own applications for credit, and removing a freeze can be cumbersome.

Protecting Your Social Security Number

One good way to minimize the risk of identity theft is to be very careful about giving out your Social Security number (SSN). Many people think they have to provide their SSN to creditors or government entities that ask for it. But this isn't always true—in some cases, you don't have to reveal it.

All government agencies that request your SSN must give you a form explaining whether the information is mandatory or optional. For many government agencies, including tax authorities, welfare offices, and state Departments of Motor Vehicles, your SSN is mandatory. But it isn't always mandatory. If it isn't, the government cannot deny you a benefit or service due to your refusal to disclose your SSN.

Employers, as well as most banks, can require that you disclose your SSN. But you are usually not required to give your SSN to private businesses. Sometimes businesses have a legitimate reason to ask for your number (for example, when you apply for credit), but, in other cases, they simply want it for general record keeping. You don't have to give a business your SSN just because they request it. Ask these questions before deciding whether to give out your number:

- Why do you need my number?
- How will my number be used?
- What law requires me to give you my number?
- What will happen if I don't give you my number?
- Can I give you an identifier other than my SSN, or just the last four digits of my SSN?
- Can my account be set up so that I can use an identifier other than my SSN (for example, a combination of letters from my last name and numbers)?

If you're filling out a form and decide not to provide your SSN, you can leave the space blank or write "refused."

But understand that a business can refuse to serve you if you don't disclose your SSN. In some situations, you may want to disclose the number to avoid hassles down the road. In other situations, you may want to take your business elsewhere.

It's a good idea to check your Social Security earnings and benefits statement each year to be sure that no one else is using your Social Security number for employment. You should receive this statement automatically each year if you have worked and are 25 or older. If the statement shows that someone else is using your Social Security number for employment, contact the Social Security Administration's fraud hotline (800-269-0271) immediately.

If you're already a victim of identity theft, consider getting a new SSN. This isn't easy. The Social Security Administration will only change your number if you fit their definition of "fraud victim." Even if you do fit within the definition, think carefully before you apply for a new SSN. A new SSN will not ensure a clean credit report, because credit bureaus may combine the credit records from your old SSN with your new records. For more information, check out the Federal Trade Commission's website at www.ftc.gov and the Social Security Administration's website at www.ssa.gov. At the very least, contact the Social Security Administration to report any fraudulent use of your SSN.

If Your Identity Is Stolen

Minimizing the disaster of identity theft depends primarily on your vigilant and constant efforts to guard your personal identification privacy, and thus be aware as quickly as possible that you've been the victim of an intrusion. As soon as you are aware of the problem, do the following:

- **File a police report and obtain a copy.** You will probably need to send copies to creditors, collection agencies, credit bureaus, banks, and the like.

- **Call each of the nationwide credit bureaus and get copies of your credit report.** Request that the credit reports be free because you believe they contain inaccurate information due to fraud. Check each report carefully when you receive it. Look for accounts that you didn't apply for or open, inquiries that you didn't initiate, and defaults and delinquencies that you didn't cause. Also, check your identifying information carefully.

- **Request that each credit bureau block the reporting of identity theft-related information on your report.** You must send the bureau proof of your identity and an "identity theft report"—an official report you have filed with a federal, state, or local law enforcement agency plus any additional information the bureau may require. You must identify the fraudulent information and include a statement that the information does not relate to any transaction by you. The bureau normally must block reporting of the information and must inform the creditor that provided the information that it has been blocked. The creditor cannot then sell, transfer, or place the debt for collection. (This is one practical reason to check your credit report and request the blocking of identity theft-related information as

soon as you learn that you may be the victim of identity theft.)

- **Contact your creditors, phone companies, utilities, and banks to find out if any of your accounts have been tampered with or if any new accounts have been opened in your name.** Ask to speak with someone in the security or fraud department, and follow up with a confirming letter. Immediately close any accounts that have been tampered with. Some advocate also closing accounts that haven't yet been affected on the theory that it's just a matter of time before the thief gets to those, too. But, before you do so, think carefully. You may have trouble getting new credit until the problems related to the identity theft are cleared. Instead, you could notify the creditors of unaffected accounts that you have been a victim of identity theft, set up a new password, and request that a fraud alert be placed on the accounts.

- **Close unused existing accounts.**

- **Contact one of the nationwide credit bureaus and request that one of the fraud alerts described here be placed in your file.**

  - **Initial alert.** You can request an initial alert if you are a victim of identity theft or other fraud or think that you may become a victim. You must submit appropriate proof of identity, which may include your Social Security number. The credit bureau receiving the alert must notify the other nationwide bureaus, and each must place an alert in your file for 90 days. The alert states that you do not authorize an additional card on an existing account, an increase in the credit limit of an existing account, or new credit (other than an extension of credit on an existing credit card account). The alert may delay your ability to get credit. Each bureau must also provide the alert each time it generates your credit score. You can get one free copy of your credit report from each bureau when you place an alert.

- **Extended alert.** If you are a victim of identity theft, you can send the credit bureau an identity theft report and request that it place an extended alert in your file. You must include appropriate proof of identity, which may include your Social Security number. The extended alert is similar to the initial alert, but it remains in place for seven years and you can get two free copies of your credit report from each bureau during the next 12 months. In addition, for five years, each bureau must exclude you from lists that it prepares for creditors or insurers with offers of credit or insurance that you did not request (so-called prescreened offers).

- **Active duty alert.** If you are on active military duty, you can add an active duty alert to your file at a major credit bureau. You must submit appropriate proof of identity, which may include your Social Security

number. The active duty alert is similar to the other alerts, but it remains in place for 12 months, the exclusion from prescreened lists lasts for two years, and you are not entitled to a free credit report.

- **Creditor's duty when alert is in place.** A creditor or other user of a credit report containing one of these alerts must take extra steps to verify the identity of the person requesting credit before it proceeds with the transaction. In the case of an extended alert, you may include a telephone number that the creditor must call to confirm that the request for credit is not the result of identity theft.

- **Fill out an FTC identity theft affidavit,** available in Appendix 3 or online at www.consumer.gov/idtheft. Creditors may accept this affidavit when you claim that you are not responsible for a new account or for transactions on an existing account. The information that you provide will enable the creditor to investigate your claim. (The creditor may require you to submit additional information or a use different form.) Follow the instructions that accompany the affidavit. Remember to send the completed affidavit by certified mail, return receipt requested, and keep the originals of any supporting documents.

- **Report stolen checks** to Telecheck (800-710-9898), International Check Services (800-526-5380), Certegy

Claims Information System (800-437-5120), CheckRite (800-766-2748), Chexsystems (800-428-9623), or CheckCenter/CrossCheck (800-843-0760).

- **Alert the post office if you suspect the thief may have filed a change of address form.** That form will be an important piece of evidence for the police to use. Fill out a "False Change of Address Complaint," available from the U.S. Postal Inspection Service at www.usps.com.

- **Alert all of your utility and phone companies.** If you're having trouble getting fraudulent phone charges removed from your account, contact your state public utility commission for local service providers. For long distance service and cellular providers, contact the Federal Communications Commission at www.fcc.gov or 888-CALL-FCC.

- **Request copies of the identity thief's application and transaction records from businesses that have provided credit, goods, or services to the thief.** Normally, the business must provide you copies when you send a properly completed written request and cannot impose a charge. Copies also must be provided to law enforcement agencies that you specify. In general, you must provide satisfactory proof of your identity, a police report, and a completed FTC identity theft affidavit. The request must be sent to the business at the address it specifies for this purpose.

- **Request businesses that have provided identity theft-related information to credit bureaus to stop providing the information.** You must send the business an identity theft report at the address that it specifies for this purpose and identify the information related to identity theft. The business normally cannot provide the information to any credit bureau after receiving such a request.

- **Keep dated, concise records of your conversations and interactions with everyone you notify of the theft.** Make copies of all correspondence you send and receive relating to the theft.

- **Contact your local Social Security office to see if your Social Security number has been used fraudulently.** (A free Social Security benefits statement is sent every year to eligible workers age 25 or older.) You can get a copy of your earnings report online at www.ssa.gov. If you notice fraudulent use of your Social Security number, call the SSA's fraud hotline at 800-269-0271.

- **If your driver's license number is being used fraudulently, you can receive a new number,** but be prepared to show proof of theft and damage.

- **If a debt collector tries to collect a debt incurred by the identity thief, tell the collector that the debt is the result of identity theft.** The collector then must tell the creditor that the debt may be the result of identity theft. The collector also must send you information that "validates" the debt. (See Chapter 3.) Send the collector a written dispute of the debt after you receive the validation, and include a copy of your police report or identity theft affidavit. Also send a copy to the creditor. Ordinarily, you will have a complete defense to a debt incurred by the identity thief and should not pay it. The information you provide the collector and creditor may cause the collector to stop collection efforts. If not, it may be helpful to consult an attorney. Consult an attorney immediately if you receive notice of legal action based on debts incurred by the identity thief.

- **File a complaint with the FTC.** The FTC can't bring criminal cases, but it can give you information about how to resolve problems that result from identity theft. Contact the FTC by calling the Identity Theft Hotline (877-ID-THEFT), visiting its website (www. consumer.gov/idtheft), or writing to Identity Theft Clearinghouse, Federal Trade Commission, 600 Pennsylvania Ave., NW, Washington, DC 20580.

You need to take control of the situation and not waste time waiting for someone else to step up and help you. Be persistent with police, credit bureaus, credit card companies, utility companies, and banks. Continue to call, write letters, and keep track of your efforts to stop the theft and reverse the damage.

 RESOURCES

More information on identity theft. The Federal Trade Commission's website on identity theft (www.consumer.gov/idtheft) has lots of useful information. The State of California's Office of Privacy Protection (www.privacy .ca.gov) has good general information on identity theft, as well as California-specific information. The nonprofit Privacy Rights Clearinghouse (www.privacyrights.org) has useful information and resources on identity theft. The nonprofit Identity Theft Resource Center has resources for victims of identity theft at www.idtheftcenter .org/local.shtml. Another good list of resources (state and federal agencies and laws) can be found at the LLRX.com website, www.llrx.com/ features/idtheft.htm.

Identity Theft Protection Products and Insurance

If you want to protect yourself from, or at least minimize, the financial losses that occur when your identity is stolen, consider buying special identity theft protection.

Many private companies (often security agencies) now sell products or packages designed to insure against identity theft damages or to protect you from becoming a victim. You can also find products on the Internet. Before you buy these services or products, however, check them out carefully. Some are scams designed to get your personal information and take advantage of you. One cheap product to consider is a paper shredder.

Also, a number of insurance companies sell identity theft protection—either as a separate insurance policy or as an option that comes with your homeowners insurance policy (some policies include this protection automatically). These policies provide compensation for common expenses associated with identity theft including lost wages, mailing costs, and attorney's fees. Some credit cards also offer an identity theft protection feature.

Law Against ID Theft

In 1998, Congress passed, and President Clinton signed, the Identity Theft and Assumption Deterrence Act (18 USC § 1028). This law makes the use of another person's identity with the intent to commit any unlawful activity under either state or federal law a federal felony. Violations of the Act are investigated by federal agencies, including the Secret Service, FBI, and Postal Inspection Service, and prosecuted by the Department of Justice. The law allows for restitution to victims.

Additionally, many states have passed or are considering laws related to identify theft. For a list of state identity theft laws, visit the Federal Trade Commission's website; go to www.ftc.gov and click on the "Fighting Back Against ID Theft" button. Use the "Law Enforcement" tab to reveal the pull-down menu, and then click on "Laws." Even if your state does not have a law specifically identified as an identity theft law, the issue is likely covered under other state laws.

In 2003, Congress amended the Fair Credit Reporting Act by adding provisions aimed at preventing identity theft, limiting its effect on consumers' credit reports, and helping victims clean up their credit reports. Some of these new provisions are described above. (See Appendix 2 for the text of the amended FCRA.)

How Creditors and Employers Use Your Credit Report

I f you've read and followed the advice in Chapter 4, you should feel confident that you've done everything you can to clean up your credit report. If you are back in good financial shape, now is the time to start thinking about rebuilding your credit. But, before you do that, it helps to understand who has access to your credit report and how creditors and employers use it to evaluate your credit.

Who Can Look at Your Credit Report

The federal Fair Credit Reporting Act (FCRA) (15 U.S.C. §§ 1681 and following) and state credit reporting laws restrict who can access your credit report and how it can be used. (Appendix 2 contains the text of the FCRA.)

The people and entities that can request your credit report include:

- **Employers,** who often use credit reports to conduct background checks of job applicants and to assess current employees for promotions or job reassignments. Before ordering your credit report, employers must first get your written authorization and provide certain disclosures. Many employers never look at credit reports. And those that do often will not be concerned about your financial problems. If you do have some negative information on your report, you might want to discuss it with the employer before he or she sees the report. (In some states, you can get a copy of your report at the same time the employer does.)

- **Government agencies,** which can request your credit report to determine whether you are eligible for public assistance. They do this to look for any hidden income or assets you might have, not to see if you have unpaid bills. The law also allows state and local government officials to get reports to help determine whether you can make child support payments. If you apply for a license issued by a government agency, it can look at your credit report if it must consider your financial status in determining your eligibility. But not all government agencies can look at your credit report. For example, district attorneys cannot look at reports to investigate criminal or civil cases, and the U.S. Citizenship and Immigration Services (formerly the INS) cannot get a report for an immigration proceeding or for reviewing citizenship applications.

- **Insurance companies,** which can look at your report if you apply for a policy. Usually, they are not interested in your credit history but instead may ask about your medical history or about any insurance claims you have filed. A credit bureau cannot provide an insurance company a credit report that contains medical information unless you consent.

- **Collection agencies,** which can look at your report when trying to collect an overdue debt from you. They mainly do this to try to locate you or find out more about your assets.

- **Judgment creditors,** who are allowed to look at credit reports in order to decide whether to begin collection efforts against you. They can also use reports for "skip tracing" (hiring someone to locate you or your assets).
- **Potential creditors,** who are allowed to review your report when you apply for credit. Although this is a broad category, there are some restrictions. For a new transaction, you must have made an offer or otherwise initiated a credit transaction before the creditor can look at your report. It is important to be careful when you are shopping around, especially for cars. Dealers will try to get you to sign an authorization so that they can look at your report and size up your financial situation before beginning their sales pitch. This request will then appear on your credit report and may negatively affect your credit. (See Chapter 4 for more information about credit inquiries.)
- **Landlords and mortgage lenders,** who you can expect to scrutinize your report very carefully before offering to lend you money to buy a home.
- **Utility companies,** which can request your credit report. However, there are special rules that prevent utility companies from denying you service in many circumstances, even if you have bad credit. Negative marks will only matter if you owe money to the particular utility company from which you seek service. Even then, most utility companies are required to offer

special payment plans and programs for people with low income that allow you to get utility service by making payments you can afford.
- **Student loan and grant lenders,** most of whom cannot deny your application because of poor credit. However, there are a few exceptions. For example, lenders are required to check the credit of parents applying for PLUS loans. Also, you cannot get a new federal loan if you are in default on another federal loan.

Apart from the entities listed above, most other people and businesses cannot legally request a copy of your credit report. Notably, your credit report cannot be used in divorce, child custody, immigration, and other legal proceedings. Government agencies are allowed to look at your report in these cases only if they get a special court order.

It's not always easy to find out if someone who should not have access to your credit report has requested, and received, one anyway. One way to detect unauthorized users is to order your credit report and look for unfamiliar names or businesses in the list of inquiries. (See Chapter 4 for information on how to order your credit report.) If someone has requested your report illegally, you may be able to sue for violation of the Fair Credit Reporting Act—you'll probably need the help of a lawyer to do this. You should also complain to state and federal government agencies. Appendix 1 includes a list of state agencies that regulate credit bureaus. The

Federal Trade Commission (at www.ftc.gov) is the primary enforcer of the federal Fair Credit Reporting Act.

How Credit Applications Are Evaluated

When you apply for credit, creditors use two primary methods to evaluate your request. They:

- weigh your three Cs—capacity, collateral, and character, and
- obtain a "risk score" based on the information in your credit report.

Your Three Cs

A creditor needs information to determine the likelihood that you will repay a loan or pay charges you incur on a line of revolving credit. This is done by evaluating the three Cs.

Capacity

Capacity refers to the amount of debts you can realistically pay given your income. Creditors look at how long you've been at your job, your income level, and the likelihood that your income will increase over time. They also look to see that you're in a stable job or at least a stable job industry. It's important when you fill out a credit application to make your job sound stable, high level, and even "professional." Are you a secretary, or are you an executive secretary or the office manager? Present yourself in the best possible light, but don't lie.

Creditors also examine your existing credit relationships, such as credit cards, bank loans, and mortgages. They want to know your credit limits (you may be denied additional credit if you already have a lot of open credit lines), your current credit balances, how long you've had each account, and your payment history—whether you pay late or on time.

Collateral

Creditors like to see that you have assets that they can take from you if you don't pay your debt. Owning a home or liquid assets such as a mutual fund may offer considerable comfort to a creditor reviewing an application. This is especially true if your credit report has negative notations in it, such as late payments.

Character

Creditors develop a feeling of your financial character through objective factors that show stability. These include the length of your residency, the length of your employment, whether you rent or own your home (you're more likely to stay put if you own), and whether you have checking and savings accounts.

These days, most creditors use credit scores (see below) to evaluate applications for credit. If the creditor considers your credit score to be good, it probably will approve your application without further evaluation. If your credit score is below the creditor's threshold for routine approval, it may review your application individually and consider your three Cs or it may simply reject you. If you are rejected, you may be able to find another creditor with different approval criteria. Be sure to get a copy of your credit report and credit score to see what the problem is.

Your Credit Score

Most credit reports include a credit score. Credit scores are numerical calculations that are supposed to indicate the risk that you will default on your payments. High credit scores indicate less risk, and low scores indicate potential problems. Most credit scores range from lows of 300 to 400 to highs of 800 to 900. The biggest credit scoring company, Fair Isaac Corporation (FICO), estimates that about 40% of Americans have scores over 750. Anything over 750 is considered to be a very good score by most lenders.

How a Credit Score Is Created

According to the Federal Trade Commission, this is how companies generate your credit score:

"Information about you and your credit experiences, such as your bill-paying history, the number and type of accounts you have, late payments, collection actions, outstanding debt, and the age of your accounts, is collected from your credit application and your credit report. Using a statistical program, creditors compare this information to the credit performance of consumers with similar profiles. A credit scoring system awards points for each factor that helps predict who is most likely to repay a debt. A total number of points — a credit score — helps predict how creditworthy you are, that is, how likely it is that you will repay a loan and make the payments when due."

Lenders use credit scores to help them determine whether you are a good credit risk for new credit, whether to increase or decrease an existing line of credit, how easy it will be to collect on an account, and even whether you are likely to file for bankruptcy. Credit scores are used in about 80% of all mortgages as well as in car loans, credit cards, and insurance policies. Your credit score not only determines whether you get a loan, but also what interest rate will be applied. If you know your Fair Isaac credit score (see below), you can visit its website (at www.myfico.com) and use your score, to find out the prevailing mortgage interest rate that most lenders charge to people with that credit score.

You now can obtain your credit score from credit bureaus that develop or distribute them for a fee of $8 to $15 (the bureau will probably try to sell you additional products, such as credit monitoring services, as well). The bureau must provide your score, the range of possible scores under the scoring model used, four key factors that affected the score, the date on which the score was created, and the name of the entity that provided the score (such as Fair Isaac). Be aware, however, that the score and scoring model that you receive may be different from those used by your lender.

If you apply for a loan on residential property, the mortgage lender must disclose your credit score, the related information just described, and a notice with contact information for the credit bureaus that provided credit scores. Lenders that evaluate loan applications using automated systems must disclose the system's score and the key factors that affected the score. In California, if you apply to an auto dealer for a loan or lease on a vehicle and the dealer obtains your credit score, the dealer must give you your score and a notice containing the range of possible scores and contact information for the credit bureau that provided the score.

To get your Fair Isaac credit score, visit www.myfico.com. You'll have to pay a $15.95 fee.

Although being able to obtain your credit score is important, the jury is still out on how helpful the score actually is. It is likely that you will get different scores from different companies. And consumer experts are not certain that the score you order online will be the same one that lenders use to determine whether they will extend credit to you.

Credit scoring companies use criteria similar to the three Cs when creating scores. Recently, Fair Isaac disclosed slightly more detail on the factors it uses in generating credit scores. Those factors include:

- Your payment history (about 35% of the score).
- Amounts you owe on credit accounts (about 30% of the score). Fair Isaac looks at the amount you owe on all accounts and whether there is a balance. They are looking to see whether you manage credit responsibly. It may view a large number of accounts on which you carry a balance as a sign that you are overextended and count it against you.
- Length of your credit history (about 15% of the score). In general, a longer credit history increases the score.
- Your new credit (about 10% of the score). Fair Isaac likes to see that you have an established credit history and that you don't have too many new accounts. Opening several accounts in a short period of time can represent greater risk.
- Types of credit (about 10% of the score). Fair Isaac is looking for a "healthy mix" of different types of credit. This factor is usually important only if there is not a lot of other

information upon which to base your score.

If you do get your credit score, and it seems lower than it should be, there may be a mistake on your credit report. (See Chapter 4 for information on how to clean up your credit report, including getting rid of errors.)

To keep up on credit scoring developments, visit www.creditscoring.com, a private website devoted to credit scoring. You can get the booklet "Understanding Your FICO Score" from Fair Isaac at www.myfico.com.

Creditors and consumers use the term FICO score generically, but there are actually three FICO scoring programs used by the major credit bureaus: Equifax's BEACON, Experian's Experian/Fair Isaac Risk Model, and TransUnion's FICO Risk Score, Classic. Your score from each bureau will vary somewhat because the scoring models are different and each bureau has

different data about you. Fair Isaac says that it makes the scores as consistent as possible between the three bureaus.

In 2006, the three major credit bureaus introduced VantageScore, a new credit scoring system that they developed jointly. A VantageScore consists of a number from 501 to 990 (higher numbers mean less risk) and a letter grade (A, B, C, F). The VantageScore is said to offer greater consistency because it uses a single scoring model and is said to do a better job of evaluating consumers with short credit histories (so-called "thin files"). Commentators point out that the new scoring system can be confusing to consumers because it differs from the more familiar FICO scoring. For example, a FICO score of 780 is good, but is only fair on the VantageScore scale.

Whether this new product catches on remains to be seen.

Tips for Raising Your Credit Score

Fair Isaac offers these tips for raising your credit score:

- Pay your bills on time.
- Make up missed payments and keep all your payments current.
- Maintain low balances on credit cards and other "revolving debt."
- Pay off debt rather than transferring it to a new account.
- Don't close unused credit card accounts just to raise your credit score.
- Don't get new credit cards that you don't need just to increase the credit available to you.
- Other tips are included in "Understanding Your FICO Score" at the Fair Isaac website, www.myfico.com.

Interestingly, Fair Isaac says that its credit scoring program does not penalize consumers who rate shop. If you're looking for a mortgage or an auto loan, each lender you contact may request your credit report. Each request will appear in the "inquiry" section of your credit report. (See Chapter 4.) Consumer advocates commonly believe that this can lower your credit score or make your credit history look less attractive to lenders. In "Understanding Your FICO Score," Fair Isaac says that you can avoid lowering your FICO score by doing your rate shopping within a short period of time (such as 14 days).

Building and Maintaining Good Credit

Establishing and keeping a good credit record is the final step in repairing your credit. This chapter covers the many ways you can build a positive credit history, including getting credit in your own name if you're married or divorced, applying for credit cards, getting a secured card, and obtaining bank loans. It also provides tips on how to maintain good credit, from using credit cards wisely to avoiding credit repair clinics. (See also "Tips for Raising Your Credit Score," in Chapter 5.) If you take the steps suggested in this chapter, you will probably be able to get a

Should You Stay Out of the Credit System?

Habitual overspending can be just as hard to overcome as excessive gambling or drinking. If you think you may be a compulsive spender, one of the worst things you can do is repair your credit and then get more. Instead, you need to get a handle on your spending habits.

Debtors Anonymous, a 12-step support program similar to Alcoholics Anonymous, has programs nationwide. If a Debtors Anonymous group or a therapist recommends that you stay out of the credit system for a while, follow that advice. Even if you don't feel you're a compulsive spender, paying as you spend may still be the way to go—because of finance charges, transaction fees, and other charges, buying on credit costs between 20% and 25% more than paying with cash.

Debtors Anonymous groups meet all over the country. If you can't find one in your area, send a self-addressed, stamped envelope to Debtors Anonymous, General Services Office, P.O. Box 920888, Needham, MA 02492-0009. Or call their office and speak to a volunteer or leave your name, address, and a request for information. The number is 781-453-2743. You can also visit their website at www. debtorsanonymous.org.

Concern about habitual overspending isn't the only reason to stay outside the credit system. Followers of a movement known as "voluntary simplicity" suggest that reliance on credit is one of the reasons people are overworked and overstressed. Credit gives us the chance to consume—and often we consume far more than we need to live comfortably and at an easy pace.

Much has been written about voluntarily downshifting. Advocates are not suggesting that we all move to the wilderness, quit our jobs, and live without electricity and running water. But they do suggest that we take a hard look at our reliance on money—and credit— to bring us happiness.

For more information on voluntary simplicity, take a look at any of these resources:
- *Simplify Your Life: 100 Ways to Slow Down and Enjoy the Things That Really Matter*, by Elaine St. James (Hyperion)
- *Get a Life: You Don't Need a Million to Retire Well*, by Ralph Warner (Nolo), and
- *Your Money or Your Life: Transforming Your Relationship With Money and Achieving Financial Independence*, by Joe Dominguez and Vicki Robin (Penguin Books).

major credit card or loan in approximately two years. And, in about four years, you may be able to qualify for a mortgage.

But, before you start this process, make sure you are financially ready to get more credit. If you get new credit too soon, while you're still in financial trouble, you're likely to dig yourself into deeper debt. First focus on stabilizing your employment, income, and debt situation. Get your high-priority debts, such as rent, mortgage, or car payments, under control. Once you're in decent financial shape, start following the strategies in this chapter to build good credit.

SKIP AHEAD

If you've never been married. Those who have never married can skip ahead to "Get Credit Cards and Use Them Wisely," below

Build Credit in Your Own Name

If you are married, separated, or divorced, and most of the credit you obtained is in your spouse's or ex-spouse's name only, you should start to get credit in your name, too.

Getting credit in your own name is also an excellent strategy for repairing your credit if:

- all or most of your financial problems can be attributed to your spouse, or
- you and your spouse have gone through financial difficulties together, but most of your credit was in your spouse's name only.

In order to understand how this works, you first must learn about which of your spouse's accounts can appear on your report. Here are the rules:

- Credit bureaus must include information about your spouse's account on your credit report in two situations: (1) you and your spouse have a joint account (that is, you both can use it), or (2) you are obligated (responsible for paying) on an account belonging to your spouse, even if your spouse is the primary signer or obligor on the account.
- Credit bureaus cannot include information about your spouse's account on your credit report if the account is not joint or you are not responsible for paying the account.

This is usually good news if you are worried that your spouse's negative credit history may reflect badly on you— delinquent accounts in your spouse's name only should not appear on your credit report. However, if you are now divorced or separated and had relied primarily on your spouse to obtain credit, so that most loans and credit cards were in your spouse's name only, you won't have a lengthy history of good credit in your report. You now need to start building good credit in your own name. If you are still married, you can start by making sure that all joint accounts and accounts that you are obligated to pay appear on your credit report, too. Then, follow the steps outlined in the rest of this chapter for building credit.

Ask Creditors to Consider Your Spouse's Credit History

Although a credit bureau cannot include information about your spouse's positive credit accounts on your credit report (unless the account meets one of the two criteria listed above), if you are applying for a loan, credit card, or other type of credit, you can always ask the creditor to consider any of your spouse's accounts that reflect favorably on your creditworthiness, too. For example, if you and your spouse make payments on your spouse's account with joint checks, bring this to the creditor's attention. A creditor doesn't have to consider this information, but it may.

Get Credit Cards and Use Them Wisely

If you survived your financial disaster and managed to hold onto one of your credit cards or a department store or gasoline card, use it and pay your bills on time. Your credit history will improve quickly. Most credit reports show payment histories for 24–36 months. If you charge something every month, no matter how small, and pay it off every month, your credit report will show steady and proper use of revolving credit.

CAUTION

Charge only a small amount each month and pay it in full. By paying in full, you will avoid incurring interest, as long as you have a card with a grace period. The average consumer who makes only the minimum payment each month ends up paying hundreds of dollars in interest charges alone. For example, if you charge $1,000 on a 17% credit card and pay it off by making the minimum payments of 2% of the balance each month, you'll take over 17 years to pay off the loan and will end up paying over $2,500 total.

Applying for Credit Cards

If you don't currently have a credit card, apply for one. Keep in mind the general guidelines under the three Cs discussion (in Chapter 5) when completing your credit application. Don't lie, but present yourself in the best possible light.

CAUTION

Don't plunge in until you're ready. Getting new credit cards before your finances are in order is a bad idea. Wait until you're out of financial trouble before you apply for credit.

It's often easiest to obtain a card from a department store or gasoline company. These companies usually open your account with a very low credit line. If you start with one credit card, charge items, and pay the bill on time, other companies will issue you a card. When you use department store and gasoline cards, try not to carry a balance from one month to the next. The interest rate on these cards can be very high.

Next, apply for a regular credit card from a bank, such as a Visa, MasterCard, or Discover card. Competition for customers is fierce, and you may be able to find a card with relatively low initial rates. Depending on how bad your credit history is, however, you may be eligible only for a low credit line or a card with a high interest rate. If you use the card and make your payments, after a year or so you can apply to increase your line of credit or reduce the interest rate.

In fact, no matter what your situation, it makes sense to call your credit card company and ask for a lower interest rate. A study conducted by the United States Public Interest Research Group in 2002 found that more than half of the consumers who complained to their credit card company were able to reduce their interest rate, usually by as much as one third. (To find out more, contact U.S. PIRG at www.uspirg .org or visit www.truthaboutcredit.org.)

It's Raining Credit Cards

If you've been through bankruptcy or other tough financial times but your problems are behind you, or you've never had credit, you may be considered an excellent candidate for a credit card. Your creditors won't tell you this. It's an industry secret they'd like to keep that way.

Credit card issuers send out approximately three billion solicitations each year to American consumers. This number represents an enormous growth since the early 1990s. While the number of American adults hasn't risen that dramatically, the number of American people now considered creditworthy has.

Credit card issuers operate in a fiercely competitive environment. People who have been through bankruptcy are now considered great credit risks—their debt is gone, they have a history of using credit, and *they can't file for bankruptcy again for another eight years.*

In fact, a Texas bankruptcy judge asked a couple who filed for bankruptcy to keep track of how many credit card solicitations they received during the two-year period after they filed their case. The total: 53, with credit limits ranging from $100 to $20,000.

And people who have been through bankruptcy aren't the only ones with stuffed mailboxes. New immigrants, low-wage earners, and others traditionally kept out of the credit world are being invited to participate, but at astronomical rates.

Beware of all these offers. They are not meant to be flattering, nor are they a sign that you can afford more credit. Don't fall into the trap of thinking, "They must think I can handle more credit or they wouldn't keep offering it to me." Credit card issuers are looking for consumers who will run up big balances and pay a lot of interest.

Tips for Applying

The following tips will help you when you apply for credit cards or an increased credit limit:

- **Be consistent with the name you use.** Use your middle initial always or never. Always use your generation (Jr., Sr., III, and so on).
- **Take advantage of preapproved credit for department store, gasoline, and bank cards.** If your credit is shot, you may not have the luxury of shopping around.
- **Be honest, but appear sympathetic.** Lenders are especially apt to ignore past credit problems that were out of your control—such as a job layoff or illness.
- **Bolster your credit application.** Don't lie, but don't denigrate yourself, either. For example, if you're an administrative assistant, don't put "clerk/typist" for your job title. Also, if you are married and your spouse has excellent credit, apply jointly or at least indicate on the credit application that you are married.
- **Apply for credit when you are most likely to get it.** For example, apply when you are working, when you've lived at the same address for at least a year, and when you don't have an unusually high number of inquiries on your credit report.
- **Apply for credit from creditors with whom you've done business.** For example, your phone company or insurance company may offer Visas or Mastercards to their customers. If you are on good terms with your bank, it may offer you a Visa or Mastercard.
- **Don't get swept up by credit card gimmicks.** Before applying for a credit card that gives you rebates, credit for future purchases, or other perks, make sure you will benefit from the offer. Some are good deals, especially cards that give you cash back. But, in general, a card with no annual fee and/or a low interest rate usually beats the cards with "deals" or any "rewards" you get by using your card.
- **Scrutinize any preapproval solicitations for nonbank cards.** A "gold" or "platinum" card with a high credit limit may be nothing more than a card that lets you purchase items through catalogues provided by the company itself. No other merchant accepts these cards, and the company won't report your charges and payments to the credit bureaus. Also, the items in the catalogues are usually high priced and poor quality.

Comparison Shop

When it comes to obtaining a new credit card, you may not have as many choices as people who already have good credit. But you should still do some comparison shopping to make sure you are getting the best deal available to you. Credit card terms and interest rates vary—and some of those variations can make a huge difference to your wallet.

Always shop for the card with the best interest rate and terms. As a general rule, if you always pay your monthly bill in full, and you don't care about perks such as free miles, look for a card that has no annual fee and a longer grace period. On the other hand, if you carry a balance from month to month, look for a card that carries a lower annual percentage rate.

Here's what you should look for in a credit card:

- **Avoid high interest rates.** Check the annual percentage rate (APR). This is the amount of interest that you will pay per year, expressed as a percentage. See "Understanding APRs," below.

- **Avoid low introductory rates.** Some cards have a low "introductory rate" (also called a "teaser rate"). After a few months, the interest rate will skyrocket. Also, sometimes the advertised rate only applies to certain people, such as those with a high income or credit score. The card company charges a much higher rate to those who don't qualify—which could mean an unpleasant surprise when your first bill arrives.

- **Understand the credit limit.** The credit limit is the total amount that you may charge on the credit card, including purchases, cash advances, balance transfers, fees, and finance charges. If you exceed the limit, you will have to pay an "over limit" fee.

- **Understand interest calculations.** Each month, the credit card company applies the APR to the balance to compute the finance charge for that month (see "Understanding APRs," below). Credit card companies may calculate the balance over one billing cycle or two (a one-cycle billing period will usually result in lower charges), and may include or exclude new purchases in the balance (excluding new purchases is usually better for consumers). The balance may be calculated in one of these three ways:

  - Adjusted balance method. The credit card company computes the finance charge by taking the amount you owed at the start of the billing cycle and subtracting any payments made during the cycle. New purchases are not included.

  - Previous balance method. The company uses the amount you owed at the beginning of the billing cycle to compute the finance charge.

  - Adjusted daily balance method. The company adds your balances for each day in the billing cycle and then divides that total by the number of days in the cycle. Payments made during the period are subtracted to get the daily amounts you owe. New purchases may or may not be included, depending on the plan. If the company uses the two-cycle average daily balance method, it uses the average daily balance for two billing cycles. New purchases may or may not be included in the total.

Understanding APRs

The APR is the percentage you will pay in interest each year. Each month, the credit card company applies the APR to the account balance to compute the finance charge for that month. The finance charge is the dollar amount you pay to use the credit. The account balance may include purchases, previous months' unpaid balances, transaction charges, and other fees. The APR is the best single indicator of the actual interest you will pay.

EXAMPLE: Suppose that you have a credit card with a whopping 28.6% APR and that your balance last month was $1,203.38. To calculate this month's finance charge, the credit card company multiplies the outstanding balance by one-twelfth of the annual rate ($1,202.38 x 2.422% = $29.15). If you make the minimum payment of $40, $29.15 pays off this month's finance charge and only $10.85 goes to reducing your outstanding balance.

A credit card may have several APRs. For example, one may apply to purchases, one to cash advances, and another to balance transfers. The APRs may be tied to different levels of outstanding balance; for example, the company may charge 14.9% on balances up to $500 and 17% on larger balances.

APRs also may be fixed or adjustable. An adjustable APR changes from time to time, and usually is tied to another interest rate, such as the prime rate or the Treasury Bill rate. The APR will change automatically when the other rate changes. Even a fixed APR may change over a period of time, but the credit card company must tell you before the rate changes.

As a general rule, look for the lowest and most stable APR that will apply to the way you plan to use the credit card. If you carry a balance from month to month, even a small difference in the APR can make a big difference in how much you'll pay over a year.

- **Review the grace period.** This is the interest-free period between the purchase date and the bill-due date. It is usually available only to those who do not carry a balance. If you pay your bill in full each month, make sure you have a grace period. Otherwise, you'll pay interest from the date of your purchase. If you carry a balance, a grace period is not as important.

- **Avoid high annual fees.** Some credit card companies charge you a flat fee (in addition to interest and other charges) for using their card. Some do not. If you pay off your balance each month, you want a card without an annual fee. If you carry a balance, a card with an annual fee but a low interest rate may be better than a card with no annual fee but a high interest rate.

- **Find out if you'll be charged higher interest rates for cash advances and late payments.** Virtually all credit cards charge higher interest rates for cash advances. And, with almost all cards, the company charges a hefty fee for late payments (up to $39) and imposes a new, much higher interest rate. If you think you might pay late once in a while (be realistic), check out these interest rates. Some are as high as 32%. Also, be aware that many credit card companies today will charge you a higher interest rate if you default on an obligation to another creditor (so-called "universal default"). Many creditors review their customers' credit reports regularly to identify "risky" cardholders. If this review makes the creditor feel insecure, it may raise your interest rate even though you have never made a late payment.

- **Watch out for extra fees.** Many, if not most, credit card companies charge a hefty fee (as high as $39) if your payment is late or you exceed your credit limit. Also look out for cash advance fees, balance transfer fees, credit limit increase fees, set-up fees, returned item fees, and fees for paying by telephone.

- **Evaluate rebates, free miles, and other perks.** Many credit cards allow you to earn cash back, free airline miles, discounts on goods and services, funds for charity, or other bonuses by using the card. Don't sign up for a card based on these perks alone—be sure to consider the other card terms as well. If you will pay high interest and high annual fees, you are better off without the perks. You can use the money you save on interest and other fees to buy airline tickets yourself or contribute to your favorite charity.

Credit card companies must disclose many of the items discussed in this section in their solicitations and applications. (You'll find a sample disclosure below) You can use disclosures like these to comparison shop among credit card offerings.

Many websites will help you shop for a credit card by surveying large numbers of credit card deals. You can compare and contrast terms and find the best card for you. A few to try are www.cardtrack.com, www.bankrate.com, and www.consumer-action.org (search for "2005 Credit Card Survey"). For more information on credit cards and how to shop for them, see the Federal Reserve Board's website at http://federalreserve.gov/pubs/shop.

Sample Disclosure Form	
Annual percentage rate (APR) for purchases	2.9% until 11/1/06 after that, **14.9%**
Other APRs	Cash advance APR: 15.9% Balance Transfer APR: 15.9% Penalty rate: 23.9% See explanation below.*
Variable-rate informtion	Your APR for purchase transactions may vary. The rate is determined monthly by adding 5.9% to the Prime Rate.**
Grace period for repayment of balances for purchases	25 days on average
Method of computing the balance for purchases	Average daily balance (excluding new purchases)
Annual fees	None
Minimum finance charge	$.50

Transaction fee for cash advances: 3% of the amount advanced
Balance transfer fee: 3% of the amount transferred
Late-payment fee: $25
Over-the-credit-limit fee: $25

* Explanation of penalty. If your payment arrives more than ten days late two times within a six-month period, the penalty rate will apply.
** The Prime Rate used to determine your APR is the rate published in the *Wall Street Journal* on the 10th day of the prior month.

Protect Yourself

Once you receive a credit card, protect yourself and your efforts to repair your credit by following these suggestions:

- **Send your creditors a change of address when you move.** Many creditors provide change of address boxes on their monthly bills. For your other creditors, you can send a letter, call the customer service phone number, or use a post office change of address post card. Don't let your monthly statements go to your old address. You may miss making payments on time, or someone may steal your statement and use your identifying information to gain access to your account or obtain credit in your name.

- **If you need an increase in your credit limit, ask for it.** Many creditors will close accounts or charge late fees on customers who exceed their credit limits. But pay close attention: If you're charging to the limit on your credit card, you may be heading for financial trouble.

- **Take steps to protect your cards.** Sign your cards as soon as they arrive. If you have a personal identification number (PIN) that allows you take cash advances, keep the number in your head and never write it down near your credit card. Make a list of your credit card issuers, the account numbers, and the issuer's phone numbers so you can quickly call if you need to report a lost or stolen card.

- **Don't give your credit card or checking account number to anyone over the phone unless you placed the call** and are certain of the company's reputation. Never, never, never give your credit card or checking account number to someone who calls you and tries to sell you something or claims to need your account number to send you a "prize." Never give your credit card number, checking account number, or personal information to a caller who says that he represents a firm you do business with and that he needs to confirm or update your account information. The same is true for Internet inquiries like this. *All of these are scams.*

Read the Fine Print: Beware of Creditors Trying to Collect Discharged Debts

If you've been through bankruptcy, you're no longer liable to pay the debts discharged in your case. Unfortunately, however, many creditors don't see it that way.

Read all credit card solicitations carefully, particularly ones that promise to restore your credit. The fine print might tell you that by signing up for the card, you voluntarily agree to repay debts you discharged in your bankruptcy case. The solicitation won't necessarily come from the original creditor whose debt you wiped out. Often the creditor sells the debt to another, so you won't recognize the new creditor (who is now the current owner of your old debt).

Attempts to have you voluntarily repay discharged debts don't come only in the form of credit card solicitations. You might also receive phone calls or dunning letters threatening legal action—"intent to file suit"—if you don't pay up.

Remind any creditor that attempts to collect discharged debts are illegal under the Bankruptcy Code (11 U.S.C. § 524) and prohibited by the Fair Debt Collection Practices Act (15 U.S.C. § 1692e).

Cosigners and Guarantors

If you can't get a credit card or loan on your own, consider asking a friend or relative to cosign or serve as guarantor on an account. A cosigner is someone who promises to repay a loan or credit card charges if the primary debtor defaults. Similarly, a guarantor promises to pay the credit grantor if the primary debtor does not. Usually, neither the cosigner's nor the guarantor's name appears on the credit account.

Although getting a cosigner or guarantor will help you get credit, it may not help you build credit in all situations. On some cosigned accounts, the creditor will report the information on the cosigner's credit report only, not on yours. The best option is to ask if you can use a guarantor instead of a cosigner. It should make no difference to the creditor.

> ⓘ CAUTION
>
> **Cosigners and guarantors should fully understand their obligations before they sign on.** For example, if the primary debtor doesn't pay the debt and erases it in bankruptcy, the cosigner or guarantor remains fully liable. The Federal Trade Commission's Credit Practices Rule requires that cosigners of credit issued by a financial institution or retail installment seller be given the following notice.

> You are being asked to guarantee this debt. Think carefully before you do so. If the borrower doesn't pay the debt, you will have to. Be sure you can afford to pay if you have to, and that you want to accept this responsibility.
>
> You may have to pay up to the full amount of the debt if the borrower does not pay. You may also have to pay late fees or collection costs, which increase this amount.
>
> The creditor can collect this debt from you without first trying to collect from the borrower. The creditor can use the same collection methods against you that can be used against the borrower, such as suing you, garnishing your wages, etc. If this debt is ever in default, that fact may become a part of your credit record.

Authorized User Accounts

Another way to repair your credit using a credit card relies on the generosity of a friend or relative you trust.

If you can find someone who is willing to add you to an account as an "authorized user," you can use the credit line but not be responsible for repaying the charges. The account holder must request that your name be added to the account and can ask that a card be issued in your name. Once your name is on the account, information about the account will probably be added to your file—and you'll be listed as an authorized user.

Of course, because the information concerning the account is reported in your credit file, this technique requires that the account holder not default. If a default occurs, that information will appear in your credit report—exactly what you don't want.

Secured Credit Cards

Many people with poor credit histories are denied regular credit cards. If your application is rejected, consider whether you truly need a credit card. Millions of people get along just fine without them. If you decide that you really need a card—for example, you travel quite a bit and need a card to reserve hotel rooms and rent cars—then you can apply for a secured credit card. With a secured credit card, you deposit a sum of money with a bank and are given a credit card with a credit limit for a percentage of the amount you deposit— as low as 50% and as high as 120%. Depending on the bank, you'll be required to deposit as little as a few hundred dollars or as much as a few thousand.

Unfortunately, secured credit cards can be expensive. Many banks charge hefty application and processing fees in addition to an annual fee. Also, the interest rate on secured credit cards can be close to 22%, while you earn only 2% or 3% on the money you deposit. And some banks have eliminated the grace period—that is, interest on your balance begins to accrue on the date you charge, not 25 days later. If you find a card with a grace period and pay your bill in full each month, you can avoid the interest charges.

Another downside of secured credit cards is that some creditors don't accept or give much weight to credit history established with a secured credit card. Ask the card issuer if it reports to the three major credit bureaus. If the issuer doesn't, you've lost an important benefit of having a secured card. Some smaller issuers don't report to the credit bureaus, but most major banks do.

Many secured credit cards have a conversion option. This lets you convert the card into a regular credit card after several months or a year if you use the secured card responsibly. Because regular credit cards typically have lower interest rates and annual fees than secured credit cards, it's usually preferable to obtain a card with a conversion option.

Use the secured credit card to make smallish purchases that you can pay off each month. Always pay on time. This will help you build your credit. After you pay on time for a year, you may be able to qualify for an unsecured credit card with a lower interest rate. Then you can use the information in "Comparison Shop," above, to find the best card you can qualify for.

To find a bank offering a secured credit card, call some local banks or do some surfing on the Internet. One source of information is www.bankrate.com.

Avoid 900 number advertisements for "instant credit" or other such offers. Obtaining a secured credit card through one of these programs will probably cost you a lot—in application fees, processing fees, and phone charges. Sometimes you call one 900 number and are told you must call a second or third number. These ads also frequently mislead consumers into thinking that their lines of credit will be higher than they actually will be. Also, be aware of secured credit cards that can be used only to purchase merchandise from the card issuer's catalogue. The merchandise often is shoddy and high priced, and the issuer probably won't report your charges and payments to the credit bureaus.

> **CAUTION**
>
> **Don't use your home as collateral.**
> If you do opt for a secured credit card, make sure it isn't secured by your home. If it is, and you get behind on your card payments, you could lose your home.

Closing Credit Card Accounts

If you want to close some accounts, here are some rules to follow:

- Close accounts you don't need. You can close an account even if you haven't paid off the balance. The card issuer will close your account, cancel your privileges, and send you monthly statements until you pay off your balance. Or contact the bank whose card you are keeping and ask it to transfer the balance on the account you are closing to the account you are keeping.

How Many Credit Cards Should You Carry?

Once you succeed in getting a credit card, you might be hungry to apply for many more cards. Not so fast. Having too much credit probably contributed to your debt problems in the first place. Ideally, you should carry one bank credit card, one department store card, and one gasoline card. Your inclination may be to charge everything on your bank card and not bother using a department store or gasoline card. When creditors look in your credit file, however, they want to see that you can handle more than one credit account at a time. Don't build up interest charges on these cards—just use them and pay the bill in full each month.

Creditors frown on applicants who have a lot of open credit. So keeping many cards may mean that you'll be turned down for other credit—perhaps credit you really need. And, if your credit applications are turned down, your file will contain inquiries from the companies that rejected you. Your credit file will look like you were desperately trying to get credit, something creditors never like to see.

- Close accounts on which you are delinquent—otherwise, the credit card issuer may close them for you. If you're delinquent on all your accounts, keep open the most current account.
- If you pay your bill in full each month—that is, you don't carry a balance—close the accounts with the highest annual fees. Make sure that the accounts you keep open have a grace period—a 20-25 day period each month in which you can pay off your bill and not incur any interest.
- If you carry a balance, close the accounts with the highest interest rates and shortest grace periods. Also, read your contract to understand the credit card company's billing practice. Interest may be calculated on the previous two months' balance, the average daily balance for the month, or your balance at the end of the billing cycle (see "Understanding APRs," above). Keep the cards that charge interest on the balance at the end of the billing cycle.
- Before you close an account, especially one you have had for a long time, consider how it may affect your credit score. Fair Isaac, the developer of the FICO credit score (see Chapter 5) recommends against closing unused credit card accounts if your purpose is to raise your FICO score. Read "What a FICO Score Considers" in "Understanding Your FICO Score," available at www.myfico.com.

How to Close a Credit Card Account

If you want to close a credit card account, make sure you do it the right way.

- Write a letter to the company and request a "hard close." If you don't do this, the company may give you a "soft close," which means new charges can go through, even though you asked that the account be closed. With a soft close, you are susceptible to credit card fraud.
- Also request, in writing, that the credit card company report to the credit bureaus that your account was "closed by consumer request." Accounts that are erroneously reported as "closed by creditor" will hurt your credit rating. Ask the company to send you written confirmation that the account was closed at your request.
- After 30 days, check your credit report to ensure that it reflects that the account in question was "closed by consumer request."

Open Deposit Accounts

Creditors look for bank accounts as a sign of stability. Quite frankly, they also look for bank accounts as a source of how you will pay your bills. If you fill out a credit application and cannot provide a checking account number, you probably won't get credit.

A savings or money market account, too, will improve your standing with creditors. Even if you never deposit additional money into the account, creditors assume that people who have savings or money market accounts use them. Having an account reassures creditors of two things: You are making an effort to build up savings, and, if you don't pay your bill and the creditor must sue you to collect, it has a source to collect its judgment.

Just because you've had poor credit history, you shouldn't be denied a bank account. Shop around and compare fees, such as check writing fees, ATM fees, monthly service charges, the minimum balance to waive the monthly charge, interest rates on savings, and the like.

You might be denied an account, however, if you have a bad check writing history. Check verification companies keep track of banks' experiences with their customers, much as credit bureaus do for creditors. Most banks will check your check writing history with a check verification company before they will open an account for you. If you are denied a bank account because of information provided by a check verification company, call the company to discuss the problem and try to provide information that resolves it. If you can't resolve the problem informally, you can dispute incomplete or inaccurate information in the company's files just as you can with a credit bureau. Some popular check verification companies include:

- Certegy (800-437-5120)
- CheckCenter/CrossCheck (800-843-0760)
- CheckRite (800-766-2748)
- Chexsystems (800-428-9623)
- International Check Services (800-526-5380), and
- Telecheck (800-710-9898).

Checking account information is not included in credit reports prepared by the three major credit bureaus.

If you open a checking account, be very careful not to bounce checks that you have written. A federal law called "Check 21" makes it harder to avoid bouncing checks. This law allows banks to process electronic images of checks instead of the paper originals. One result is that checks clear much faster than most of us are used to. Consumer representatives urge consumers not to write a check unless the funds are already in the account to cover it. (For more information on Check 21, go to www.consumersunion.org/finance/ckclear1002.htm.)

If you bounce a check to a creditor, it most likely will report a late or missed payment to a credit bureau, jeopardizing your hard work to repair your credit. A history of bounced checks also may make it harder to open bank accounts in the future.

To learn more about ATM and other bank fees, visit the following websites: www.uspirg.org (U.S. Public Interest Research Group), www.consumersunion.org (Consumers Union), www.consumer-action.org (Consumer Action), and www.ftc.gov (Federal Trade Commission).

Work With Local Merchants

Another way to repair your credit is to approach a local merchant (such as an electronics or furniture store) and arrange to purchase an item on credit. Many local stores will work with you to set up a payment schedule, but be prepared to put down a deposit of up to 30% or to pay a high rate of interest. If you still don't qualify, the merchant might agree to give you credit if you get someone to cosign or guarantee the loan. Or you may be able to get credit by first buying an item on layaway.

Even if a local merchant won't extend you credit, it may very well let you make a purchase on a layaway plan. When you purchase an item on layaway, the seller keeps the merchandise until you fully pay for it. Only then are you entitled to pick it up. One advantage of layaway is that you don't pay interest. One disadvantage is that it may be months before you actually get the item. This might be fine if you're buying a dress for your cousin's wedding that is eight months away. It isn't so fine if your mattress is so shot that you wake up with a backache every morning.

Layaway purchases are not reported to credit bureaus. If you purchase an item on layaway and make all the payments on time, however, the store may be willing to issue you a store credit card or store credit privileges.

Obtain a Bank Loan

One way to repair your credit is to take some money you've saved and open a savings account. You ask the bank to give you a loan against the money in your account. In exchange, you have no access to your money—you give your passbook to the bank and the bank won't give you an ATM card for the account—so there's no risk to the bank if you fail to make the payments. If the bank doesn't offer these types of loans, apply for a personal loan and offer either to get a cosigner or to secure it against some collateral you own (*not* your house).

No matter what kind of loan you get, be sure you know the following:

- **Does the bank report these loan payments to credit bureaus?** This is key; the whole reason you take out the loan is to repair your credit. If the bank doesn't report your payments to a credit bureau, there's no reason to take out a loan.

- **What is the minimum deposit amount required for loans?** Some banks won't give you a loan unless you have $3,000 in an account; others will lend you money on $50. Find a bank that fits your budget.

- **What is the interest rate?** The interest rate on the loan is usually much higher than what people with good credit pay. You will probably pay between 8% and 12% interest on the loan. Yes, this means you'll lose a little money on the transaction, but it can be worth it if you're determined to repair your credit.

- **What is the maximum amount you can borrow?** On passbook loans, banks won't lend you 100% of what's in your account; most will lend you between 80% and 90%.
- **What is the repayment schedule?** Banks usually give you one to three years to repay the loan. Some banks have no minimum monthly repayment amount on passbook loans; you could pay nothing for nearly the entire loan period and then pay the entire balance in the last month. Although you can pay the loan back in only one or two payments, don't. Pay it off over at least 12 months so that monthly installment payments appear in your credit file.

And, no matter what, *do not miss a loan payment.* This is extremely important: If you miss a loan payment, the bank will report the late or missed payment to a credit bureau, and you will have set back your efforts to repair your credit.

Avoid Credit Repair Clinics

You've probably seen ads for companies that claim they can fix your credit, qualify you for a loan, or get you a credit card. Their pitches are tempting, especially if your credit is bad and you desperately want to buy a car or house.

Avoid these outfits. They are a bad idea, for two reasons: First, they charge you for doing what you can do yourself or with the help of a nonprofit debt counselor (see Appendix 1). Some of them are more interested in helping themselves to your money than in doing you any good—they'll take your fee and disappear, paying just a few of your creditors or none. Second, some of them are extremely shady or outright criminal. Many of their practices are fraudulent, deceptive, and even illegal. For example, some suggest that you create a new identity by applying for an IRS Employer Identification number (EIN), a nine-digit number that resembles a Social Security number, and use it instead of your Social Security number when you apply for credit. This is illegal. It's a federal crime to make false statements on an application for a loan or credit. It's also a federal crime to misrepresent your Social Security number and to obtain an EIN from the IRS under false pretenses. If that's not bad enough, using an EIN instead of your Social Security number won't even help you repair your credit—and will prevent you from earning Social Security benefits. This scam is called "Credit File Segregation" or "File Segregation"; you'll see it advertised in classified ads, TV, radio, and the Internet.

Credit repair clinics devise new schemes as often as consumer protection agencies catch onto their previous ones.

Even assuming that a credit repair company is legitimate, don't listen to its pitches. These companies can't do anything for you that you can't do yourself. What they will do, however, is charge you between $250 and $5,000 for their unnecessary services. Here's what credit repair clinics claim to be able to do for you:

- **Remove incorrect information from your credit file.** You can do that yourself under the Fair Credit Reporting Act. See Chapter 4.

- **Remove correct, but negative, information from your credit file.** Negative items in your credit file can legally stay there for seven or ten years, as long as they are correct. No one can wave a wand and make them go away. One tactic of credit repair services is to try to take advantage of the law requiring credit bureaus to verify information if the customer disputes it. Credit repair clinics do this by challenging every item in a credit file—negative, positive, or neutral— with the hope of overwhelming the credit bureau into removing information without verifying it. Credit bureaus are aware of this tactic and often dismiss these challenges on the ground that they are frivolous, a right credit bureaus have under the Fair Credit Reporting Act. You are better off getting your report and selectively challenging items that are incomplete or inaccurate. Even if the credit bureau removes information that the bureau had the right to include in your file, it's no doubt only a temporary removal. Most correct information reappears after 30 to 60 days, when the creditor that first reported the information to the credit bureaus rereports it.

- **Get outstanding debt balances and court judgments removed from your credit file.** Credit repair clinics often advise debtors to pay outstanding debts if the creditor agrees to remove the negative information from your credit file. This is certainly a negotiation tactic you want to consider (see Chapter 3), but you don't need to pay a credit repair clinic for this advice.

- **Get a major credit card.** Credit repair clinics can give you a list of banks that offer secured credit cards. While this information is helpful in rebuilding credit, it's not worth hundreds or thousands of dollars—you can get a list yourself for little or nothing.

The federal Credit Repair Organizations Act (CROA) (15 U.S.C. §§1679–1679j) regulates for-profit credit repair clinics (the text is included in Appendix 2). Some dubious credit repair clinics have tried to get around these regulations by setting themselves up as nonprofits, but they still take your money and provide poor results— or do nothing for you that you couldn't do for yourself.

Under the federal law, a credit repair clinic must:

- inform you of your rights under the Fair Credit Reporting Act
- accurately represent what it can and cannot do
- not collect any money until all promised services are performed
- provide a written contract, and
- let you cancel the contract within three business days of signing.

Any contract that doesn't comply with the CROA's requirements is void, and you cannot waive (sign away) these rights. Any lawsuit you bring against a credit repair clinic for violation of this law must be

Additional State Protections Concerning Credit Repair Clinics

Arizona

Ariz. Rev. Stat. Ann. §§ 44-1701 to 44-1712

Credit repair service may not charge or collect a fee for referring consumer to a retail seller who will or may extend credit that is on substantially the same terms as those available to the general public.

Arkansas

Ark. Code Ann. §§ 4-91-101 to 4-91-109

Credit repair service may not charge or collect a fee for referring consumer to a retail seller who will or may extend credit that is on substantially the same terms as those available to the general public.

Cancellation rights. May cancel contract within 5 days of signing. Any payment must be returned within 10 days of receipt of cancellation notice.

California

Cal. Civ. Code §§ 1789.10 to 1789.22

Credit repair service may not charge or collect a fee for referring consumer to a retail seller who will or may extend credit that is on substantially the same terms as those available to the general public or on the same terms that would have been extended without the assistance of the credit repair organization; submit a debtor's dispute to a consumer credit reporting agency without the debtor's knowledge; or use a consumer credit reporting agency's telephone system or toll-free number to represent the caller as the debtor without the debtor's authorization.

Cancellation rights. May cancel contract within 5 working days of signing.

Time limit for performing services. 6 months.

Colorado

Colo. Rev. Stat. §§ 12-14.5-101 to 12-14.5-113

Cancellation rights. May cancel contract within 5 working days of signing.

Connecticut

Conn. Gen. Stat. Ann. § 36a-700

State protections do not exceed federal laws.

Delaware

Del. Code Ann. tit. 6, §§ 2401 to 2414

Credit repair service may not charge or collect a fee for referring consumer to a retail seller who will or may extend credit that is on substantially the same terms as those available to the general public.

Credit repair service must disclose a complete and accurate statement of the availability of nonprofit credit counseling services.

Time limit for performing services. 180 days.

District of Columbia

D.C. Code Ann. §§ 28-4601 to 28-4608

Credit repair service may not charge or collect a fee for referring consumer to a retail seller who will or may extend credit that is on substantially the same terms as those available to the general public.

Cancellation rights. May cancel contract within 5 calendar days of signing. Must be reimbursed within 10 days of receipt of cancellation notice.

Additional State Protections Concerning Credit Repair Clinics (continued)

Florida

Fla. Stat. Ann. §§ 817.701 to 817.706

Credit repair service may not charge or collect a fee for referring consumer to a retail seller who will or may extend credit that is on substantially the same terms as those available to the general public.

Cancellation rights. May cancel contract within 5 days of signing. Any payment must be returned within 10 days of receipt of cancellation notice.

Georgia

Ga. Code Ann. §§ 16-9-59, 18-5-1 to 18-5-3

Credit repair service may not charge more than 7.5% of the amount the debtor provides each month for distribution to creditors.

Who may provide service. Only nonprofit organizations or federally regulated banks may offer credit repair services; attorneys and real estate brokers may provide credit repair services incidental to their regular business practice.

Hawaii

Haw. Rev. Stat. § 481B-12

State protections do not exceed federal laws.

Idaho

Idaho Code §§ 26-2222, 26-2223

Who may provide service. Only nonprofit organizations may provide credit counseling or other debt management services.

Illinois

815 Ill. Comp. Stat. §§ 605/1 to 605/16

Credit repair service may not charge or collect a fee for referring consumer to a retail seller who will or may extend credit that is on substantially the same terms as those available to the general public.

Cancellation rights. Any payment must be returned within 10 days of receipt of cancellation notice.

Indiana

Ind. Code Ann. §§ 24-5-15-1 to 24-5-15-11

Credit repair service may not charge or collect a fee for referring consumer to a retail seller who will or may extend credit that is on substantially the same terms as those available to the general public.

Credit repair service must disclose a complete and accurate statement of the availability of nonprofit credit counseling services.

Cancellation rights. Any payment must be returned within 10 days of receipt of cancellation notice or any other written notice.

Iowa

Iowa Code §§ 538A.1 to 538A.14

Credit repair service may not charge or collect a fee for referring consumer to a retail seller who will or may extend credit that is on substantially the same terms as those available to the general public.

Cancellation rights. Any payment must be returned within 10 days of receipt of cancellation notice.

Additional State Protections Concerning Credit Repair Clinics (continued)

Kansas

Kan. Stat. Ann. §§ 50-1116 to 50-1135

Credit repair service must comply with an extensive list of requirements, including educating debtors, specifying the scope of an agreement, itemizing fees, and disclosing the consumer's rights.

Credit repair service may not delay payments, make false promises or deceptive statements, give or receive compensation for referrals, or collect fees above $20 per month from the customer (after a $50 initial consultation fee).

For more information contact your state's consumer protection agency, listed in Appendix A.

Kentucky

Ky. Rev. Stat. Ann. §§ 380.010 to 390.990

Who may provide service. Debt adjustment services may be provided only by a nonprofit organization, attorney, debtor's regular full-time employee, creditor providing service at no cost, or lender who, at the debtor's request, adjusts debts at no additional cost as part of disbursing the loan funds.

Louisiana

La. Rev. Stat. Ann. §§ 9:3573.1 to 9:3573.17

Credit repair service must disclose a complete and accurate statement of the availability of nonprofit credit counseling services, disclose all payments expected from the consumer, give estimated completion date, and wait for payment until services are complete.

Cancellation rights. May cancel contract within 5 days of signing. Any payment must be returned within 10 days of receipt of cancellation notice.

Maine

Me. Rev. Stat. Ann. tit. 9-A, §§ 10-101 to 10-401

Credit repair service is required to keep consumer fees in an escrow account separate from any operating accounts of the business, pending completion of services offered.

Maryland

Md. Code Ann. [Com. Law] §§ 14-1901 to 14-1916

Credit repair service may not charge or collect a fee for referring consumer to a retail seller who will or may extend credit that is on substantially the same terms as those available to the general public or assist a consumer to obtain credit at a rate of interest which is in violation of federal or state maximum rate.

Cancellation rights. Any payment must be returned within 10 days of receipt of cancellation notice.

Massachusetts

Mass. Gen. Laws ch. 93, §§ 68A to 68E

Credit repair service may not charge or collect a fee for referring consumer to a retail seller who will or may extend credit that is on substantially the same terms as those available to the general public.

Cancellation rights. Any payment must be returned within 10 days of receipt of cancellation notice.

Additional State Protections Concerning Credit Repair Clinics (continued)

Michigan

Mich. Comp. Laws §§ 445.1821 to 445.1825

Credit repair service may not charge or collect a fee for referring consumer to a retail seller who will or may extend credit that is on substantially the same terms as those available to the general public, submit a debtor's dispute to a consumer credit reporting agency without the debtor's knowledge, or provide a service that is not pursuant to a written contract.

Time limit for performing services. 90 days.

Minnesota

Minn. Stat. Ann. §§ 332.52 to 332.60

Credit repair service may not charge or collect a fee for referring consumer to a retail seller who will or may extend credit that is on substantially the same terms as those available to the general public.

Credit repair service must disclose the name and address of any person who directly or indirectly owns or controls a 10% or greater interest in the credit services organization; any litigation or unresolved complaint filed within the preceding 5 years with the state, any other state, or the U.S., or a notarized statement that there has been no such litigation or complaint; and the percentage of customers during the past year for whom the credit services organization fully and completely performed the services it agreed to provide.

Cancellation rights. May cancel contract within 5 days of signing. Any payment must be returned within 10 days of receipt of cancellation notice.

Mississippi

Mississippi Nonprofit Debt Management Services Act, Miss. Code Ann. §§ 81-22-1 to 81-22-29

Who may provide service. Only a nonprofit organization may operate as a licensed Debt Management Service.

Credit repair service may not purchase any debt, lend money or provide credit, operate as a debt collector, or structure a negative amortization agreement for the consumer.

Credit repair service is required to maintain separate account records for each consumer. May not commingle trust accounts with any business operating accounts

Fees. May not charge more than a one-time fee of $75.00 for setting up a debt management plan, $30.00 per month to maintain plan, $15.00 for obtaining an individual credit report, or $25.00 for a joint report. Educational courses and products may be offered for a fee, but consumer must be informed that purchasing them is not mandatory for receiving debt management services.

Missouri

Mo. Rev. Stat. §§ 407.635 to 407.644

Credit repair service may not charge or collect a fee for referring consumer to a retail seller who will or may extend credit that is on substantially the same terms as those available to the general public.

Credit repair service must disclose a complete and accurate statement of the availability of nonprofit credit counseling services.

Additional State Protections Concerning Credit Repair Clinics (continued)

Cancellation rights. Any payment must be returned within 10 days of receipt of cancellation notice.

Time limit for performing services. 180 days.

Nebraska

Neb. Rev. Stat. §§ 45-801 to 45-815

Credit repair service may not charge or collect a fee for referring consumer to a retail seller who will or may extend credit that is on substantially the same terms as those available to the general public.

Cancellation rights. Any payment must be returned within 10 days of receipt of cancellation notice.

Nevada

Nev. Rev. Stat. Ann. §§ 598.741 to 598.787

Credit repair service may not charge or collect a fee for referring consumer to a retail seller who will or may extend credit that is on substantially the same terms as those available to the general public, submit a debtor's dispute to a consumer credit reporting agency without the debtor's knowledge, or call a consumer credit reporting agency and represent the caller as the debtor.

Credit repair service must disclose a complete and accurate statement of the availability of nonprofit credit counseling services, including toll-free numbers if available.

Cancellation rights. May cancel contract within 5 days of signing.

New Hampshire

N.H. Rev. Stat. Ann. §§ 359-D:1 to 359-D:11

Credit repair service may not charge or collect a fee for referring consumer to a retail seller who will or may extend credit that is on substantially the same terms as those available to the general public.**Cancellation rights.** May cancel contract within 5 days of signing. Any payment must be returned within 5 days of receipt of cancellation notice.

New Jersey

N.J. Stat. Ann. §§ 17:16G-1 to 17:16G-6; N.J. Admin. Code tit. 3, § 25-1.2

Who may provide service. Only nonprofit organizations may provide credit counseling or debt adjustment services. No more than 40% of the board of directors can be employed by a corporation or institution which offers credit to the general public.

Fees. Monthly debt adjustment fee cannot exceed one percent of the debtor's gross monthly income or $25, whichever is less. Credit counseling services fee cannot exceed $60 per month.

New Mexico

N.M. Stat. Ann. §§ 56-2-1 to 56-2-4

Who may provide service. Nonprofit corporations organized as a community effort to assist debtors may provide debt adjustment services. Exceptions: attorney; regular, full-time employee of a debtor who does it as part of job; person authorized by court or state or federal law; creditor who provides debt adjustment without cost; and lender who, at the debtor's request, adjusts debts at no additional cost as part of disbursing the loan funds.

Additional State Protections Concerning Credit Repair Clinics (continued)

New York

N.Y. Gen. Bus. Law §§ 458-a to 458-k

Credit repair service is required to annex a copy of the consumer's current credit report to the contract and clearly mark the adverse entries proposed to be modified.

North Carolina

N.C. Gen. Stat. §§ 66-220 to 66-226

Credit repair service may not charge or collect a fee for referring consumer to a retail seller who will or may extend credit that is on substantially the same terms as those available to the general public.**Cancellation rights.** Any payment must be returned within 10 days of receipt of cancellation notice.

North Dakota

N.D. Cent. Code §§ 13-06-01 to 13-06-03, 13-07-01 to 13-07-07

Credit repair service may not enter into an agreement with a debtor unless a thorough written budget analysis indicates that the debtor can reasonably meet the requirements of the financial adjustment plan and will benefit from it.

Credit repair service is required to credit any interest accrued as a result of payments deposited in a trust account to debt management education programs.

Fees. May charge an origination fee of up to $50; may take up to 15% of any sum deposited by the debtor for distribution as partial payment of the service's total fee.

Ohio

Ohio Rev. Code Ann. §§ 4712.01 to 4712.99

Credit repair service may not charge or collect a fee for referring consumer to a person that extends credit, except when credit has actually been extended as a result of the referral; submit the debtor's disputes to a consumer reporting agency without the debtor's signed, written authorization and positive identification; or contact a consumer reporting agency to submit or obtain information about a debtor, stating or implying to be the debtor or debtor's attorney, guardian, or other legal representative.

Credit repair service must disclose a complete and accurate statement of the availability of nonprofit budget and debt counseling services; the percentage of customers during the past year for whom the credit services organization fully and completely performed the services it agreed to provide.

Time limit for performing service. 60 days.

Oklahoma

Okla. Stat. Ann. tit. 24, §§ 131 to 139

Credit repair service may not charge or collect a fee for referring consumer to a retail seller who will or may extend credit that is on substantially the same terms as those available to the general public.

Cancellation rights. May cancel contract within 5 days of signing. Any payment must be returned within 10 days of receipt of cancellation notice.

Additional State Protections Concerning Credit Repair Clinics (continued)

Oregon

Or. Rev. Stat. §§ 646.380 to 646.396

Credit repair service may not charge or collect a fee for referring consumer to a retail seller who will or may extend credit that is on substantially the same terms as those available to the general public.

Credit repair service is required to print all contracts in at least 10-point type.

Pennsylvania

73 Pa. Cons. Stat. Ann. §§ 2181 to 2192

Credit repair service may not charge or collect a fee for referring consumer to a retail seller who will or may extend credit that is on substantially the same terms as those available to the general public.

Cancellation rights. May cancel contract within 5 days of signing. Any payment must be returned within 15 days of receipt of cancellation notice.

Tennessee

Tenn. Code Ann. §§ 47-18-1001 to 47-18-1011

Credit repair service may not charge or collect a fee for referring consumer to a retail seller who will or may extend credit that is on substantially the same terms as those available to the general public; use a program or plan which charges installment payments directly to a credit card prior to full and complete performance of the services it has agreed to perform.

Credit repair service must disclose a complete and accurate statement of the availability of nonprofit budget and debt counseling services.

Cancellation rights. May cancel contract within 5 business days of signing. Any payment must be returned within 10 days of receipt of cancellation notice.

Texas

Tex. Fin. Code Ann. §§ 393.001 to 393.505

Credit repair service may not charge or collect a fee for referring consumer to a retail seller who will or may extend credit that is on substantially the same terms as those available to the general public.

Credit repair service must disclose a complete and accurate statement of the availability of nonprofit budget and debt counseling services.

Cancellation rights. Any payment must be returned within 10 days of receipt of cancellation notice.

Time limit for performing service. 180 days.

Utah

Utah Code Ann. §§ 13-21-1 to 13-21-7

Credit repair service may not charge or collect a fee for referring consumer to a retail seller who will or may extend credit that is on substantially the same terms as those available to the general public.

Cancellation rights. May cancel contract within 5 days of signing. Any payment must be returned within 10 days of receipt of cancellation notice.

Additional State Protections Concerning Credit Repair Clinics (continued)

Vermont

Vt. Stat. Ann. tit. 8, §§ 4861 to 4876

Credit repair service must state in writing all services it will perform and all fees consumers will pay; state that debt adjustment plans are not suitable for all debtors; disclose if creditors may compensate the licensee; disclose the right to cancel within 3 days, without penalty; and make these disclosures in the language used to negotiate the agreement.

Credit repair service may not engage in false or deceptive advertising or communications, threaten to disclose information about debt, or charge more than a $50 initial fee plus ten percent of payments received from the debtor for distribution to creditors.

For more information contact your state's consumer protection agency, listed in Appendix A, Section F.

Virginia

Va. Code Ann. §§ 59.1-335.1 to 59.1-335.12

Credit repair service may not charge or collect a fee for referring consumer to a retail seller who will or may extend credit that is on substantially the same terms as those available to the general public.

Credit repair service must disclose. Information statement must include the following notice in at least 10-point bold type: "You have no obligation to pay any fees or charges until all services have been performed completely for you." The notice must also be conspicuously posted on a sign in the repair service's place of business, so that it is noticeable and readable when consumers are being interviewed.

Cancellation rights. Any payment must be returned within 10 days of receipt of cancellation notice.

Washington

Wash. Rev. Code Ann. §§ 19.134.010 to 19.134.900

Credit repair service may not charge or collect a fee for referring consumer to a retail seller who will or may extend credit that is on substantially the same terms as those available to the general public.

Cancellation rights. May cancel contract within 5 days of signing. Any payment must be returned within 10 days of receipt of cancellation notice.

West Virginia

W. Va. Code §§ 46A-6C-1 to 46A-6C-12

Credit repair service may not charge or collect a fee for referring consumer to a retail seller who will or may extend credit that is on substantially the same terms as those available to the general public.

Credit repair service must disclose a complete and accurate statement of the availability of nonprofit budget and debt counseling services.

Cancellation rights. Any payment must be returned within 10 days of receipt of cancellation notice.

Time limit for performing service. 180 days.

Additional State Protections Concerning Credit Repair Clinics (continued)

Wisconsin

Wis. Stat. Ann. §§ 422.501 to 422.506

Credit repair service may not charge or collect a fee for referring consumer to a retail seller who will or may extend credit that is on substantially the same terms as those available to the general public.

Cancellation rights. May cancel contract within 5 days of signing. Any payment must be returned within 15 days of receipt of cancellation notice.

Wyoming

Who may provide service. Only nonprofits and attorneys may offer debt adjustment services.

Current as of January 2007

filed within five years of the violation. A court may award actual damages, punitive damages (meant to punish), and attorneys' fees.

A few states provide additional protections to consumers who use credit repair clinics. For example, some states give you more than three days to cancel the credit repair contract, require the credit repair clinic to perform the promised services within a specific amount of time, and require that the credit repair clinic inform you about available nonprofit credit counseling services.

The chart, "Additional State Protections Concerning Credit Repair Clinics," lists additional protections and the code section where you can find the text of these provisions. To find your state law, visit your public library or local law library. Or, visit the legal research section of Nolo's website, at www.nolo.com/statute/index.cfm, and click on the "State Law" tab.

If you're still tempted to use a credit repair organization (whether or not it claims to be a nonprofit), do the following:

- Ask whether the company is bonded. A company that is bonded has posted money in the event it goes out of business or goes bankrupt and dissatisfied consumers seek a refund. A legitimate company should be willing to give you the name of the company through which it is bonded. Call the bonding company for verification. Some states (California, for example) require that credit repair companies post a bond and be registered with the state. If your state has these requirements, never use a credit repair company that has not complied with them.

- Ask to see a copy of the contract before you sign. Carefully check the company's fees, its claims of what it can do, and your right to a refund.

Avoid any company that won't give you a written agreement or the right to cancel if you change your mind.

- Call your local Better Business Bureau and your state consumer affairs office (a list is in Appendix 1) to see if either has complaints on file for the company.
- Ask for the names and phone numbers of satisfied customers. Be wary of any satisfied customers you speak to whose claims sound exactly like the claims of the company. These people are probably phonies—people who pose as satisfied customers but who never used the company's service and are simply paid to say good things about the company.

Avoid Credit Discrimination

When you're trying to build good credit, the last thing you need is to be denied credit for a reason other than poor creditworthiness. Unfortunately, some people are denied credit for reasons entirely unrelated to their ability to pay, such as their race, gender, or age.

Fortunately, several powerful federal laws and some state laws prohibit discrimination in credit transactions. This section discusses the laws prohibiting credit discrimination and provides information on what to do if you think a creditor has discriminated against you.

Laws Prohibiting Credit Discrimination

Two federal laws, the Equal Credit Opportunity Act (ECOA) and the Fair Housing Act (FHA), prohibit credit discrimination.

The ECOA (15 U.S.C. §§ 1691 and following) is quite broad in scope. It prohibits discrimination in any part of a credit transaction, including:

- applications for credit
- credit evaluation
- restrictions in granting credit, such as requiring collateral or security deposits
- credit terms
- loan servicing
- treatment upon default, and
- collection procedures.

The ECOA requires a creditor to give you notice when it denies your credit application revokes your credit, changes the terms of an existing credit arrangement, or refuses to grant credit or terms substantially as requested. If the creditor denies you credit, it must give you a written notice that tells you either the specific reasons for rejecting you or that you can request those reasons within 60 days. An acceptable reason might be "Your income is too low;" an unacceptable reason would be "You don't meet our minimum standards."

The ECOA prohibits a creditor from refusing to grant credit because of your:

- race or color
- national origin
- sex
- marital status

- religion
- age, or
- public assistance status.

The federal Fair Housing Act (FHA) (42 U.S.C.§§ 3601 and following) prohibits discrimination in residential real estate transactions. It covers loans to purchase, improve, or maintain your home, or loans for which your home is used as collateral. The FHA also prohibits discrimination in the rental housing market. Like the ECOA, the FHA prohibits discrimination based on race, color, religion, national origin, and sex. In addition, the FHA prohibits discrimination based on:

- familial status, and
- disability.

Other federal laws provide protections in addition to the ECOA and FHA. For example, the Community Reinvestment Act (12 U.S.C. §§ 2901 and following) can be used to combat discrimination by banks and lenders. And, often, state antidiscrimination laws provide even more protection than federal laws; for example, some states prohibit discrimination based on occupation, personal characteristics, or sexual orientation. Below, we discuss in detail some of the important categories in which credit discrimination is prohibited.

Race Discrimination

In general, lenders are prohibited from asking a person's race on a credit application or from ascertaining it from any means other than personal observation by a loan officer (for example, by looking for race information on a credit file). There is one important exception to this law: A mortgage lender may ask applicants to voluntarily disclose their race for the sole purpose of monitoring home mortgage applications. Other creditors may ask for this information, but only to monitor their own practices for discrimination. Creditors may not use the information to make a credit decision.

Unfortunately, laws prohibiting race discrimination have not eradicated the practice. In fact, lenders are accused of getting around race discrimination prohibitions by "redlining"—that is, denying credit to residents of predominantly nonwhite neighborhoods. More recently, consumer advocates have charged lenders with reverse redlining, which involves aggressively marketing their highest-priced loan products to communities of color.

National Origin Discrimination

Discrimination based on national origin is prohibited under the ECOA, the FHA, and most state credit discrimination laws. The exact definition of "national origin" is often unclear, but it generally refers to an individual's ancestry. A creditor might be discriminating based on national origin if it treats people with Latino or Asian surnames differently from people with European surnames. This category has also been interpreted to include discrimination against non-English speakers. However, it does not necessarily include noncitizens. A creditor is allowed to consider an applicant's residency status in the United States in certain circumstances.

Sex Discrimination

The ECOA, FHA, and many state laws prohibit credit discrimination based on sex. This category often overlaps with the "marital status" category.

Specific examples of prohibited sex discrimination include:

- rating female-specific jobs (such as waitress) lower than male-specific jobs (such as waiter) for the purpose of obtaining credit
- denying credit because an applicant's income comes from sources historically associated with women—for example, part-time jobs, alimony, or child support (however, a creditor may ask you to prove that you have received alimony, child support, or separate maintenance income consistently)
- requiring married women who apply for credit alone to provide information about their husbands while not requiring married men to provide information about their wives, and
- denying credit to a pregnant woman who anticipates taking a maternity leave.

However, a creditor is allowed to ask your sex when you apply for a real estate loan. The federal government collects this information for statistical purposes. Other creditors may ask for this information as well, although you can refuse to provide it.

Marital Status Discrimination

The ECOA and many state laws prohibit discrimination based on marital status. The FHA has a similar provision that prohibits discrimination based on familial status.

These laws require that a married person be allowed to apply for credit in his or her name only. A creditor cannot require an applicant's spouse to cosign when the applicant requests an individual account, as long as no jointly held or community property is involved and the applicant can meet the creditor's standards on his or her own.

Creditors can only ask about your spouse or former spouse when you apply for your own credit in any of the following cases:

- Your spouse will be permitted to use the account.
- Your spouse will be liable on the account.
- You are relying on your spouse's income to repay the credit.
- You live in a community property state (Arizona, California, Idaho, Louisiana, Nevada, New Mexico, Texas, Washington, or Wisconsin) or you are relying on property located in a community property state to establish your creditworthiness.
- You are relying on alimony, child support, or other maintenance payments from a spouse to repay the creditor—but you are not required to reveal this income if you don't want the creditor to consider it in evaluating your application. A creditor may ask if you are obligated to pay alimony, child support, or separate maintenance.

Sexual Orientation Discrimination

No federal law specifically prohibits credit discrimination based on sexual orientation.

However, a few states prohibit this type of discrimination.

Age Discrimination

The ECOA and many state laws prohibit credit discrimination based on age. This is mostly meant to protect the elderly (defined in the ECOA as people who are at least 62 years old). Creditors are allowed to consider age in order to give more favorable treatment to an older person (for example, considering an older person's long payment history that a younger person hasn't had time to build yet). However, age cannot be used to an older person's detriment. For example, a creditor cannot automatically refuse to consider income often associated with the elderly, such as part-time employment or retirement benefits.

Other Discrimination Prohibited by State Law

A few states have enacted laws barring credit discrimination on grounds other than those covered by the federal laws. Check with your state consumer protection office or do some research on your own to see if there are additional grounds in your state.

RESOURCES

Legal research help. For tips on doing your own legal research, see *Legal Research: How to Find & Understand the Law,* by Stephen R. Elias and Susan Levinkind (Nolo).

Postbankruptcy Discrimination

If you're considering filing for bankruptcy or you've been through bankruptcy, you may be worried that you'll suffer discrimination. There are two categories of legal protection against this kind of discrimination, depending on whether you are dealing with a private person or a governmental entity.

Private employers may not fire you or otherwise discriminate against you solely because you filed for bankruptcy. (11 U.S.C. § 525(b).) It's unclear whether the act prohibits employers from not hiring you because you went through bankruptcy.

Unfortunately, however, other forms of discrimination in the private sector are not illegal. If you seek to rent an apartment and the landlord does a credit check and refuses to rent to you because you filed for bankruptcy, there's not much you can do other than try to show that you'll pay your rent and be a responsible tenant. If a bank refuses to give you a loan because it perceives you as a poor credit risk, you may have little recourse.

All federal, state, and local governmental entities are prohibited from denying, revoking, suspending, or refusing to renew a license, permit, charter, franchise, or other similar grant solely because you filed for bankruptcy. (11 U.S.C. § 525(a).) Judges interpreting this law have ruled that the government cannot:

- deny you a job or fire you
- deny or terminate your public benefits
- deny or refuse to renew your state liquor license
- withhold your college transcript

- deny you a driver's license, or
- deny you a contract, such as a contract for a construction project.

In general, courts have ruled that the intent of the statute is to prohibit a government entity from standing in your way of pursuing a livelihood involving a license, permit, charter, or franchise, but that it does not mean that a government agency must extend you credit, such as a government-backed home loan. However, a government agency cannot exclude you from a student loan program if you have filed for bankruptcy. (11 USC § 525(c).)

In addition, once any government-related debt has been canceled in bankruptcy, all acts against you that arise out of that debt must also end. For example, if a state university has withheld your transcript because you haven't paid back your student loan, once the loan is discharged, you must be given your transcript.

Keep in mind that only government denials based on your bankruptcy are prohibited. You may be denied a loan, job, or apartment for reasons unrelated to the bankruptcy (for example, you earn too much to qualify for public housing) or for reasons related to your future credit-worthiness (for instance, the government concludes you won't be able to repay a student loan).

What to Do If a Creditor Discriminates Against You

If you think that a creditor has discriminated against you on a prohibited basis, you should complain to the creditor, your state attorney general (see Appendix 1), the Federal Trade Commission (www.ftc.gov), and the federal agency that regulates the particular creditor. If the discrimination is related to housing, contact the Department of Housing and Urban Development (www. hud.gov). You may also want to contact an attorney for help.

You can learn more from these websites:

- www.innercitypress.org
- www.communitychange.org (Nonprofit Center for Community Change), and
- www.usdoj.gov (U.S. Department of Justice).   ■

Resources

Below are organizations, agencies, and publications that can provide valuable help in your efforts to repair your credit.

Credit and Debt Counseling Agencies

Credit and debt counseling agencies are organizations funded primarily by major creditors, such as department stores, credit card companies, and banks, who can work with you to help you repay your debts and improve your financial picture. Many are nonprofit companies, but some are not.

To use a credit or debt counseling agency to help you pay your debts, you must have some disposable income. A counselor contacts your creditors to let them know that you've sought assistance and need more time to pay. Based on your income and debts, the counselor, with your creditors, decides on how much you will pay. You then make one payment each month to the counseling agency, which in turn pays your creditors. The agency asks the creditors to return a small percentage of the money to fund its work. This arrangement is generally referred to as a "debt management program."

Some creditors will make concessions to help you when you're on a debt management program. But few creditors will make interest concessions, such as waiving a portion of the accumulated interest to help you repay the principal. More likely, you'll get late fees dropped and the opportunity to reinstate your credit if you successfully complete a debt management program.

Participating in a credit or debt counseling agency's debt management program is a little bit like filing for Chapter 13 bankruptcy. (See Chapter 1.) Working with a credit or debt counseling agency has one advantage: No bankruptcy will appear on your credit record.

But a debt management program also has two disadvantages when compared to Chapter 13 bankruptcy. First, if you miss a payment, Chapter 13 protects you from creditors who would otherwise start collection actions. A debt management program has no such protection, and any one creditor can pull the plug on your plan. Also, a debt management program plan usually requires that your debts be paid in full. In Chapter 13 bankruptcy, the amount you have to pay depends on your disposable income and the value of your nonexempt property; you may end up paying back only a small percentage of your unsecured debt.

The combination of high consumer debt and easy access to information (via the Internet) has led to an explosion in the number of credit and debt counseling agencies ready to offer you help. Some provide limited services, such as budgeting and debt repayment, while others offer a range of services, from debt counseling to financial planning.

When choosing a credit or debt counseling agency, look for a company that is truly a nonprofit. Many for-profit outfits use names that sound like a nonprofit, such as "foundation," to confuse you. And, your inquiry shouldn't stop there. Many of the unscrupulous credit and debt counseling

Questions to Ask a Credit or Debt Counseling Agency

Myvesta.org (formerly Debt Counselors of America) suggests that you ask the following questions before using any counseling agency (the explanations below are paraphrased from Myvesta's website):

1. **Will you send me information about your organization and programs?** An agency should be willing to give you information about its services—and you shouldn't have to provide account numbers, debt amounts, or other information to get it. If an agency won't give you information up front about its programs, consider it a warning sign.

2. **Is there a minimum amount of debt I have to have in order to work with you?** An agency should not turn you away because you have less than a certain amount of debt.

3. **Will you help me with all my debts?** Most credit counseling agencies work only with credit card debt because secured lenders (those that offer mortgages and car loans, for example) won't make automatic reductions in rates and terms. Some agencies will make payments on secured debts as a convenience to you, however. If this is important to you, ask about it.

4. **Can you still help me if I cannot afford the minimum payment in a debt management program?** Avoid agencies that turn you away or tell you to file for bankruptcy because you can't meet their requirements. A good agency should be able to guide you to other resources that can help.

5. **How high are the fees?** Look for a group with low or no fees. Some agencies charge steep up-front fees just to participate in their program. Ask for information about set-up fees, monthly fees, and other charges, and make sure the agency doesn't charge a fee to close your account.

6. **What kind of security measures do you have to protect my information?** Make sure the agency you use has sufficient security in place to protect your Social Security number and other confidential information.

7. **Can I get up-to-date, regular reports of the status of my account?** You want to be able to check your account status at any time. Look for secure, encrypted Web access to your account. If access is by phone only, find out whether someone will be available to answer your questions when you call.

8. **Will you sell my name or address to outside parties?** Get a copy of the agency's privacy policy and read it. Make sure that the agency doesn't disclose your confidential information to inappropriate third parties. Ask whether your name and address will be included on mailing lists sold to outside organizations.

9. **Does counseling affect my report?** Although credit counseling agencies don't report your participation to the credit bureaus, many creditors do. Ask the agency to explain what effect this might have on your credit report.

Questions to Ask a Credit or Debt Counseling Agency (Continued)

10. **How often do you send payments to creditors?** Look for an agency that sends payments out at least weekly. If an agency pays only once a month and your payment is late, it might sit at the agency for weeks before the creditor receives it.

11. **What are my payment options?** Find an agency that gives you some convenient payment choices.

12. **Does your organization have accreditation?** Look for an agency that has been accredited by an independent organization, such as BSI Management Systems.

13. **What kind of training do your counselors have?** A good counseling agency provides both internal training and training with outside experts.

14. **Are you comfortable?** You might be in this program for years, so make sure you feel comfortable with the people you'll be dealing with. Look for friendly, courteous staff who are willing to answer your questions.

---

companies have nonprofit status. These companies often try to get you to pay "voluntary contributions" up front or pay other fees. At a minimum, always ask about fees before agreeing to give your business to a particular counselor. And review the "Questions to Ask a Credit or Debt Counseling Agency," below.

Some experts caution against using even the legitimate nonprofit credit and debt counseling agencies companies. Critics point out that these agencies get most of their funding from creditors. Therefore, say critics, counselors cannot be objective in counseling debtors to file for bankruptcy if they know the agency won't receive funds from its supporters. (Some offices also receive grants from private agencies, such as the United Way, and federal agencies, including the Department of Housing and Urban Development.)

In response to this and other consumer concerns, credit and debt counseling agencies accredited by the National Foundation for Consumer Credit (the majority of agencies are) reached an agreement with the Federal Trade Commission to disclose the following to consumers:

- that creditors fund a large portion of the cost of their operations
- that the credit agency must balance the ability of the debtor to make payments with the requirements of the creditors that fund the office, and
- a reliable estimate of how long it will take a debtor to repay his or her debts under a debt management program.

CAUTION

Make sure your bills get paid. If you sign up for a debt management plan, keep paying your bills directly until you know that your creditors have approved the plan. Make sure the agency's schedule will allow it to pay your debts before they are due each month. Call each of your creditors the first month to make sure the agency paid them on time.

Consumer Credit Counseling Service

Consumer Credit Counseling Service (CCCS) is the oldest credit or debt counseling agency in the country. Actually, CCCS isn't one agency. CCCS is the primary operating name of many credit and debt counseling agencies affiliated with the National Foundation for Consumer Credit (NFCC).

CCCS may charge you a small start-up fee (about $20) and a monthly fee (an average of about $11) for setting up a repayment plan. CCCS also helps people make monthly budgets, for a small fee of about $12, or sometimes free. If you can't afford the fee, CCCS will waive it. In most CCCS offices, the primary service offered is a debt management program. A few offices have additional services, such as helping you save money toward buying a house or reviewing your credit report.

CCCS has more than 1,100 offices, located in every state. Look in the phone book to find the one nearest you or contact the main office at 801 Roeder Road, Suite 900, Silver Spring, MD 20910, 800-388-2227 (voice) or at www.nfcc.org.

Other Credit and Debt Counseling Agencies

With a few exceptions, all bankruptcy filers are now required to get credit counseling. Filers must get this counseling from a nonprofit agency that meets a number of requirements and has been approved by the Office of the U.S. Trustee. If you decide to get help with a repayment plan, you would do well to choose one of these agencies— the U.S. Trustee's office oversees their operation, which gives you some protection against fraudulent practices. You can find a list of approved agencies at the U.S. Trustee's website, at www.usdoj.gov/ust.

Debtors Anonymous

Debtors Anonymous is a 12-step support program which uses many of the guidelines of Alcoholics Anonymous. Debtors Anonymous groups meet all over the country. If you can't find one in your area, send a self-addressed, stamped envelope to Debtors Anonymous, General Services Office, P.O. Box 920888, Needham, MA 02492-0009. Or call their office and speak to a volunteer or leave your name and address and a request for information. Their number is 781-453-2743. You can also visit their website at www.debtorsanonymous.org.

Nolo Publications

Several Nolo publications can provide you with information to supplement this book.

Solve Your Money Troubles: Get Debt Collectors Off Your Back & Regain Financial Freedom, by Robin Leonard and John Lamb, provides extensive information on prioritizing your debts, negotiating with creditors, and deciding whether or not bankruptcy is for you.

How to File for Chapter 7 Bankruptcy, by Stephen R. Elias, Albin Renauer, and Robin Leonard, is a detailed, thorough how-to guide for filing for Chapter 7 bankruptcy. Recommendedfor readers who are certain they want to file for Chapter 7.

Chapter 13 Bankruptcy: Repay Your Debts, by Stephen Elias and Robin Leonard, explains Chapter 13 bankruptcy and includes the forms and instructions necessary to file a Chapter 13 bankruptcy case.

The New Bankruptcy: Will It Work for You?, by Stephen Elias, answers the most common—and not so common—questions about Chapter 7 bankruptcy and Chapter 13 bankruptcy, to help you decide if bankruptcy is right for you.

Stand Up to the IRS, by Frederick W. Daily, guides taxpayers through the ins and outs of an audit, self-representation in tax court, challenging tax bills, and setting up repayment plans for tax bills they do owe. This book was named one of the top three personal finance books by *Money* magazine.

Everybody's Guide to Small Claims Court, by Ralph Warner, is an indispensable guide for anyone wanting to sue a credit bureau or collection agency in small claims court or to defend against a small claims court action filed by a collector.

Divorce and Money: How to Make the Best Financial Decisions During Divorce, by Violet Woodhouse with Dale Fetherling, is a thorough workbook for people making financial decisions while ending their marriage. Divorce is a time when you are at risk of damaging your credit. This book gives tips on dividing the assets and allocating the debts while protecting your precious credit rating.

Other Publications

Publications from non-Nolo publishers have a wealth of information beyond what is in this book.

The Ultimate Credit Handbook: How to Cut Your Debt and Have a Lifetime of Great Credit, by Gerri Detweiler (Plume Books), covers everything you'd want to know about credit ratings, credit cards, completing credit applications, protecting your credit privacy, and many other topics.

NCLC Guide to Surviving Debt: A Guide for Consumers, by the National Consumer Law Center (NCLC). NCLC is a nonprofit organization that normally publishes books to assist lawyers. NCLC uses its years of experience in counseling low-income debtors across the country to offer tips on all kinds of debts and income sources, including government benefits, defenses to collection lawsuits, and strategies when your house is in foreclosure. Order this guide from NCLC, Publications Department, 77 Summer Street, 10th Floor, Boston, MA 02110, 617-542-9595 or on NCLC's website, at www.nclc.org/ publications/guides/ surviving_debt.shtml.

What Every Credit Card User Needs to Know, by Howard Strong (Owl Books), includes almost everything you need to know about selecting and using credit cards. It also contains many useful sample letters.

Online Resources

If you have access to the Internet, you can find a good deal of information using your computer. But you can't do it all—not every court decision or state statute is available online. Furthermore, unless you know what you are looking for—the case name and citation or the code section—you may have difficulty finding it.

Still, there are a number of useful sites. For legal research, visit:

- **www.nolo.com/statute/index.cfm**
  Nolo's website provides a legal research page with links to each state's online legal information (including state statutes) plus links to federal statues, regulations, and the U.S. Constitution.

Specific debt, credit, finance, consumer protection and bankruptcy information is available at a few sites, including the following:

- **www.nolo.com**
  Nolo's online site includes legal information for consumers, such as frequently asked questions and articles on legal issues (click on the "property & money" category).

- **www.myvesta.org**
  Myvesta.org, a nonprofit online resource dedicated to helping people get out of debt, maintains a website designed to help you deal with your financial problems. Their advice covers budgeting, financial recovery, debt management, and debt payoff. The site is updated daily; is free; lists software, publications, and information; contains special programs to help you get out of debt; and has a debt forum where you can post your specific questions for myvesta.org's counselors to answer.

- **www.ftc.gov**
  The Federal Trade Commission's website provides free publications on many consumer topics, including credit repair. It also provides links to the full text of numerous consumer protection laws (click on "Rules & Acts" in any of the consumer topics).

- **www.pueblo.gsa.gov**
  The Federal Citizen Information Center provides the latest in consumer news as well as many publications of interest to consumers, including the Consumer Information Catalog.

- **www.fdic.gov**
  www.federalreserve.gov
  The Federal Deposit Insurance Corporation and Federal Reserve Board websites have consumer information and resources for understanding and researching banks and financial institutions.

- **www.irs.gov**
  The Internal Revenue Service provides tax information, forms, and publications.
- **www.fraud.org**
  The National Fraud Information Center's website provides lots of information on how to protect yourself from telemarketing and Internet scams and how to report fraud.
- **www.bbb.org**
  The Better Business Bureau has information on a number of consumer topics and links to local BBB offices. Use this site to check with your local BBB for complaints about businesses in the area before doing business with them.

State Consumer Protection Agencies

The state agencies listed below enforce consumer protection laws and provide consumer protection information. Many of these agencies regulate credit bureaus, accept complaints about credit bureaus in the state, and provide free information about your rights as they relate to collection bureaus.

If your state can't or won't help you, contact the Federal Trade Commission, www.ftc.gov.

Alabama
Consumer Affairs Division
Office of Attorney General
Alabama State House
11 South Union Street, Third Floor
Montgomery, AL 36130
334-242-7335
800-392-5658
www.ago.state.al.us

Alaska
Consumer Protection Unit
Fair Business Practices Section
Office of the Attorney General
1031 West 4th Avenue, Suite 200
Anchorage AK 99501-5903
907-269-5100
www.law.state.ak.us/consumer

Arizona
Consumer Information and Complaints
Office of Attorney General
1275 West Washington Street
Phoenix, AZ 85007-2926
602-542-5763
800-352-8431
602-542-5002 (TTY)
www.ag.state.az.us

Arkansas
Consumer Protection Division
Office of the Attorney General
323 Center Street, Suite 200
Little Rock, AR 72201
501-682-2341
800-482-8982
501-682-6073 (TTY)
www.ag.state.ar.us

California

Public Inquiry Unit
Office of the Attorney General
Department of Justice
P.O. Box 944255
Sacramento, CA 94244-2550
916-322-3360
800-952-5225
916-324-5564 (TDY)
http://ag.ca.gov/consumers

Colorado

Consumer Protection Section
Office of Attorney General
1525 Sherman Street
Fifth Floor
Denver, CO 80203-1768
303-866-5189
800-222-4444
www.ago.state.co.us/consumer_
  protection.cfm

Connecticut

Department of Consumer Protection
165 Capitol Avenue
Hartford, CT 06106-1630
860-713-6300
800-831-7225
860-713-7240 (TDD)
www.ct.gov/dcp

Delaware

Consumer Protection Unit
Office of the Attorney General
820 North French Street
Carvel State Building
Wilmington, DE 19801
302-577-8600
800-220-5424
www.state.de.us/attgen/fraud/consumerpro-
  tection/consumerprotection.htm

District of Columbia

Department of Consumer and Regulatory Affairs
941 North Capitol Street, NE
Washington, DC 20002
202-442-4400
202-442-9480 (TDD-TTY)
www.dcra.dc.gov/dcra

Florida

Division of Consumer Services
Department of Agriculture and Consumer
  Services
2005 Apalachee Parkway
Tallahassee, FL 32399-6500
850-488-2221
800-435-7352
www.doacs.state.fl.us or www.800helpfla.com

Georgia

Governor's Office of Consumer Affairs
2 Martin Luther King, Jr. Drive, Suite 356
Atlanta, GA 30334
404-651-8600
800-869-1123
www2.state.ga.us/gaoca

Hawaii

Office of Consumer Protection
235 S. Beretonia Street
Suite 801
Leiopapa A Kamehameha Building
Honolulu, HI 96813
808-587-3222
808-586-2630
www.state.hi.us/dcca/areas/ocp

Idaho

Consumer Protection Unit
Office of Attorney General
700 W. Jefferson Street
P.O. Box 83720
Boise, ID 83720-0010
208-334-2400
800-432-3545
www.state.id.us/ag/consumer

Illinois

Consumer Protection Division
Office of Attorney General
100 W. Randolph Street
Chicago, IL 60601
312-814-3000
800-386-5438
800-964-3013 (TTY)
www.ag.state.il.us/consumers

Indiana

Consumer Credit Division
Department of Financial Institutions
30 South Meridian Street, Suite 300
Indianapolis, IN 46204
317-232-3955
800-382-4880
www.in.gov/dfi

Iowa

Consumer Protection Division
Office of Attorney General
1305 E. Walnut Street
Des Moines, IA 50319
515-281-5926
www.state.ia.us/government/ag/
   consumer.html

Kansas

Consumer Protection and Antitrust Division
Office of Attorney General
120 S.W. Tenth Avenue
Topeka, KS 66612-1597
785-296-3751
800-432-2310
785-291-3767 (TTY)
www.ksag.org/Divisions/consumer/
   main.htm

Kentucky

Consumer Protection Division
Office of the Attorney General
The Capitol, Suite 118
700 Capitol Ave.
Frankfort, KY 40601
502-696-5389
888-423-9257
www.ag.ky.gov/cp

Louisiana

Consumer Protection Section
Office of the Attorney General
P.O. Box 94095
Baton Rouge, LA 70804-9095
225-326-6465
800-351-4889
www.ag.state.la.us/consumers.aspx

Maine

Consumer Information and Mediation Service
Public Protection Division
Office of the Attorney General
6 State House Station
Augusta, ME 04333-0006
207-626-8800
207-626-8865 (TTY)
www.maine.gov/ag/?r=protection

Maryland

Consumer Protection Division
Office of Attorney General
200 St. Paul Place
Baltimore, MD 21202-2022
410-576-6550
888-743-0023
www.oag.state.md.us/consumer

Massachusetts

Office of Consumer Affairs and Business Regulation
lation
10 Park Plaza, Suite 5170
Boston, MA 02116
617-973-8787 (hotline)
617-973-8700
888-283-3757
www.mass.gov/consumer

Michigan

Consumer Protection Division
Office of Attorney General
P.O. Box 30212
Lansing, MI 48909
517-373-1140
877-765-8388
www.ag.state.mi.us/cp

Minnesota

Consumer Protection Division
Office of Attorney General
1400 Bremer Tower
445 Minnesota Street
St. Paul, MN 55101-2130
651-296-3353
800-657-3787
651-297-7206 (TTY)
800-366-4812 (TTY)
www.ag.state.mn.us

Mississippi

Consumer Protection Division
Office of the Attorney General
P.O. Box 22947
Jackson, MS 39225-2947
601-359-4230
800-281-4418
www.ago.state.ms.us/divisions/ consumer

Missouri

Consumer Protection Division
Attorney General's Office
P.O. Box 899
Jefferson City, MO 65102
573-751-3321
800-392-8222
www.ago.state.mo.gov/divisions/
consumerprotection.htm

Montana

Consumer Protection Office
1219 Eighth Avenue
P.O. Box 200151
Helena, MT 59620-0151
406-444-4500
http://doj.mt.gov/consumer

Nebraska

Consumer Protection Division
Office of Attorney General
2115 State Capitol Building
Lincoln, NE 68509-8920
402-471-2682
800-727-6432
www.ago.state.ne.us

Nevada

Consumer Affairs Division

Department of Business and Industry

1850 E. Sahara Avenue, Suite 101

Las Vegas, NV 89104

702-486-7355

[or]

4600 Kietzke Lane

Building B, Suite 113

Reno, NV 89502

775-688-1800

www.fyiconsumer.org

New Hampshire

Consumer Protection and Antitrust Bureau

Department of Justice

33 Capitol Street

Concord, NH 03301-6397

603-271-3658

www.nh.gov/nhdoj/consumer

New Jersey

Division of Consumer Affairs

Department of Law and Public Safety

124 Halsey Street

Newark, NJ 07102

973-504-6200

800-242-5846

973-504-6588 (TDD)

www.njconsumeraffairs.gov

New Mexico

Consumer Protection Division

Office of Attorney General

P.O. Drawer 1508

Santa Fe, NM 87504-1508

505-827-6060

800-678-1508

www.ago.state.nm.us/divs/cons/cons.htm

New York

Consumer Protection Board

5 Empire State Plaza, Suite 2101

Albany, NY 12223-1556

518-474-3514

518-474-8583 (Complaint Unit)

800-697-1220

800-788-9898 (TTY)

www.consumer.state.ny.us

North Carolina

Consumer Protection Division

Department of Justice, Attorney General's Office

9001 Mail Service Center

Raleigh, NC 27699-9001

919-716-6400

877-566-7226

www.ncdoj.com/consumer protection/cp_
about.jsp

North Dakota

Consumer Protection Division

Office of Attorney General

600 East Boulevard Avenue

Dept. 125

Bismarck, ND 58505-0040

701-328-3404

800-472-2600

www.ag.state.nd.us/CPAT/CPAT.htm

Ohio

Consumer Protection Division

Office of Attorney General

State Office Tower

30 East Broad Street, 17th Floor

Columbus, OH 43215-3428

614-466-4320

800-282-0515

www.ag.state.oh.us/citizen/
consumerindex.asp

Oklahoma

Consumer Protection Unit
Office of the Attorney General
4545 N. Lincoln Boulevard, Suite 112
Oklahoma City, OK 73105-3498
405-521-3921
www.oag.state.ok.us/oagweb.nsf/consumer

Oregon

Financial Fraud/Consumer Protection Section
1162 Court Street, NE
Salem, OR 97301-4096
503-378-4320
503-229-5576 (Portland toll-free)
877-877-9392
www.doj.state.or.us/FinFraud/index.shtml

Pennsylvania

Bureau of Consumer Protection
Office of Attorney General
Strawberry Square, 14th Floor
Harrisburg, PA 17120
717-787-9707
800-441-2555
www.attorneygeneral.gov/consumers.asp

Rhode Island

Consumer Protection Unit
Department of Attorney General
150 S. Main Street
Providence, RI 02903
401-274-4400
800-852-7776
401-453-0410 (TTY)
www.riag.state.ri.us/civil/unit.
    php?name=consumer

South Carolina

Department of Consumer Affairs
P.O. Box 5757
3600 Forest Drive, 3rd Floor
Columbia, SC 29250
803-734-4200
800-922-1594
www.ssconsumer.gov

South Dakota

Division of Consumer Protection
Office of the Attorney General
1302 E. Hwy. 14, Suite 3
Pierre, SD 57501-5070
605-773-4400
800-300-1986
www.state.sd.us/attorney/office/ divisions/
    consumer

Tennessee

Division of Consumer Affairs
Department of Commerce and Insurance
500 James Robertson Parkway
Nashville, TN 37243-0600
615-741-4737
800-342-8385
http://state.tn.us/consumer

Texas

Consumer Protection Division
Office of the Attorney General
P.O. Box 12548
Austin, TX 78711-2548
512-463-2185
800-621-0508
www.oag.state.tx.us/consumer/
    consumer.shtml

Utah

Division of Consumer Protection
Department of Commerce
160 E. 300 South
SM Box 146704
Salt Lake City, UT 84114-6704
801-530-6601
800-721-7233
http://consumerprotection.utah.gov

Vermont

Consumer Assistance Program
Office of Attorney General
104 Morrill Hall, UVM
Burlington, VT 05405-0106
802-656-3183
800-649-2424
www.atg.state.vt.us/disply.
    php?pubsec=0&smod=8

Virginia

Office of Consumer Affairs
Department of Agriculture and Consumer
    Services
102 Governor St.
Richmond, VA 23219
804-786-2042
800-552-9963
www.vdacs.virginia.gov/consumers

Washington

Consumer Resource Center
Office of the Attorney General
P.O. Box 40100
1125 Washington Street SE
Olympia, WA 98504-0100
360-753-6200
800-551-4636
800-276-9883 (TDD)
www.atg.wa.gov/consumerintro.shtml

West Virginia

Consumer Protection Division
Office of the Attorney General
1900 Kanawha Boulevard
Room 26E
Charleston, WV 25305-9924
304-558-8986
800-368-8808
www.wvag.us

Wisconsin

Bureau of Consumer Protection
Department of Agriculture, Trade, and
    Consumer Protection
P.O. Box 8911
Madison, WI 53708-8911
608-221-4949
800-422-7128
608-224-5058 (TTY)
www.datcp.state.wi.us

Wyoming

Consumer Protection Unit
Attorney General's Office
123 Capitol
200 W. 24th Street
Cheyenne, WY 82002
307-777-7874
800-438-5799
http://attorneygeneral.state.wy.us/
    consumer.htm

Where to Complain About Credit Discrimination

If you believe you have been a victim of credit discrimination, here are the appropriate government agencies to contact:

- Consumer Response Center
  Federal Trade Commission
  Washington, DC 20580

  Contact the FTC if you have been discriminated against by a store, mortgage company, small loan and finance company, oil company, public utility, state credit union, government lending program, or travel and expense credit card company. Although the FTC doesn't intervene in individual disputes, the information you provide may show a pattern of violations on which it can act.

- Comptroller of the Currency
  Compliance Management
  Mail Stop 7-5
  Washington, DC 20219

  Use this address if your complaint is about a nationally chartered bank ("National" or "N.A." will be in its name).

- Federal Deposit Insurance Corporation
  Consumer Affairs Division
  Washington, DC 20429

  Contact the FDIC if your complaint is about a state-chartered bank that is insured by the FDIC but is not a member of the Federal Reserve System.

- Office of Thrift Supervision
  Consumer Affairs Program
  Washington, DC 20552

  Use this address to complain about a federally chartered or federally-insured savings and loan association.

- National Credit Union Administration
  Consumer Affairs Division
  Washington, DC 20456

  Use the address if your complaint is about a federally chartered credit union.

- Department of Justice
  Civil Rights Division
  Washington, DC 20530

  You can complain to the Justice Department about any type of creditor. ■

Federal Credit Reporting and Credit Repair Laws

This appendix contains many of the rules regulating credit bureaus. You'll find the federal government's rules in the Fair Credit Reporting Act (FCRA). In addition, most states have enacted laws related to credit reporting and credit bureaus. To get your state law, contact your state consumer protection agency (listed in Appendix 1). This appendix also includes the text of the Federal Credit Repair Organizations Act—the law that regulates credit repair clinics. A summary of state laws that govern credit repair clinics is found in Chapter 6.

The text of these statutes was current as of January 2007. To check for changes in the law, see Nolo's website (www.nolo.com) for updates to this book, obtain a copy of the statute in question, online (see www.nolo.com/statute/index.cfm), or visit your local law library.

If a credit bureau violates the federal FCRA, you can register a complaint with the Federal Trade Commission (contact information is in Chapter 4). You can also sue for negligent or willful noncompliance with the federal FCRA within two years of the bureau's violation. You can sue for actual damages, such as court costs, attorney's fees, lost wages, and, if applicable, infliction of emotional distress. In cases of truly outrageous behavior, you can ask for punitive damages—damages meant to punish for malicious or willful conduct.

If a credit bureau violates a state law, you can register a complaint with the appropriate state agency (addresses and phone numbers are in Appendix 1). You can probably also sue for noncompliance with the state law. If you are thinking about suing, however, you'll need to find the full state law and read it carefully. (Look for the law at a local law library, at a large public library, or on the Internet.)

These lawsuits can probably be filed in small claims court without the help of an attorney. (See *Everybody's Guide to Small Claims Court*, by Ralph Warner (Nolo) for information on suing in small claims court.) If you plan to ask for punitive damages, you'll probably need a lawyer's help to file a lawsuit in a regular civil court.

Text of the Federal Fair Credit Reporting Act

15 U.S.C. § 1681. Congressional findings and statement of purpose

(a) Accuracy and fairness of credit reporting
The Congress makes the following findings:

(1) The banking system is dependent upon fair and accurate credit reporting. Inaccurate credit reports directly impair the efficiency of the banking system, and unfair credit reporting methods undermine the public confidence which is essential to the continued functioning of the banking system.

(2) An elaborate mechanism has been developed for investigating and

evaluating the credit worthiness, credit standing, credit capacity, character, and general reputation of consumers.

(3) Consumer reporting agencies have assumed a vital role in assembling and evaluating consumer credit and other information on consumers.

(4) There is a need to insure that consumer reporting agencies exercise their grave responsibilities with fairness, impartiality, and a respect for the consumer's right to privacy.

(b) Reasonable procedures

It is the purpose of this subchapter to require that consumer reporting agencies adopt reasonable procedures for meeting the needs of commerce for consumer credit, personnel, insurance, and other information in a manner which is fair and equitable to the consumer, with regard to the confidentiality, accuracy, relevancy, and proper utilization of such information in accordance with the requirements of this subchapter.

15 U.S.C. § 1681a. Definitions; rules of construction

(a) Definitions and rules of construction set forth in this section are applicable for the purposes of this subchapter.

(b) The term "person" means any individual, partnership, corporation, trust, estate, cooperative, association, government or governmental subdivision or agency, or other entity.

(c) The term "consumer" means an individual.

(d) Consumer report.

(1) In general.

The term "consumer report" means any written, oral, or other communication of any information by a consumer reporting agency bearing on a consumer's credit worthiness, credit standing, credit capacity, character, general reputation, personal characteristics, or mode of living which is used or expected to be used or collected in whole or in part for the purpose of serving as a factor in establishing the consumer's eligibility for—

(A) credit or insurance to be used primarily for personal, family, or household purposes;

(B) employment purposes; or

(C) any other purpose authorized under section 1681b of this title.

(2) Exclusions.

Except as provided in paragraph (3), the term "consumer report" does not include—

(A) subject to section 1681s-3 of this title, any—

(i) report containing information solely as to transactions or experiences between the consumer and the person making the report;

(ii) communication of that information among persons related by common ownership or affiliated by corporate control; or

(iii) communication of other information among persons related by common ownership or affiliated by corporate control, if it is clearly and conspicuously disclosed to the consumer that the information may be communicated among such persons and the consumer is given the opportunity, before the time that the information is initially communicated, to direct that such information not be communicated among such persons;

(B) any authorization or approval of a specific extension of credit directly or indirectly by the issuer of a credit card or similar device;

(C) any report in which a person who has been requested by a third party to make a specific extension of credit directly or indirectly to a consumer conveys his or her decision with respect to such request, if the third party advises the consumer of the name and address of the person to whom the request was made, and such person makes the disclosures to the consumer required under section 1681m of this title; or

(D) a communication described in subsection (o) or (x) of this section.

(3) Restriction on sharing of medical information Except for information or any communication of information disclosed as provided in section 1681b(g)(3) of this title, the exclusions in paragraph (2) shall not apply with respect to information disclosed to any person related by common ownership or affiliated by corporate control, if the information is—

(A) medical information;

(B) an individualized list or description based on the payment transactions of the consumer for medical products or services; or

(C) an aggregate list of identified consumers based on payment transactions for medical products or services.

(e) The term "investigative consumer report" means a consumer report or portion thereof in which information on a consumer's character, general reputation, personal characteristics, or mode of living is obtained through personal interviews with neighbors, friends, or associates of the consumer reported on or with others with whom he is acquainted or who may have knowledge concerning any such items of information. However, such information shall not include specific factual information on a consumer's credit record obtained directly from a creditor of the consumer or from a consumer reporting agency when such information was obtained directly from a creditor of the consumer or from the consumer.

(f) The term "consumer reporting agency" means any person which, for monetary fees, dues, or on a cooperative nonprofit basis, regularly engages in whole or in part in the practice of assembling or evaluating consumer credit information or other information on consumers for the purpose of furnishing consumer reports to third parties, and which uses any means or facility of interstate commerce for the purpose of preparing or furnishing consumer reports.

(g) The term "file," when used in connection with information on any consumer, means all of the information on that consumer recorded and retained by a consumer reporting agency regardless of how the information is stored.

(h) The term "employment purposes" when used in connection with a consumer report means a report used for the purpose of evaluating a consumer for employment, promotion, reassignment, or retention as an employee.

(i) Medical information

The term "medical information"—

(1) means information or data, whether oral or recorded, in any form or medium, created by or derived from a health care provider or the consumer, that relates to—

(A) the past, present, or future physical, mental, or behavioral health or condition of an individual;

(B) the provision of health care to an individual; or

(C) the payment for the provision of health care to an individual.

(2) does not include the age or gender of a consumer, demographic

information about the consumer, including a consumer's residence address or e-mail address, or any other information about a consumer that does not relate to the physical, mental, or behavioral health or condition of a consumer, including the existence or value of any insurance policy.

(j) Definitions relating to child support obligations

(1) Overdue support

The term "overdue support" has the meaning given to such term in section 666(e) of Title 42.

(2) State or local child support enforcement agency

The term "State or local child support enforcement agency" means a State or local agency which administers a State or local program for establishing and enforcing child support obligations.

(k) Adverse action.

(1) Actions included.

The term "adverse action"—

(A) has the same meaning as in section 1691(d)(6) of this title; and

(B) means—

(i) a denial or cancellation of, an increase in any charge for, or a reduction or other adverse or unfavorable change in the terms of coverage or amount of, any insurance, existing or applied for, in connection with the underwriting of insurance;

(ii) a denial of employment or any other decision for employment purposes that adversely affects any current or prospective employee;

(iii) a denial or cancellation of, an increase in any charge for, or any other adverse or unfavorable change in the terms of, any license or benefit described in section 1681b(a)(3)(D) of this title; and

(iv) an action taken or determination that is—

    (I) made in connection with an application that was made by, or a transaction that was initiated by, any consumer, or in connection with a review of an account under section 1681b(a)(3)(F)(ii) of this title; and

    (II) adverse to the interests of the consumer.

(2) Applicable findings, decisions, commentary, and orders.

For purposes of any determination of whether an action is an adverse action under paragraph (1)(A), all appropriate final findings, decisions, commentary, and orders issued under section 1691(d)(6) of this title by the Board of Governors of the Federal Reserve System or any court shall apply.

(l) Firm offer of credit or insurance. The term "firm offer of credit or insurance" means any offer of credit or insurance to a consumer that will be honored if the consumer is determined, based on information in a consumer report on the consumer, to meet the specific criteria used to select the consumer for the offer, except that the offer may be further conditioned on one or more of the following:

(1) The consumer being determined, based on information in the consumer's application for the credit or insurance, to meet specific criteria bearing on credit worthiness or insurability, as applicable, that are established—

    (A) before selection of the consumer for the offer; and

    (B) for the purpose of determining whether to extend credit or insurance pursuant to the offer.

(2) Verification

    (A) that the consumer continues to meet the specific criteria used to select the consumer for the offer, by using information in a consumer report on the consumer, information in the consumer's application for the credit or insurance, or other information bearing on the credit worthiness or insurability of the consumer; or

    (B) of the information in the consumer's application for the credit or insurance, to determine that the consumer meets the specific criteria bearing on credit worthiness or insurability.

(3) The consumer furnishing any collateral that is a requirement for the extension of the credit or insurance that was—

    (A) established before selection of the consumer for the offer of credit or insurance; and

    (B) disclosed to the consumer in the offer of credit or insurance.

(m) Credit or insurance transaction that is not initiated by the consumer.

The term "credit or insurance transaction that is not initiated by the consumer" does not include the use of a consumer report by a person with which the consumer has an account or insurance policy, for purposes of—

(1) reviewing the account or insurance policy; or

(2) collecting the account.

(n) State.

The term "State" means any State, the Commonwealth of Puerto Rico, the District of Columbia, and any territory or possession of the United States.

(o) Excluded communications.

A communication is described in this subsection if it is a communication—

(1) that, but for subsection (d)(2)(D) of this section, would be an investigative consumer report;

(2) that is made to a prospective employer for the purpose of—

    (A) procuring an employee for the employer; or

    (B) procuring an opportunity for a natural person to work for the employer;

(3) that is made by a person who regularly performs such procurement;

(4) that is not used by any person for any purpose other than a purpose described in subparagraph (A) or (B) of paragraph (2); and

(5) with respect to which—

    (A) the consumer who is the subject of the communication—

        (i) consents orally or in writing to the nature and scope of the communication, before the collection of any information for the purpose of making the communication;

        (ii) consents orally or in writing to the making of the communication to a prospective employer, before the making of the communication; and

        (iii) in the case of consent under clause (i) or (ii) given orally, is provided written confirmation of that consent by the person making the communication, not later than 3 business days after the receipt of the consent by that person;

    (B) the person who makes the communication does not, for the purpose of making the communication, make any inquiry that if made by a prospective employer of the consumer who is the subject of the communication would violate any applicable Federal or State equal employment opportunity law or regulation; and

(C) the person who makes the communication—

    (i) discloses in writing to the consumer who is the subject of the communication, not later than 5 business days after receiving any request from the consumer for such disclosure, the nature and substance of all information in the consumer's file at the time of the request, except that the sources of any information that is acquired solely for use in making the communication and is actually used for no other purpose, need not be disclosed other than under appropriate discovery procedures in any court of competent jurisdiction in which an action is brought; and

    (ii) notifies the consumer who is the subject of the communication, in writing, of the consumer's right to request the information described in clause (i).

(p) Consumer reporting agency that compiles and maintains files on consumers on a nationwide basis. The term "consumer reporting agency that compiles and maintains files on consumers on a nationwide basis" means a consumer reporting agency that regularly engages in the practice of assembling or evaluating, and maintaining, for the purpose of furnishing consumer reports to third parties bearing on a consumer's credit worthiness, credit standing, or credit capacity, each of the following regarding consumers residing nationwide:

(1) Public record information.

(2) Credit account information from persons who furnish that information regularly and in the ordinary course of business.

(q) Definitions relating to fraud alerts

(1) Active duty military consumer
The term "active duty military consumer" means a consumer in military service who—

    (A) is on active duty (as defined in section 101(d)(1) of Title 10) or is a reservist performing duty under a call or order to active duty under a provision of law referred to in section 101(a)(13) of Title 10; and

    (B) is assigned to service away from the usual duty station of the consumer.

(2) Fraud alert; active duty alert
The terms "fraud alert" and "active duty alert" mean a statement in the file of a consumer that—

    (A) notifies all prospective users of a consumer report relating to the consumer that the consumer may be a victim of fraud, including identity theft, or is an active duty military consumer, as applicable; and

(B) is presented in a manner that facilitates a clear and conspicuous view of the statement described in subparagraph (A) by any person requesting such consumer report.

(3) Identity theft

The term "identity theft" means a fraud committed using the identifying information of another person, subject to such further definition as the Commission may prescribe, by regulation.

(4) Identity theft report

The term "identity theft report" has the meaning given that term by rule of the Commission, and means, at a minimum, a report—

(A) that alleges an identity theft;

(B) that is a copy of an official, valid report filed by a consumer with an appropriate Federal, State, or local law enforcement agency, including the United States Postal Inspection Service, or such other government agency deemed appropriate by the Commission; and

(C) the filing of which subjects the person filing the report to criminal penalties relating to the filing of false information if, in fact, the information in the report is false.

(5) New credit plan

The term "new credit plan" means a new account under an open end credit plan (as defined in section 1602(i) of this title) or a new credit

transaction not under an open end credit plan.

(r) Credit and debit related terms

(1) Card issuer

The term "card issuer" means—

(A) a credit card issuer, in the case of a credit card; and

(B) a debit card issuer, in the case of a debit card.

(2) Credit card

The term "credit card" has the same meaning as in section 1602 of this title.

(3) Debit card

The term "debit card" means any card issued by a financial institution to a consumer for use in initiating an electronic fund transfer from the account of the consumer at such financial institution, for the purpose of transferring money between accounts or obtaining money, property, labor, or services.

(4) Account and electronic fund transfer

The terms "account" and "electronic fund transfer" have the same meanings as in section 1693a of this title.

(5) Credit and creditor

The terms "credit" and "creditor" have the same meanings as in section 1691a of this title.

(s) Federal banking agency

The term "Federal banking agency" has the same meaning as in section 1813 of Title 12.

(t) Financial institution

The term "financial institution" means a State or National bank, a State or Federal savings and loan association, a mutual savings bank, a State or Federal credit union, or any other person that, directly or indirectly, holds a transaction account (as defined in section 461(b) of Title 12) belonging to a consumer.

(u) Reseller

The term "reseller" means a consumer reporting agency that—

(1) assembles and merges information contained in the database of another consumer reporting agency or multiple consumer reporting agencies concerning any consumer for purposes of furnishing such information to any third party, to the extent of such activities; and

(2) does not maintain a database of the assembled or merged information from which new consumer reports are produced.

(v) Commission

The term "Commission" means the Federal Trade Commission.

(w) Nationwide specialty consumer reporting agency

The term "nationwide specialty consumer reporting agency" means a consumer reporting agency that compiles and maintains files on consumers on a nationwide basis relating to—

(1) medical records or payments;

(2) residential or tenant history;

(3) check writing history;

(4) employment history; or

(5) insurance claims.

(x) Exclusion of certain communications for employee investigations

(1) Communications described in this subsection

A communication is described in this subsection if—

(A) but for subsection (d)(2)(D) of this section, the communication would be a consumer report;

(B) the communication is made to an employer in connection with an investigation of—

(i) suspected misconduct relating to employment; or

(ii) compliance with Federal, State, or local laws and regulations, the rules of a self-regulatory organization, or any preexisting written policies of the employer;

(C) the communication is not made for the purpose of investigating a consumer's credit worthiness, credit standing, or credit capacity; and

(D) the communication is not provided to any person except—

(i) to the employer or an agent of the employer;

(ii) to any Federal or State officer, agency, or department, or any officer, agency, or department of a unit of general local government;

(iii) to any self-regulatory organization with regulatory authority over the activities of the employer or employee;

(iv) as otherwise required by law; or

(v) pursuant to section 1681f of this title.

(2) Subsequent disclosure

After taking any adverse action based in whole or in part on a communication described in paragraph (1), the employer shall disclose to the consumer a summary containing the nature and substance of the communication upon which the adverse action is based, except that the sources of information acquired solely for use in preparing what would be but for subsection (d)(2)(D) of this section an investigative consumer report need not be disclosed.

(3) Self-regulatory organization defined

For purposes of this subsection, the term "self-regulatory organization" includes any self-regulatory organization (as defined in section 78c(a)(26) of this title), any entity established under title I of the Sarbanes-Oxley Act of 2002, any board of trade designated by the Commodity Futures Trading Commission, and any futures association registered with such Commission.

15 U.S.C. § 1681b. Permissible purposes of consumer reports

(a) In general

Subject to subsection (c) of this section, any consumer reporting agency may furnish a consumer report under the following circumstances and no other:

(1) In response to the order of a court having jurisdiction to issue such an order, or a subpoena issued in connection with proceedings before a Federal grand jury.

(2) In accordance with the written instructions of the consumer to whom it relates.

(3) To a person which it has reason to believe—

(A) intends to use the information in connection with a credit transaction involving the consumer on whom the information is to be furnished and involving the extension of credit to, or review or collection of an account of, the consumer; or

(B) intends to use the information for employment purposes; or

(C) intends to use the information in connection with the underwriting of insurance involving the consumer; or

(D) intends to use the information in connection with a determination of the consumer's eligibility for a license or other benefit granted by a governmental instrumentality required by law to consider an applicant's financial responsibility or status; or

(E) intends to use the information, as a potential investor or servicer, or current insurer, in connection with a valuation of, or an assessment of the credit or prepayment risks associated with, an existing credit obligation; or

(F) otherwise has a legitimate business need for the information—

    (i) in connection with a business transaction that is initiated by the consumer; or

    (ii) to review an account to determine whether the consumer continues to meet the terms of the account.

(4) In response to a request by the head of a State or local child support enforcement agency (or a State or local government official authorized by the head of such an agency), if the person making the request certifies to the consumer reporting agency that—

    (A) the consumer report is needed for the purpose of establishing an individual's capacity to make child support payments or determining the appropriate level of such payments;

    (B) the paternity of the consumer for the child to which the obligation relates has been established or acknowledged by the consumer in accordance with State laws under which the obligation arises (if required by those laws);

    (C) the person has provided at least 10 days' prior notice to the consumer whose report is requested, by certified or registered mail to the last known address of the consumer, that the report will be requested; and

    (D) the consumer report will be kept confidential, will be used solely for a purpose described in subparagraph (A), and will not be used in connection with any other civil, administrative, or criminal proceeding, or for any other purpose.

(5) To an agency administering a State plan under section 654 of Title 42 for use to set an initial or modified child support award.

(6) To the Federal Deposit Insurance Corporation or the National Credit Union Administration as part of its preparation for its appointment or as part of its exercise of powers, as conservator, receiver, or liquidating agent for an insured depository institution or insured credit union under the Federal Deposit Insurance Act or the Federal Credit Union Act, or other applicable Federal or State law, or in connection with the resolution or liquidation of a failed or failing insured depository institution or insured credit union, as applicable.

(b)   Conditions for furnishing and using consumer reports for employment purposes

(1) Certification from user

A consumer reporting agency may furnish a consumer report for employment purposes only if—

    (A) the person who obtains such report from the agency certifies to the agency that—

        (i) the person has complied with paragraph (2) with respect to the consumer report, and the person will comply with paragraph (3) with respect to the consumer report if paragraph (3) becomes applicable; and

(ii) information from the consumer report will not be used in violation of any applicable Federal or State equal employment opportunity law or regulation; and

(B) the consumer reporting agency provides with the report, or has previously provided, a summary of the consumer's rights under this subchapter, as prescribed by the Federal Trade Commission under section 1681g(c)(3) of this title.

(2) Disclosure to consumer

(A) In general

Except as provided in subparagraph (B), a person may not procure a consumer report, or cause a consumer report to be procured, for employment purposes with respect to any consumer, unless—

(i) a clear and conspicuous disclosure has been made in writing to the consumer at any time before the report is procured or caused to be procured, in a document that consists solely of the disclosure, that a consumer report may be obtained for employment purposes; and

(ii) the consumer has authorized

in writing (which authorization may be made on the document referred to in clause (i)) the procurement of the report by that person.

(B) Application by mail, telephone, computer, or other similar means

If a consumer described in subparagraph (C) applies for employment by mail, telephone, computer, or other similar means, at any time before a consumer report is procured or caused to be procured in connection with that application—

(i) the person who procures the consumer report on the consumer for employment purposes shall provide to the consumer, by oral, written, or electronic means, notice that a consumer report may be obtained for employment purposes, and a summary of the consumer's rights under section 1681m(a)(3) of this title; and

(ii) the consumer shall have consented, orally, in writing, or electronically to the procurement of the report by that person.

(C) Scope

Subparagraph (B) shall apply to a person procuring a consumer report on a consumer in connection with the consumer's application for employment only if—

(i) the consumer is applying for a position over which the Secretary of Transportation has the power to establish qualifications and maximum hours of service pursuant to the provisions of section 31502 of Title 49, or a position subject to safety regulation by a State transportation agency; and

(ii) as of the time at which the person procures the report or causes the report to be procured the only interaction between the consumer and the person in connection with that employment application has been by mail, telephone, computer, or other similar means.

(3) Conditions on use for adverse actions

(A) In general

Except as provided in subparagraph (B), in using a consumer report for employment purposes, before taking any adverse action based in whole or in part on the report, the person intending to take such adverse action shall provide to the consumer to whom the report relates—

(i) a copy of the report; and

(ii) a description in writing of the rights of the consumer under this subchapter, as prescribed by the Federal Trade Commission under section 1681g(c)(3) of this title.

(B) Application by mail, telephone, computer, or other similar means

(i) If a consumer described in subparagraph (C) applies for employment by mail, telephone, computer, or other similar means, and if a person who has procured a consumer report on the consumer for employment purposes takes adverse action on the employment application based in whole or in part on the report, then the person must provide to the consumer to whom the report relates, in lieu of the notices required under subparagraph (A) of this section and under section 1681m(a) of this title, within 3 business days of taking such action, an oral, written, or electronic notification—

(I) that adverse action has been taken based in whole or in part on a consumer report received from a consumer reporting agency;

(II) of the name, address, and telephone number of the consumer reporting agency that furnished the consumer report (including a toll-free telephone number established by the agency if the agency compiles and maintains files on consumers on a nationwide basis);

(III) that the consumer reporting agency did not make the decision to take the adverse action and is unable to provide to the consumer the specific reasons why the adverse action was taken; and

(IV) that the consumer may, upon providing proper identification, request a free copy of a report and may dispute with the consumer reporting agency the accuracy or completeness of any information in a report.

(ii) If, under clause (B)(i)(IV), the consumer requests a copy of a consumer report from the person who procured the report, then, within 3 business days of receiving the consumer's request, together with proper identification, the person must send or provide to the consumer a copy of a report and a copy of the consumer's rights as prescribed by the Federal Trade Commission under section 1681g(c)(3) of this title.

(C) Scope

Subparagraph (B) shall apply to a person procuring a consumer report on a consumer in connection with the consumer's application for employment only if—

(i) the consumer is applying for a position over which the Secretary of Transportation has the power to establish qualifications and maximum hours of service pursuant to the provisions of section 31502 of Title 49, or a position subject to safety regulation by a State transportation agency; and

(ii) as of the time at which the person procures the report or causes the report to be procured the only interaction between the consumer and the person in connection with that employment application has been by mail, telephone, computer, or other similar means.

(4) Exception for national security investigations

(A) In general

In the case of an agency or department of the United States Government which seeks to obtain and use a consumer report for employment purposes, paragraph (3) shall not apply to any adverse action by such agency or department which is based in part on such consumer report, if the head of such agency or department makes a written finding that—

(i) the consumer report is relevant to a national security investigation of such agency or department;

(ii) the investigation is within the jurisdiction of such agency or department;

(iii) there is reason to believe that compliance with paragraph (3) will—

(I) endanger the life or physical safety of any person;

(II) result in flight from prosecution;

(III) result in the destruction of, or tampering with, evidence relevant to the investigation;

(IV) result in the intimidation of a potential witness relevant to the investigation;

(V) result in the compromise of classified information; or

(VI) otherwise seriously jeopardize or unduly delay the investigation or another official proceeding.

(B) Notification of consumer upon conclusion of investigation

Upon the conclusion of a national security investigation described in subparagraph (A), or upon the determination that the exception under subparagraph (A) is no longer required for the reasons set forth in such subparagraph, the official exercising the authority in such subparagraph shall provide to the consumer who is the subject of the consumer report with regard to which such finding was made—

(i) a copy of such consumer report with any classified information redacted as necessary;

(ii) notice of any adverse action which is based, in part, on the consumer report; and

(iii) the identification with reasonable specificity of the nature of the investigation for which the consumer report was sought.

(C) Delegation by head of agency or department

For purposes of subparagraphs (A) and (B), the head of any agency or department of the United States Government may delegate his or her authorities under this paragraph to an official of such agency or department who has personnel security responsibilities and is a member of the Senior Executive Service or equivalent civilian or military rank.

(D) Definitions

For purposes of this paragraph, the following definitions shall apply:

(i) Classified information. The term "classified information" means information that is protected from unauthorized disclosure under Executive Order No. 12958 or successor orders.

(ii) National security investigation. The term "national security investigation" means any official inquiry by an agency or department of the United States Government to determine the eligibility of a consumer to receive access or continued access to classified information or to determine whether classified information has been lost or compromised.

(E) Repealed. Pub.L. 108-177, Title III, § 361(j), Dec. 13, 2003, 117 Stat. 2625

(F) Redesignated (D)

(c) Furnishing reports in connection with credit or insurance transactions that are not initiated by the consumer

(1) In general

A consumer reporting agency may furnish a consumer report relating to any consumer pursuant to subparagraph (A) or (C) of subsection (a)(3) of this section in connection with any credit or insurance transaction that is not initiated by the consumer only if—

(A) the consumer authorizes the agency to provide such report to such person; or

(B)

(i) the transaction consists of a firm offer of credit or insurance;

(ii) the consumer reporting agency has complied with subsection (e) of this section; and

(iii) there is not in effect an election by the consumer, made in accordance with subsection (e) of this section, to have the consumer's name and address excluded from lists of names provided by the agency pursuant to this paragraph.

(2) Limits on information received under paragraph (1)(B)

A person may receive pursuant to paragraph (1)(B) only—

(A) the name and address of a consumer;

(B) an identifier that is not unique to the consumer and that is used by the person solely for the purpose of verifying the identity of the consumer; and

(C) other information pertaining to a consumer that does not identify the relationship or experience of the consumer with respect to a particular creditor or other entity.

(3) Information regarding inquiries
Except as provided in section 1681g(a)(5) of this title, a consumer reporting agency shall not furnish to any person a record of inquiries in connection with a credit or insurance transaction that is not initiated by a consumer.

(d) Reserved

(e) Election of consumer to be excluded from lists

(1) In general
A consumer may elect to have the consumer's name and address excluded from any list provided by a consumer reporting agency under subsection (c)(1)(B) of this section in connection with a credit or insurance transaction that is not initiated by the consumer, by notifying the agency in accordance with paragraph (2) that the consumer does not consent to any use of a consumer report relating to the consumer in connection with any credit or insurance transaction that is not initiated by the consumer.

(2) Manner of notification
A consumer shall notify a consumer reporting agency under paragraph (1)—

(A) through the notification system maintained by the agency under paragraph (5); or

(B) by submitting to the agency a signed notice of election form issued by the agency for purposes of this subparagraph.

(3) Response of agency after notification through system
Upon receipt of notification of the election of a consumer under paragraph (1) through the notification system maintained by the agency under paragraph (5), a consumer reporting agency shall—

(A) inform the consumer that the election is effective only for the 5-year period following the election if the consumer does not submit to the agency a signed notice of election form issued by the agency for purposes of paragraph (2)(B); and

(B) provide to the consumer a notice of election form, if requested by the consumer, not later than 5 business days after receipt of the notification of the election through the system established under paragraph (5), in the case of a request made at the time the consumer provides notification through the system.

(4) Effectiveness of election
An election of a consumer under paragraph (1)—

(A) shall be effective with respect to a consumer reporting agency beginning 5 business days after the date on which the consumer notifies the agency in accordance with paragraph (2);

(B) shall be effective with respect to a consumer reporting agency—

(i) subject to subparagraph (C), during the 5-year period beginning 5 business days after the date on which the consumer notifies the agency of the election, in the case of an election for which a consumer notifies the agency only in accordance with paragraph (2)(A); or

(ii) until the consumer notifies the agency under subparagraph (C), in the case of an election for which a consumer notifies the agency in accordance with paragraph (2)(B);

(C) shall not be effective after the date on which the consumer notifies the agency, through the notification system established by the agency under paragraph (5), that the election is no longer effective; and

(D) shall be effective with respect to each affiliate of the agency.

(5) Notification system

(A) In general

Each consumer reporting agency that, under subsection (c)(1)(B) of this section, furnishes a consumer report in connection with a credit or insurance transaction that is not initiated by a consumer, shall—

(i) establish and maintain a notification system, including a toll-free telephone number, which permits any consumer whose consumer report is maintained by the agency to notify the agency, with appropriate identification, of the consumer's election to have the consumer's name and address excluded from any such list of names and addresses provided by the agency for such a transaction; and

(ii) publish by not later than 365 days after September 30, 1996, and not less than annually thereafter, in a publication of general circulation in the area served by the agency—

(I) a notification that information in consumer files maintained by the agency may be used in connection with such transactions; and

(II) the address and toll-free telephone number for consumers to use to notify the agency of the consumer's election under clause (i).

(B) Establishment and maintenance as compliance Establishment and maintenance of a notification system (including a toll-free telephone number) and publication by a consumer reporting agency on the agency's own behalf and on behalf of any of its affiliates in accordance with this paragraph is deemed to be compliance with this paragraph by each of those affiliates.

(6) Notification system by agencies that operate nationwide

Each consumer reporting agency that compiles and maintains files on consumers on a nationwide basis shall establish and maintain a notification system for purposes of paragraph (5) jointly with other such consumer reporting agencies.

(f) Certain use or obtaining of information prohibited

A person shall not use or obtain a consumer report for any purpose unless—

(1) the consumer report is obtained for a purpose for which the consumer report is authorized to be furnished under this section; and

(2) the purpose is certified in accordance with section 1681e of this title by a prospective user of the report through a general or specific certification.

(g) Protection of medical information

(1) Limitation on consumer reporting agencies

A consumer reporting agency shall not furnish for employment purposes, or in connection with a credit or insurance transaction, a consumer report that contains medical information (other than medical contact information treated in the manner required under section 605(a)(6) of this title) about a consumer, unless—

(A) if furnished in connection with an insurance transaction, the consumer affirmatively consents to the furnishing of the report;

(B) if furnished for employment purposes or in connection with a credit transaction—

(i) the information to be furnished is relevant to process or effect the employment or credit transaction; and

(ii) the consumer provides specific written consent for the furnishing of the report that describes in clear and conspicuous language the use for which the information will be furnished; or

(C) the information to be furnished pertains solely to transactions, accounts, or balances relating to debts arising from the receipt of medical services, products, or devises, where such information, other than account status or amounts, is restricted or reported using codes that do not identify, or do not provide information sufficient to infer, the specific provider or the nature of such services, products, or devices, as provided in section 1681c(a)(6) of this title.

(2) Limitation on creditors

Except as permitted pursuant to paragraph (3)(C) or regulations prescribed under paragraph (5)(A), a creditor shall not obtain or use medical information (other than medical information treated in the manner required under section 605(a)(6) of this title) pertaining to a consumer in connection with any determination of the consumer's eligibility, or continued eligibility, for credit.

(3) Actions authorized by Federal law, insurance activities, and regulatory determinations Section 1681a(d)(3) of this title shall not be construed so as to treat information or any communication of information as a consumer report if the information or communication is disclosed—

  (A) in connection with the business of insurance or annuities, including the activities described in section 18B of the model Privacy of Consumer Financial and Health Information Regulation issued by the National Association of Insurance Commissioners (as in effect on January 1, 2003);

  (B) for any purpose permitted without authorization under the Standards for Individually Identifiable Health Information promulgated by the Department of Health and Human Services pursuant to the Health Insurance Portability and Accountability Act of 1996, or referred to under section 1179 of such Act [sic; probably should be "section 1179 of the Social Security Act"], or

described in section 6802(e) of this title; or

  (C) as otherwise determined to be necessary and appropriate, by regulation or order and subject to paragraph (6), by the Commission, any Federal banking agency, or the National Credit Union Administration (with respect to any financial institution subject to the jurisdiction of such agency or Administration under paragraph (1), (2), or (3) of section 1681s(b) of this title), or the applicable State insurance authority (with respect to any person engaged in providing insurance or annuities).

(4) Limitation on redisclosure of medical information
Any person that receives medical information pursuant to paragraph (1) or (3) shall not disclose such information to any other person, except as necessary to carry out the purpose for which the information was initially disclosed, or as otherwise permitted by statute, regulation, or order.

(5) Regulations and effective date for paragraph (2)

  (A) Regulations required
Each Federal banking agency and the National Credit Union Administration shall, subject to paragraph (6) and after notice and opportunity for comment, prescribe regulations that permit

transactions under paragraph (2) that are determined to be necessary and appropriate to protect legitimate operational, transactional, risk, consumer, and other needs (and which shall include permitting actions necessary for administrative verification purposes), consistent with the intent of paragraph (2) to restrict the use of medical information for inappropriate purposes.

  (B) Final regulations required
    The Federal banking agencies and the National Credit Union Administration shall issue the regulations required under subparagraph (A) in final form before the end of the 6-month period beginning on the December 4, 2003.

(6) Coordination with other laws
  No provision of this subsection shall be construed as altering, affecting, or superseding the applicability of any other provision of Federal law relating to medical confidentiality.

15 U.S.C. § 1681c. Requirements relating to information contained in consumer reports

(a) Information excluded from consumer reports
  Except as authorized under subsection (b) of this section, no consumer reporting agency may make any consumer report containing any of the following items of information:

(1) Cases under Title 11 or under the Bankruptcy Act that, from the date of entry of the order for relief or the date of adjudication, as the case may be, antedate the report by more than 10 years.

(2) Civil suits, civil judgments, and records of arrest that, from date of entry, antedate the report by more than seven years or until the governing statute of limitations has expired, whichever is the longer period.

(3) Paid tax liens which, from date of payment, antedate the report by more than seven years.

(4) Accounts placed for collection or charged to profit and loss which antedate the report by more than seven years.

(5) Any other adverse item of information, other than records of convictions of crimes which antedates the report by more than seven years.

(6) The name, address, and telephone number of any medical information furnisher that has notified the agency of its status, unless—

  (A) such name, address, and telephone number are restricted or reported using codes that do not identify, or provide information sufficient to infer, the specific provider or the nature of such services, products, or devices to a person other than the consumer; or

  (B) the report is being provided to an insurance company for a purpose relating to engaging in the business of insurance other than property and casualty insurance.

(b) Exempted cases

The provisions of paragraphs (1) through (5) of subsection (a) of this section are not applicable in the case of any consumer credit report to be used in connection with—

(1) a credit transaction involving, or which may reasonably be expected to involve, a principal amount of $150,000 or more;

(2) the underwriting of life insurance involving, or which may reasonably be expected to involve, a face amount of $150,000 or more; or

(3) the employment of any individual at an annual salary which equals, or which may reasonably be expected to equal $75,000, or more.

(c) Running of reporting period

(1) In general. The 7-year period referred to in paragraphs (4) and (6) of subsection (a) of this section shall begin, with respect to any delinquent account that is placed for collection (internally or by referral to a third party, whichever is earlier), charged to profit and loss, or subjected to any similar action, upon the expiration of the 180-day period beginning on the date of the commencement of the delinquency which immediately preceded the collection activity, charge to profit and loss, or similar action.

(2) Effective date. Paragraph (1) shall apply only to items of information added to the file of a consumer on or after the date that is 455 days after September 30, 1996.

(d) Disclosed

(1) Title 11 information

Any consumer reporting agency that furnishes a consumer report that contains information regarding any case involving the consumer that arises under Title 11 shall include in the report an identification of the chapter of such Title 11 under which such case arises if provided by the source of the information. If any case arising or filed under Title 11 is withdrawn by the consumer before a final judgment, the consumer reporting agency shall include in the report that such case or filing was withdrawn upon receipt of documentation certifying such withdrawal.

(2) Key factor in credit score information

Any consumer reporting agency that furnishes a consumer report that contains any credit score or any other risk score or predictor on any consumer shall include in the report a clear and conspicuous statement that a key factor (as defined in section 1681g(f)(2)(B) of this title) that adversely affected such score or predictor was the number of enquiries, if such a predictor was in fact a key factor that adversely affected such score. This paragraph shall not apply to a check services company, acting as such, which issues authorizations for the purpose of approving or processing negotiable instruments, electronic fund transfers, or similar methods of payments, but only to the extent that such company is engaged in such activities.

(e) Indication of closure of account by consumer

If a consumer reporting agency is notified pursuant to section 1681s-2(a)(4) of this title that a credit account of a consumer was voluntarily closed by the consumer, the agency shall indicate that fact in any consumer report that includes information related to the account.

(f) Indication of dispute by consumer

If a consumer reporting agency is notified pursuant to section 1681s-2(a)(3) of this title that information regarding a consumer who was furnished to the agency is disputed by the consumer, the agency shall indicate that fact in each consumer report that includes the disputed information.

(g) Truncation of credit card and debit card numbers

(1) In general

Except as otherwise provided in this subsection, no person that accepts credit cards or debit cards for the transaction of business shall print more than the last 5 digits of the card number or the expiration date upon any receipt provided to the cardholder at the point of the sale or transaction.

(2) Limitation

This subsection shall apply only to receipts that are electronically printed, and shall not apply to transactions in which the sole means of recording a credit card or debit card account number is by handwriting or by an imprint or copy of the card.

(3) Effective date

This subsection shall become effective—

(A) 3 years after December 4, 2003, with respect to any cash register or other machine or device that electronically prints receipts for credit card or debit card transactions that is in use before January 1, 2005; and

(B) 1 year after December 4, 2003, with respect to any cash register or other machine or device that electronically prints receipts for credit card or debit card transactions that is first put into use on or after January 1, 2005.

(h) Notice of discrepancy in address

(1) In general

If a person has requested a consumer report relating to a consumer from a consumer reporting agency described in section 1681a(p) of this title, the request includes an address for the consumer that substantially differs from the addresses in the file of the consumer, and the agency provides a consumer report in response to the request, the consumer reporting agency shall notify the requester of the existence of the discrepancy.

(2) Regulations

    (A) Regulations required

        The Federal banking agencies, the National Credit Union Administration, and the Commission shall jointly, with respect to the entities that are subject to their respective enforcement authority under section 1681s of this title, prescribe regulations providing guidance regarding reasonable policies and procedures that a user of a consumer report should employ when such user has received a notice of discrepancy under paragraph (1).

    (B) Policies and procedures to be included

        The regulations prescribed under subparagraph (A) shall describe reasonable policies and procedures for use by a user of a consumer report—

        (i) to form a reasonable belief that the user knows the identity of the person to whom the consumer report pertains; and

        (ii) if the user establishes a continuing relationship with the consumer, and the user regularly and in the ordinary course of business furnishes information to the consumer reporting agency from which the notice of discrepancy pertaining to the consumer was obtained, to reconcile the address of the consumer with the consumer reporting agency by furnishing such address to such consumer reporting agency as part of information regularly furnished by the user for the period in which the relationship is established.

15 U.S.C. § 1681c-1. Identity theft prevention; fraud alerts and active duty alerts

(a) One-call fraud alerts

    (1) Initial alerts

        Upon the direct request of a consumer, or an individual acting on behalf of or as a personal representative of a consumer, who asserts in good faith a suspicion that the consumer has been or is about to become a victim of fraud or related crime, including identity theft, a consumer reporting agency described in section 1681a(p) of this title that maintains a file on the consumer and has received appropriate proof of the identity of the requester shall—

        (A) include a fraud alert in the file of that consumer, and also provide that alert along with any credit score generated in using that file, for a period of not less than 90 days, beginning on the date of such request, unless the consumer or such representative requests that such fraud alert be removed before the end of such period, and the agency has received appropriate proof of the identity of the requester for such purpose; and

(B) refer the information regarding the fraud alert under this paragraph to each of the other consumer reporting agencies described in section 1681a(p) of this title, in accordance with procedures developed under section 1681s(f) of this title.

(2) Access to free reports

In any case in which a consumer reporting agency includes a fraud alert in the file of a consumer pursuant to this subsection, the consumer reporting agency shall—

(A) disclose to the consumer that the consumer may request a free copy of the file of the consumer pursuant to section 1681j(d) of this title; and

(B) provide to the consumer all disclosures required to be made under section 1681a of this title, without charge to the consumer, not later than 3 business days after any request described in subparagraph (A).

(b) Extended alerts

(1) In general

Upon the direct request of a consumer, or an individual acting on behalf of or as a personal representative of a consumer, who submits an identity theft report to a consumer reporting agency described in section 1681a(p) of this title that maintains a file on the consumer, if the agency has received appropriate proof of the identity of the requester, the agency shall—

(A) include a fraud alert in the file of that consumer, and also provide that alert along with any credit score generated in using that file, during the 7-year period beginning on the date of such request, unless the consumer or such representative requests that such fraud alert be removed before the end of such period and the agency has received appropriate proof of the identity of the requester for such purpose;

(B) during the 5-year period beginning on the date of such request, exclude the consumer from any list of consumers prepared by the consumer reporting agency and provided to any third party to offer credit or insurance to the consumer as part of a transaction that was not initiated by the consumer, unless the consumer or such representative requests that such exclusion be rescinded before the end of such period; and

(C) refer the information regarding the extended fraud alert under this paragraph to each of the other consumer reporting agencies described in section 1681a(p) of this title, in accordance with procedures developed under section 1681s(f) of this title.

(2) Access to free reports

In any case in which a consumer reporting agency includes a fraud alert in the file of a consumer pursuant to this subsection, the consumer reporting agency shall—

   (A) disclose to the consumer that the consumer may request 2 free copies of the file of the consumer pursuant to section 1681j(d) of this title during the 12-month period beginning on the date on which the fraud alert was included in the file; and

   (B) provide to the consumer all disclosures required to be made under section 1681g of this title, without charge to the consumer, not later than 3 business days after any request described in subparagraph (A).

(c) Active duty alerts

Upon the direct request of an active duty military consumer, or an individual acting on behalf of or as a personal representative of an active duty military consumer, a consumer reporting agency described in section 1681a(p) of this title that maintains a file on the active duty military consumer and has received appropriate proof of the identity of the requester shall—

   (1) include an active duty alert in the file of that active duty military consumer, and also provide that alert along with any credit score generated in using that file, during a period of not less than 12 months, or such longer period as the Commission shall determine, by regulation, beginning on the date of the request, unless the active duty military consumer or such representative requests that such fraud alert be removed before the end of such period, and the agency has received appropriate proof of the identity of the requester for such purpose;

   (2) during the 2-year period beginning on the date of such request, exclude the active duty military consumer from any list of consumers prepared by the consumer reporting agency and provided to any third party to offer credit or insurance to the consumer as part of a transaction that was not initiated by the consumer, unless the consumer requests that such exclusion be rescinded before the end of such period; and

   (3) refer the information regarding the active duty alert to each of the other consumer reporting agencies described in section 1681a(p) of this title, in accordance with procedures developed under section 1681s(f) of this title.

(d) Procedures

Each consumer reporting agency described in section 1681a(p) of this title shall establish policies and procedures to comply with this section, including procedures that inform consumers of the availability of initial, extended, and active duty alerts and procedures that allow consumers and active duty military consumers to request initial, extended, or active duty alerts (as applicable) in a simple and easy manner, including by telephone.

(e) Referrals of alerts

Each consumer reporting agency described in section 1681a(p) of this title that receives a referral of a fraud alert or active duty alert from another consumer reporting agency pursuant to this section shall, as though the agency received the request from the consumer directly, follow the procedures required under—

(1) paragraphs (1)(A) and (2) of subsection (a) of this section, in the case of a referral under subsection (a)(1)(B) of this section;

(2) paragraphs (1)(A), (1)(B), and (2) of subsection (b) of this section, in the case of a referral under subsection (b)(1)(C) of this section; and

(3) paragraphs (1) and (2) of subsection (c) of this section, in the case of a referral under subsection (c)(3) of this section.

(f) Duty of reseller to reconvey alert

A reseller shall include in its report any fraud alert or active duty alert placed in the file of a consumer pursuant to this section by another consumer reporting agency.

(g) Duty of other consumer reporting agencies to provide contact information

If a consumer contacts any consumer reporting agency that is not described in section 1681a(p) of this title to communicate a suspicion that the consumer has been or is about to become a victim of fraud or related crime, including identity theft, the agency shall provide information to the consumer on how to contact the Commission and the consumer reporting agencies described in section 1681a(p) of this title to obtain more detailed information and request alerts under this section.

(h) Limitations on use of information for credit extensions

(1) Requirements for initial and active duty alerts

(A) Notification

Each initial fraud alert and active duty alert under this section shall include information that notifies all prospective users of a consumer report on the consumer to which the alert relates that the consumer does not authorize the establishment of any new credit plan or extension of credit, other than under an open-end credit plan (as defined in section 1602(i) of this title), in the name of the consumer, or issuance of an additional card on an existing credit account requested by a consumer, or any increase in credit limit on an existing credit account requested by a consumer, except in accordance with subparagraph (B).

(B) Limitation on users

(i) In general

No prospective user of a consumer report that in-cludes an initial fraud alert or an active duty alert in accordance with this section may establish a new credit plan or extension of credit, other than under an open-end credit plan (as defined in section 1602(i) of this title), in the name of the consumer, or issue an additional card on an existing credit account requested by a consumer, or grant any increase in credit limit on an existing credit account requested by a consumer, unless the user utilizes reasonable policies and procedures to form a reasonable belief that the user knows the identity of the person making the request.

(ii) Verification

If a consumer requesting the alert has specified a telephone number to be used for identity verification purposes, before authorizing any new credit plan or extension described in clause (i) in the name of such consumer, a user of such consumer report shall contact the consumer using that telephone number or take reasonable steps to verify the consumer's identity and confirm that the application for a new credit plan is not the result of identity theft.

(2) Requirements for extended alerts

(A) Notification

Each extended alert under this section shall include information that provides all prospective users of a consumer report relating to a consumer with—

(i) notification that the consumer does not authorize the establishment of any new credit plan or extension of credit described in clause (i), other than under an open-end credit plan (as defined in section 1602(i) of this title), in the name of the consumer, or issuance of an additional card on an existing credit account requested by a consumer, or any increase in credit limit on an existing credit account requested by a consumer, except in accordance with subparagraph (B); and

(ii) a telephone number or other reasonable contact method designated by the consumer.

(B) Limitation on users

No prospective user of a consumer report or of a credit score generated using the information in the file of a consumer that includes an extended fraud alert in accordance with this section may establish a new credit plan or extension of credit, other than under an open-end credit plan (as defined in section

1602(i) of this title), in the name of the consumer, or issue an additional card on an existing credit account requested by a consumer, or any increase in credit limit on an existing credit account requested by a consumer, unless the user contacts the consumer in person or using the contact method described in subparagraph (A)(ii) to confirm that the application for a new credit plan or increase in credit limit, or request for an additional card, is not the result of identity theft.

15 U.S.C. § 1681c-2. Block of information resulting from identity theft

(a) Block

Except as otherwise provided in this section, a consumer reporting agency shall block the reporting of any information in the file of a consumer that the consumer identifies as information that resulted from an alleged identity theft, not later than 4 business days after the date of receipt by such agency of—

(1) appropriate proof of the identity of the consumer;

(2) a copy of an identity theft report;

(3) the identification of such information by the consumer; and

(4) a statement by the consumer that the information is not information relating to any transaction by the consumer.

(b) Notification

A consumer reporting agency shall promptly notify the furnisher of information identified by the consumer under subsection (a) of this section—

(1) that the information may be a result of identity theft;

(2) that an identity theft report has been filed;

(3) that a block has been requested under this section; and

(4) of the effective dates of the block.

(c) Authority to decline or rescind

(1) In general

A consumer reporting agency may decline to block, or may rescind any block, of information relating to a consumer under this section, if the consumer reporting agency reasonably determines that—

(A) the information was blocked in error or a block was requested by the consumer in error;

(B) the information was blocked, or a block was requested by the consumer, on the basis of a material misrepresentation of fact by the consumer relevant to the request to block; or

(C) the consumer obtained possession of goods, services, or money as a result of the blocked transaction or transactions.

(2) Notification to consumer

If a block of information is declined or rescinded under this subsection, the affected consumer shall be notified promptly, in the same manner as consumers are notified of the reinsertion of information under section 1681i(a)(5)(B) of this title.

(3) Significance of block

For purposes of this subsection, if a consumer reporting agency rescinds a block, the presence of information in the file of a consumer prior to the blocking of such information is not evidence of whether the consumer knew or should have known that the consumer obtained possession of any goods, services, or money as a result of the block.

(d) Exception for resellers

(1) No reseller file

This section shall not apply to a consumer reporting agency, if the consumer reporting agency—

(A) is a reseller;

(B) is not, at the time of the request of the consumer under subsection (a) of this section, otherwise furnishing or reselling a consumer report concerning the information identified by the consumer; and

(C) informs the consumer, by any means, that the consumer may report the identity theft to the Commission to obtain consumer information regarding identity theft.

(2) Reseller with file

The sole obligation of the consumer reporting agency under this section, with regard to any request of a consumer under this section, shall be to block the consumer report maintained by the consumer

reporting agency from any subsequent use, if—

(A) the consumer, in accordance with the provisions of subsection (a) of this section, identifies, to a consumer reporting agency, information in the file of the consumer that resulted from identity theft; and

(B) the consumer reporting agency is a reseller of the identified information.

(3) Notice

In carrying out its obligation under paragraph (2), the reseller shall promptly provide a notice to the consumer of the decision to block the file. Such notice shall contain the name, address, and telephone number of each consumer reporting agency from which the consumer information was obtained for resale.

(e) Exception for verification companies

The provisions of this section do not apply to a check services company, acting as such, which issues authorizations for the purpose of approving or processing negotiable instruments, electronic fund transfers, or similar methods of payments, except that, beginning 4 business days after receipt of information described in paragraphs (1) through (3) of subsection (a) of this section, a check services company shall not report to a national consumer reporting agency described in section 1681a(p) of this title, any information identified in the subject identity theft report as resulting from identity theft.

(f) Access to blocked information by law enforcement agencies

No provision of this section shall be construed as requiring a consumer reporting agency to prevent a Federal, State, or local law enforcement agency from accessing blocked information in a consumer file to which the agency could otherwise obtain access under this title.

15 U.S.C. § 1681d. Disclosure of investigative consumer reports

(a) Disclosure of fact of preparation

A person may not procure or cause to be prepared an investigative consumer report on any consumer unless—

(1) it is clearly and accurately disclosed to the consumer that an investigative consumer report including information as to his character, general reputation, personal characteristics, and mode of living, whichever are applicable, may be made, and such disclosure (A) is made in a writing mailed, or otherwise delivered, to the consumer, not later than three days after the date on which the report was first requested, and (B) includes a statement informing the consumer of his right to request the additional disclosures provided for under subsection (b) of this section and the written summary of the rights of the consumer prepared pursuant to section 1681g(c) of this title; and

(2) the person certifies or has certified to the consumer reporting agency that—

(A) the person has made the disclosures to the consumer required by paragraph (1); and

(B) the person will comply with subsection (b) of this section.

(b) Disclosure on request of nature and scope of investigation

Any person who procures or causes to be prepared an investigative consumer report on any consumer shall, upon written request made by the consumer within a reasonable period of time after the receipt by him of the disclosure required by subsection (a)(1) of this section, make a complete and accurate disclosure of the nature and scope of the investigation requested. This disclosure shall be made in a writing mailed, or otherwise delivered, to the consumer not later than five days after the date on which the request for such disclosure was received from the consumer or such report was first requested, whichever is the later.

(c) Limitation on liability upon showing of reasonable procedures for compliance with provisions

No person may be held liable for any violation of subsection (a) or (b) of this section if he shows by a preponderance of the evidence that at the time of the violation he maintained reasonable procedures to assure compliance with subsection (a) or (b) of this section.

(d) Prohibitions

(1) Certification. A consumer reporting agency shall not prepare or furnish an investigative consumer report unless the agency has received a

certification under subsection (a)(2) of this section from the person who requested the report.

(2) Inquiries. A consumer reporting agency shall not make an inquiry for the purpose of preparing an investigative consumer report on a consumer for employment purposes if the making of the inquiry by an employer or prospective employer of the consumer would violate any applicable Federal or State equal employment opportunity law or regulation.

(3) Certain public record information. Except as otherwise provided in section 1681k of this title, a consumer reporting agency shall not furnish an investigative consumer report that includes information that is a matter of public record and that relates to an arrest, indictment, conviction, civil judicial action, tax lien, or outstanding judgment, unless the agency has verified the accuracy of the information during the 30-day period ending on the date on which the report is furnished.

(4) Certain adverse information. A consumer reporting agency shall not prepare or furnish an investigative consumer report on a consumer that contains information that is adverse to the interest of the consumer and that is obtained through a personal interview with a neighbor, friend, or associate of the consumer or with another person with whom the consumer is acquainted or who

has knowledge of such item of information, unless—

   (A) the agency has followed reasonable procedures to obtain confirmation of the information, from an additional source that has independent and direct knowledge of the information; or

   (B) the person interviewed is the best possible source of the information.

15 U.S.C. § 1681e. Compliance procedures

(a) Identity and purposes of credit users

Every consumer reporting agency shall maintain reasonable procedures designed to avoid violations of section 1681c of this title and to limit the furnishing of consumer reports to the purposes listed under section 1681b of this title. These procedures shall require that prospective users of the information identify themselves, certify the purposes for which the information is sought, and certify that the information will be used for no other purpose. Every consumer reporting agency shall make a reasonable effort to verify the identity of a new prospective user and the uses certified by such prospective user prior to furnishing such user a consumer report. No consumer reporting agency may furnish a consumer report to any person if it has reasonable grounds for believing that the consumer report will not be used for a purpose listed in section 1681b of this title.

(b) Accuracy of report

Whenever a consumer reporting agency prepares a consumer report it shall follow reasonable procedures to assure maximum possible accuracy of the information concerning the individual about whom the report relates.

(c) Disclosure of consumer reports by users allowed

A consumer reporting agency may not prohibit a user of a consumer report furnished by the agency on a consumer from disclosing the contents of the report to the consumer, if adverse action against the consumer has been taken by the user based in whole or in part on the report.

(d) Notice to users and furnishers of information

(1) Notice requirement. A consumer reporting agency shall provide to any person—

(A) who regularly and in the ordinary course of business furnishes information to the agency with respect to any consumer; or

(B) to whom a consumer report is provided by the agency; a notice of such person's responsibilities under this subchapter.

(2) Content of notice. The Federal Trade Commission shall prescribe the content of notices under paragraph (1), and a consumer reporting agency shall be in compliance with this subsection if it provides a notice under paragraph (1) that is substantially similar to the Federal Trade Commission prescription under this paragraph.

(e) Procurement of consumer report for resale

(1) Disclosure. A person may not procure a consumer report for purposes of reselling the report (or any information in the report) unless the person discloses to the consumer reporting agency that originally furnishes the report—

(A) the identity of the end-user of the report (or information); and

(B) each permissible purpose under section 1681b of this title for which the report is furnished to the end-user of the report (or information).

(2) Responsibilities of procurers for resale. A person who procures a consumer report for purposes of reselling the report (or any information in the report) shall—

(A) establish and comply with reasonable procedures designed to ensure that the report (or information) is resold by the person only for a purpose for which the report may be furnished under section 1681b of this title, including by requiring that each person to which the report (or information) is resold and that resells or provides the report (or information) to any other person—

(i) identifies each end user of the resold report (or infor-mation);

(ii) certifies each purpose for which the report (or information) will be used; and

    (iii) certifies that the report (or information) will be used for no other purpose; and

(B) before reselling the report, make reasonable efforts to verify the identifications and certifications made under subparagraph (A).

(3) Resale of consumer report to a federal agency or department. Notwithstanding paragraph (1) or (2), a person who procures a consumer report for purposes of reselling the report (or any information in the report) shall not disclose the identity of the end-user of the report under paragraph (1) or (2) if—

(A) the end user is an agency or department of the United States Government which procures the report from the person for purposes of determining the eligibility of the consumer concerned to receive access or continued access to classified information (as defined in section 1681b(b)(4)(E)(i) of this title); and

(B) the agency or department certifies in writing to the person reselling the report that nondisclosure is necessary to protect classified information or the safety of persons employed by or contracting with, or undergoing investigation for work or contracting with the agency or department.

15 U.S.C. § 1681f. Disclosures to governmental agencies

Notwithstanding the provisions of section 1681b of this title, a consumer reporting agency may furnish identifying information respecting any consumer, limited to his name, address, former addresses, places of employment, or former places of employment, to a governmental agency.

15 U.S.C. § 1681g. Disclosures to consumers

(a) Information on file; sources; report recipient

    Every consumer reporting agency shall, upon request, and subject to section 1681h(a)(1) of this title, clearly and accurately disclose to the consumer:

(1) All information in the consumer's file at the time of the request, except that—

    (A) if the consumer to whom the file relates requests that the first 5 digits of the social security number (or similar identification number) of the consumer not be included in the disclosure and the consumer reporting agency has received appropriate proof of the identity of the requester, the consumer reporting agency shall so truncate such number in such disclosure; and

    (B) nothing in this paragraph shall be construed to require a consumer reporting agency to disclose to a consumer any information concerning credit scores or any other risk scores or predictors relating to the consumer.

(2) The sources of the information; except that the sources of information acquired solely for use in preparing an investigative consumer report and actually used for no other purpose need not be disclosed: Provided, that in the event an action is brought under this subchapter, such sources shall be available to the plaintiff under appropriate discovery procedures in the court in which the action is brought.

(3)

   (A) Identification of each person (including each end-user identified under section 1681e(e)(1) of this title) that procured a consumer report—

      (i) for employment purposes, during the 2-year period preceding the date on which the request is made; or

      (ii) for any other purpose, during the 1-year period preceding the date on which the request is made.

   (B) An identification of a person under subparagraph (A) shall include—

      (i) the name of the person or, if applicable, the trade name (written in full) under which such person conducts business; and

      (ii) upon request of the consumer, the address and telephone number of the person.

   (C) Subparagraph (A) does not apply if—

      (i) the end user is an agency or department of the United States Government that procures the report from the person for purposes of determining the eligibility of the consumer to whom the report relates to receive access or continued access to classified information (as defined in section 1681b(b)(4)(E)(i) of this title); and

      (ii) the head of the agency or department makes a written finding as prescribed under section 1681b(b)(4)(A) of this title.

(4) The dates, original payees, and amounts of any checks upon which is based any adverse characterization of the consumer, included in the file at the time of the disclosure.

(5) A record of all inquiries received by the agency during the 1-year period preceding the request that identified the consumer in connection with a credit or insurance transaction that was not initiated by the consumer.

(6) If the consumer requests the credit file and not the credit score, a statement that the consumer may request and obtain a credit score.

(b) Exempt information

The requirements of subsection (a) of this section respecting the disclosure of sources of information and the recipients of consumer reports do not apply to information received or consumer reports furnished prior to the effective date of this subchapter except to the extent that the matter involved is contained in the files of the consumer reporting agency on that date.

(c) Summary of rights to obtain and dispute information in consumer reports and to obtain credit scores

  (1) Commission summary of rights required

    (A) In general

      The Commission shall prepare a model summary of the rights of consumers under this subchapter.

    (B) Content of summary

      The summary of rights prepared under subparagraph (A) shall include a description of—

      (i) the right of a consumer to obtain a copy of a consumer report under subsection (a) of this section from each consumer reporting agency;

      (ii) the frequency and circumstances under which a consumer is entitled to receive a consumer report without charge under section 1681j of this title;

      (iii) the right of a consumer to dispute information in the file of the consumer under section 1681i of this title;

      (iv) the right of a consumer to obtain a credit score from a consumer reporting agency, and a description of how to obtain a credit score;

      (v) the method by which a consumer can contact, and obtain a consumer report from, a consumer reporting agency without charge, as provided in the regulations of the Commission prescribed under section 211(c) [sic; probably should be section 211(d)] of the Fair and Accurate Credit Transactions Act of 2003; and

      (vi) the method by which a consumer can contact, and obtain a consumer report from, a consumer reporting agency described in section 1681a(w) of this title, as provided in the regulations of the Commission prescribed under section 1681j(a)(1)(C) of this title.

    (C) Availability of summary of rights

      The Commission shall—

      (i) actively publicize the availability of the summary of rights prepared under this paragraph;

      (ii) conspicuously post on its Internet website the availability of such summary of rights; and

      (iii) promptly make such summary of rights available to consumers, on request.

  (2) Summary of rights required to be included with agency disclosures

A consumer reporting agency shall provide to a consumer, with each written disclosure by the agency to the consumer under this section—

(A) the summary of rights prepared by the Commission under paragraph (1);

(B) in the case of a consumer reporting agency described in section 1681a(p) of this title, a toll-free telephone number established by the agency, at which personnel are accessible to consumers during normal business hours;

(C) a list of all Federal agencies responsible for enforcing any provision of this subchapter, and the address and any appropriate phone number of each such agency, in a form that will assist the consumer in selecting the appropriate agency;

(D) a statement that the consumer may have additional rights under State law, and that the consumer may wish to contact a State or local consumer protection agency or a State attorney general (or the equivalent thereof) to learn of those rights; and

(E) a statement that a consumer reporting agency is not required to remove accurate derogatory information from the file of a consumer, unless the information is outdated under section 1681c of this title or cannot be verified.

(d) Summary of rights of identity theft victims

(1) In general

The Commission, in consultation with the Federal banking agencies and the National Credit Union Administration, shall prepare a model summary of the rights of consumers under this subchapter with respect to the procedures for remedying the effects of fraud or identity theft involving credit, an electronic fund transfer, or an account or transaction at or with a financial institution or other creditor.

(2) Summary of rights and contact information

Beginning 60 days after the date on which the model summary of rights is prescribed in final form by the Commission pursuant to paragraph (1), if any consumer contacts a consumer reporting agency and expresses a belief that the consumer is a victim of fraud or identity theft involving credit, an electronic fund transfer, or an account or transaction at or with a financial institution or other creditor, the consumer reporting agency shall, in addition to any other action that the agency may take, provide the consumer with a summary of rights that contains all of the information required by the Commission under paragraph (1), and information on how to contact the Commission to obtain more detailed information.

(e) Information available to victims

(1) In general

For the purpose of documenting fraudulent transactions resulting from identity theft, not later than 30 days after the date of receipt of a request from a victim in accordance with paragraph (3), and subject to verification of the identity of the victim and the claim of identity theft in accordance with paragraph (2), a business entity that has provided credit to, provided for consideration products, goods, or services to, accepted payment from, or otherwise entered into a commercial transaction for consideration with, a person who has allegedly made unauthorized use of the means of identification of the victim, shall provide a copy of application and business transaction records in the control of the business entity, whether maintained by the business entity or by another person on behalf of the business entity, evidencing any transaction alleged to be a result of identity theft to—

(A) the victim;

(B) any Federal, State, or local government law enforcement agency or officer specified by the victim in such a request; or

(C) any law enforcement agency investigating the identity theft and authorized by the victim to take receipt of records provided under this subsection.

(2) Verification of identity and claim

Before a business entity provides any information under paragraph (1), unless the business entity, at its discretion, otherwise has a high degree of confidence that it knows the identity of the victim making a request under paragraph (1), the victim shall provide to the business entity—

(A) as proof of positive identification of the victim, at the election of the business entity—

(i) the presentation of a government-issued identification card;

(ii) personally identifying information of the same type as was provided to the business entity by the unauthorized person; or

(iii) personally identifying information that the business entity typically requests from new applicants or for new transactions, at the time of the victim's request for information, including any documentation described in clauses (i) and (ii); and

(B) as proof of a claim of identity theft, at the election of the business entity—

(i) a copy of a police report evidencing the claim of the victim of identity theft; and

(ii) a properly completed—

(I) copy of a standardized affidavit of identity theft developed and made available by the Commission; or

(II) an affidavit of fact that is acceptable to the business entity for that purpose.

(3) Procedures

The request of a victim under paragraph (1) shall—

(A) be in writing;

(B) be mailed to an address specified by the business entity, if any; and

(C) if asked by the business entity, include relevant information about any transaction alleged to be a result of identity theft to facilitate compliance with this section including—

  (i) if known by the victim (or if readily obtainable by the victim), the date of the application or transaction; and

  (ii) if known by the victim (or if readily obtainable by the victim), any other identifying information such as an account or transaction number.

(4) No charge to victim

Information required to be provided under paragraph (1) shall be so provided without charge.

(5) Authority to decline to provide information

A business entity may decline to provide information under paragraph (1) if, in the exercise of good faith, the business entity determines that—

(A) this subsection does not require disclosure of the information;

(B) after reviewing the information provided pursuant to paragraph (2), the business entity does not have a high degree of confidence in knowing the true identity of the individual requesting the information;

(C) the request for the information is based on a misrepresentation of fact by the individual requesting the information relevant to the request for information; or

(D) the information requested is Internet navigational data or similar information about a person's visit to a website or online service.

(6) Limitation on liability

Except as provided in section 1681s of this title, sections 1681n and 1681o of this title do not apply to any violation of this subsection.

(7) Limitation on civil liability

No business entity may be held civilly liable under any provision of Federal, State, or other law for disclosure, made in good faith pursuant to this subsection.

(8) No new recordkeeping obligation

Nothing in this subsection creates an obligation on the part of a business entity to obtain, retain, or maintain information or records that are not otherwise required to be obtained, retained, or maintained in the ordinary course of its business or under other applicable law.

(9) Rule of construction

(A) In general

No provision of subtitle A of title V of Public Law 106-102, prohibiting the disclosure of financial information by a business entity to third parties shall be used to deny disclosure of information to the victim under this subsection.

(B) Limitation

Except as provided in subparagraph (A), nothing in this subsection permits a business entity to disclose information, including information to law enforcement under subparagraphs (B) and (C) of paragraph (1), that the business entity is otherwise prohibited from disclosing under any other applicable provision of Federal or State law.

(10) Affirmative defense

In any civil action brought to enforce this subsection, it is an affirmative defense (which the defendant must establish by a preponderance of the evidence) for a business entity to file an affidavit or answer stating that—

(A) the business entity has made a reasonably diligent search of its available business records; and

(B) the records requested under this subsection do not exist or are not reasonably available.

(11) Definition of victim

For purposes of this subsection, the term "victim" means a consumer whose means of identification or financial information has been used or transferred (or has been alleged to have been used or transferred) without the authority of that consumer, with the intent to commit, or to aid or abet, an identity theft or a similar crime.

(12) Effective date

This subsection shall become effective 180 days after December 4, 2003.

(13) Effectiveness study

Not later than 18 months after December 4, 2003, the Comptroller General of the United States shall submit a report to Congress assessing the effectiveness of this provision.

(f) Disclosure of credit scores

(1) In general

Upon the request of a consumer for a credit score, a consumer reporting agency shall supply to the consumer a statement indicating that the information and credit scoring model may be different than the credit score that may be used by the lender, and a notice which shall include—

(A) the current credit score of the consumer or the most recent credit score of the consumer that was previously calculated by the credit reporting agency for a purpose related to the extension of credit;

(B) the range of possible credit scores under the model used;

(C) all of the key factors that adversely affected the credit score of the consumer in the model used, the total number of which shall not exceed 4, subject to paragraph (9);

(D) the date on which the credit score was created; and

(E) the name of the person or entity that provided the credit score or credit file upon which the credit score was created.

(2) Definitions

For purposes of this subsection, the following definitions shall apply:

(A) Credit score

The term "credit score"—

(i) means a numerical value or a categorization derived from a statistical tool or modeling system used by a person who makes or arranges a loan to predict the likelihood of certain credit behaviors, including default (and the numerical value or the categorization derived from such analysis may also be referred to as a "risk predictor" or "risk score"); and

(ii) does not include—

(I) any mortgage score or rating of an automated underwriting system that considers one or more factors in addition to credit information, including the loan to value ratio, the amount

of down payment, or the financial assets of a consumer; or

(II) any other elements of the underwriting process or underwriting decision.

(B) Key factors

The term "key factors" means all relevant elements or reasons adversely affecting the credit score for the particular individual, listed in the order of their importance based on their effect on the credit score.

(3) Timeframe and manner of disclosure

The information required by this subsection shall be provided in the same timeframe and manner as the information described in subsection (a) of this section.

(4) Applicability to certain uses

This subsection shall not be construed so as to compel a consumer reporting agency to develop or disclose a score if the agency does not—

(A) distribute scores that are used in connection with residential real property loans; or

(B) develop scores that assist credit providers in understanding the general credit behavior of a consumer and predicting the future credit behavior of the consumer.

(5) Applicability to credit scores developed by another person

(A) In general

This subsection shall not be

construed to require a consumer reporting agency that distributes credit scores developed by another person or entity to provide a further explanation of them, or to process a dispute arising pursuant to section 1681i of this title, except that the consumer reporting agency shall provide the consumer with the name and address and website for contacting the person or entity who developed the score or developed the methodology of the score.

(B) Exception

This paragraph shall not apply to a consumer reporting agency that develops or modifies scores that are developed by another person or entity.

(6) Maintenance of credit scores not required

This subsection shall not be construed to require a consumer reporting agency to maintain credit scores in its files.

(7) Compliance in certain cases

In complying with this subsection, a consumer reporting agency shall—

(A) supply the consumer with a credit score that is derived from a credit scoring model that is widely distributed to users by that consumer reporting agency in connection with residential real property loans or with a credit score that assists the consumer in understanding the credit scoring

assessment of the credit behavior of the consumer and predictions about the future credit behavior of the consumer; and

(B) a statement indicating that the information and credit scoring model may be different than that used by the lender.

(8) Fair and reasonable fee

A consumer reporting agency may charge a fair and reasonable fee, as determined by the Commission, for providing the information required under this subsection.

(9) Use of enquiries as a key factor

If a key factor that adversely affects the credit score of a consumer consists of the number of enquiries made with respect to a consumer report, that factor shall be included in the disclosure pursuant to paragraph (1)(C) without regard to the numerical limitation in such paragraph.

(g) Disclosure of credit scores by certain mortgage lenders

(1) In general

Any person who makes or arranges loans and who uses a consumer credit score, as defined in subsection (f) of this section, in connection with an application initiated or sought by a consumer for a closed end loan or the establishment of an open end loan for a consumer purpose that is secured by 1 to 4 units of residential real property (hereafter in this subsection referred to as the "lender") shall provide the following to the consumer as soon as reasonably practicable:

(A) Information required under subsection (f)—

    (i) In general

        A copy of the information identified in subsection (f) of this section that was obtained from a consumer reporting agency or was developed and used by the user of the information.

    (ii) Notice under subparagraph (D)

        In addition to the information provided to it by a third party that provided the credit score or scores, a lender is only required to provide the notice contained in subparagraph (D).

(B) Disclosures in case of automated underwriting system

    (i) In general

        If a person that is subject to this subsection uses an automated underwriting system to underwrite a loan, that person may satisfy the obligation to provide a credit score by disclosing a credit score and associated key factors supplied by a consumer reporting agency.

    (ii) Numerical credit score

        However, if a numerical credit score is generated by an automated underwriting system used by an enterprise, and that score is disclosed to the person, the score shall be disclosed to the consumer consistent with subparagraph (C).

    (iii) Enterprise defined

        For purposes of this subparagraph, the term "enterprise" has the same meaning as in paragraph (6) of section 4502 of Title 12.

(C) Disclosures of credit scores not obtained from a consumer reporting agency

    A person that is subject to the provisions of this subsection and that uses a credit score, other than a credit score provided by a consumer reporting agency, may satisfy the obligation to provide a credit score by disclosing a credit score and associated key factors supplied by a consumer reporting agency.

(D) Notice to home loan applicants

    A copy of the following notice, which shall include the name, address, and telephone number of each consumer reporting agency providing a credit score that was used:

NOTICE TO THE HOME LOAN APPLICANT

In connection with your application for a home loan, the lender must disclose to you the score that a consumer reporting agency distributed to users and the lender used in connection with your home loan, and the key factors affecting your credit scores.

The credit score is a computer generated summary calculated at the time of the request and based on information that a consumer reporting agency or lender has on file. The scores are based on data about your credit history and payment patterns. Credit scores are important because they are used to assist the lender in determining whether you will obtain a loan. They may also be used to determine what interest rate you may be offered on the mortgage. Credit scores can change over time, depending on your conduct, how your credit history and payment patterns change, and how credit scoring technologies change. Because the score is based on information in your credit history, it is very important that you review the credit-related information that is being furnished to make sure it is accurate. Credit records may vary from one company to another.

If you have questions about your credit score or the credit information that is furnished to you, contact the consumer reporting agency at the address and telephone number provided with this notice, or contact the lender, if the lender developed or generated the credit score. The consumer reporting agency plays no part in the decision to take any action on the loan application and is unable to provide you with specific reasons for the decision on a loan application.

If you have questions concerning the terms of the loan, contact the lender.

(E) Actions not required under this subsection
This subsection shall not require any person to—
  (i) explain the information provided pursuant to subsection (f) of this section;
  (ii) disclose any information other than a credit score or key factors, as defined in subsection (f) of this section;
  (iii) disclose any credit score or related information obtained by the user after a loan has closed;
  (iv) provide more than 1 disclosure per loan transaction; or
  (v) provide the disclosure required by this subsection when another person has made the disclosure to the consumer for that loan transaction.

(F) No obligation for content
  (i) In general
The obligation of any person pursuant to this subsection shall be limited solely to providing a copy of the information that was received from the consumer reporting agency.
  (ii) Limit on liability
No person has liability under this subsection for the content of that information or for the omission of any information within the report

provided by the consumer reporting agency.

(G) Person defined as excluding enterprise

As used in this subsection, the term "person" does not include an enterprise (as defined in paragraph (6) of section 4502 of Title 12).

(2) Prohibition on disclosure clauses null and void

(A) In general

Any provision in a contract that prohibits the disclosure of a credit score by a person who makes or arranges loans or a consumer reporting agency is void.

(B) No liability for disclosure under this subsection

A lender shall not have liability under any contractual provision for disclosure of a credit score pursuant to this subsection.

15 U.S.C. § 1681h. Conditions and form of disclosure to consumers

(a) In general

(1) Proper identification. A consumer reporting agency shall require, as a condition of making the disclosures required under section 1681g of this title, that the consumer furnish proper identification.

(2) Disclosure in writing. Except as provided in subsection (b) of this section, the disclosures required to be made under section 1681(g) of this title shall be provided under that section in writing.

(b) Other forms of disclosure

(1) In general. If authorized by a consumer, a consumer reporting agency may make the disclosures required under 1681g of this title—

(A) other than in writing; and

(B) in such form as may be—

(i) specified by the consumer in accordance with paragraph (2); and

(ii) available from the agency.

(2) Form. A consumer may specify pursuant to paragraph (1) that disclosures under section 1681g of this title shall be made—

(A) in person, upon the appearance of the consumer at the place of business of the consumer reporting agency where disclosures are regularly provided, during normal business hours, and on reasonable notice;

(B) by telephone, if the consumer has made a written request for disclosure by telephone;

(C) by electronic means, if available from the agency; or

(D) by any other reasonable means that is available from the agency.

(c) Trained personnel

Any consumer reporting agency shall provide trained personnel to explain to the consumer any information furnished to him pursuant to section 1681g of this title.

(d) Persons accompanying consumer

The consumer shall be permitted to be accompanied by one other person of his choosing, who shall furnish reasonable identification. A consumer reporting agency may require the consumer to furnish a written statement granting permission to the consumer reporting agency to discuss the consumer's file in such person's presence.

(e) Limitation of liability

Except as provided in sections 1681n and 1681o of this title, no consumer may bring any action or proceeding in the nature of defamation, invasion of privacy, or negligence with respect to the reporting of information against any consumer reporting agency, any user of information, or any person who furnishes information to a consumer reporting agency, based on information disclosed pursuant to section 1681g, 1681h, or 1681m of this title, or based on information disclosed by a user of a consumer report to or for a consumer against whom the user has taken adverse action, based in whole or in part on the report except as to false information furnished with malice or willful intent to injure such consumer.

15 U.S.C. § 1681i. Procedure in case of disputed accuracy

(a) Reinvestigations of disputed information

   (1) Reinvestigation required.—

      (A) In general. Subject to subsection (f) of this section, if the completeness or accuracy of any item of information contained in a consumer's file at a consumer reporting agency is disputed by the consumer and the consumer notifies the agency directly, or

indirectly through a reseller, of such dispute, the agency shall, free of charge, conduct a reasonable reinvestigation to determine whether the disputed information is inaccurate and record the current status of the disputed information, or delete the item from the file in accordance with paragraph (5), before the end of the 30-day period beginning on the date on which the agency receives the notice of the dispute from the consumer or reseller.

      (B) Extension of period to reinvestigate.

Except as provided in subparagraph (C), the 30-day period described in subparagraph (A) may be extended for not more than 15 additional days if the consumer reporting agency receives information from the consumer during that 30-day period that is relevant to the reinvestigation.

      (C) Limitations on extension of period to reinvestigate.

Subparagraph (B) shall not apply to any reinvestigation in which, during the 30-day period described in subparagraph (A), the information that is the subject of the reinvestigation is found to be inaccurate or incomplete or the consumer reporting agency determines that the information cannot be verified.

(2) Prompt notice of dispute to furnisher of information.—

(A) In general. Before the expiration of the 5-business-day period beginning on the date on which a consumer reporting agency receives notice of a dispute from any consumer or a reseller in accordance with paragraph (1), the agency shall provide notification of the dispute to any person who provided any item of information in dispute, at the address and in the manner established with the person. The notice shall include all relevant information regarding the dispute that the agency has received from the consumer or reseller.

(B) Provision of other information. The consumer reporting agency shall promptly provide to the person who provided the information in dispute all relevant information regarding the dispute that is received by the agency from the consumer or the reseller after the period referred to in subparagraph (A) and before the end of the period referred to in paragraph (1)(A).

(3) Determination that dispute is frivolous or irrelevant.—

(A) In general. Notwithstanding paragraph (1), a consumer reporting agency may terminate a reinvestigation of information disputed by a consumer under that paragraph if the agency reasonably determines that the dispute by the consumer is frivolous or irrelevant, including by reason of a failure by a consumer to provide sufficient information to investigate the disputed information.

(B) Notice of determination. Upon making any determination in accordance with subparagraph (A) that a dispute is frivolous or irrelevant, a consumer reporting agency shall notify the consumer of such determination not later than 5 business days after making such determination, by mail or, if authorized by the consumer for that purpose, by any other means available to the agency.

(C) Contents of notice. A notice under subparagraph (B) shall include—

(i) the reasons for the determination under subparagraph (A); and

(ii) identification of any information required to investigate the disputed information, which may consist of a standardized form describing the general nature of such information.

(4) Consideration of consumer information. In conducting any reinvestigation under paragraph (1)

with respect to disputed information in the file of any consumer, the consumer reporting agency shall review and consider all relevant information submitted by the consumer in the period described in paragraph (1)(A) with respect to such disputed information.

(5) Treatment of inaccurate or unverifiable information.—

(A) In general. If, after any reinvestigation under paragraph (1) of any information disputed by a consumer, an item of the information is found to be inaccurate or incomplete or cannot be verified, the consumer reporting agency shall—

(i) promptly delete that item of information from the file of the consumer, or modify that item of information, as appropriate, based on the results of the reinvestigation; and

(ii) promptly notify the furnisher of that information that the information has been modified or deleted from the file of the consumer.

(B) Requirements relating to reinsertion of previously deleted material.—

(i) Certification of accuracy of information. If any information is deleted from a consumer's file pursuant to subparagraph (A), the information may not be reinserted in the file by the consumer reporting agency unless the person who furnishes the information certifies that the information is complete and accurate.

(ii) Notice to consumer. If any information that has been deleted from a consumer's file pursuant to subparagraph (A) is reinserted in the file, the consumer reporting agency shall notify the consumer of the reinsertion in writing not later than 5 business days after the reinsertion or, if authorized by the consumer for that purpose, by any other means available to the agency.

(iii) Additional information. As part of, or in addition to, the notice under clause (ii), a consumer reporting agency shall provide to a consumer in writing not later than 5 business days after the date of the reinsertion—

(I) a statement that the disputed information has been reinserted;

(II) the business name and address of any furnisher of information contacted and the telephone number of such furnisher, if reasonably available, or of any furnisher of information that contacted the consumer reporting agency, in connection with the reinsertion of such information; and

(III) a notice that the consumer has the right to add a statement to the consumer's file disputing the accuracy or completeness of the disputed information.

(C) Procedures to prevent reappearance. A consumer reporting agency shall maintain reasonable procedures designed to prevent the reappearance in a consumer's file, and in consumer reports on the consumer, of information that is deleted pursuant to this paragraph (other than information that is reinserted in accordance with subparagraph (B)(i)).

(D) Automated reinvestigation system. Any consumer reporting agency that compiles and maintains files on consumers on a nationwide basis shall implement an automated system through which furnishers of information to that consumer reporting agency may report the results of a reinvestigation that finds incomplete or inaccurate information in a consumer's file to other such consumer reporting agencies.

(6) Notice of results of reinvestigation.—

(A) In general. A consumer reporting agency shall provide written notice to a consumer of the results of a reinvestigation under this subsection not later than 5 business days after the completion of the reinvestigation, by mail or, if authorized by the consumer for that purpose, by other means available to the agency.

(B) Contents. As part of, or in addition to, the notice under subparagraph (A), a consumer reporting agency shall provide to a consumer in writing before the expiration of the 5-day period referred to in subparagraph (A)—

(i) a statement that the reinvestigation is completed;

(ii) a consumer report that is based upon the consumer's file as that file is revised as a result of the reinvestigation;

(iii) a notice that, if requested by the consumer, a description of the procedure used to determine the accuracy and completeness of the information shall be provided to the consumer by the agency, including the business name and address of any furnisher of information contacted in connection with such information and the telephone number of such furnisher, if reasonably available;

(iv) a notice that the consumer has the right to add a statement to the consumer's file disputing the accuracy or completeness of the information; and

(v) a notice that the consumer has the right to request under subsection (d) of this section that the consumer reporting agency furnish notifications under that subsection.

(7) Description of reinvestigation procedure. A consumer reporting agency shall provide to a consumer a description referred to in paragraph (6)(B)(iii) by not later than 15 days after receiving a request from the consumer for that description.

(8) Expedited dispute resolution. If a dispute regarding an item of information in a consumer's file at a consumer reporting agency is resolved in accordance with paragraph (5)(A) by the deletion of the disputed information by not later than 3 business days after the date on which the agency receives notice of the dispute from the consumer in accordance with paragraph (1)(A), then the agency shall not be required to comply with paragraphs (2), (6), and (7) with respect to that dispute if the agency—

(A) provides prompt notice of the deletion to the consumer by telephone;

(B) includes in that notice, or in a written notice that accompanies a confirmation and consumer report provided in accordance with subparagraph (C), a statement of the consumer's right to request under subsection (d) of this section that the agency furnish notifications under that subsection; and

(C) provides written confirmation of the deletion and a copy of a consumer report on the consumer that is based on the consumer's file after the deletion, not later than 5 business days after making the deletion.

(b) Statement of dispute

If the reinvestigation does not resolve the dispute, the consumer may file a brief statement setting forth the nature of the dispute. The consumer reporting agency may limit such statements to not more than one hundred words if it provides the consumer with assistance in writing a clear summary of the dispute.

(c) Notification of consumer dispute in subsequent consumer reports

Whenever a statement of a dispute is filed, unless there is reasonable grounds to believe that it is frivolous or irrelevant, the consumer reporting agency shall, in any subsequent consumer report containing the information in question, clearly note that it is disputed by the consumer and provide either the consumer's statement or a clear and accurate codification or summary thereof.

(d) Notification of deletion of disputed information

Following any deletion of information which is found to be inaccurate or whose accuracy can no longer be verified or any notation as to disputed information, the consumer reporting agency shall, at the request of the consumer, furnish notification that the item has been deleted or the statement, codification, or summary pursuant to subsection (b) or (c) of this section to any person specifically designated by the consumer who has within two years prior thereto received a consumer report for employment purposes, or within six months prior thereto received a consumer report for any other purpose, which contained the deleted or disputed information.

(e) Treatment of complaints and report to Congress

(1) In general

The Commission shall—

(A) compile all complaints that it receives that a file of a consumer that is maintained by a consumer reporting agency described in section 1681a(p) of this title contains incomplete or inaccurate information, with respect to which, the consumer appears to have disputed the completeness or accuracy with the consumer reporting agency or otherwise utilized the procedures provided by subsection (a) of this section; and

(B) transmit each such complaint to each consumer reporting agency involved.

(2) Exclusion

Complaints received or obtained by the Commission pursuant to its investigative authority under the Federal Trade Commission Act shall not be subject to paragraph (1).

(3) Agency responsibilities

Each consumer reporting agency described in section 1681a(p) of this title that receives a complaint transmitted by the Commission pursuant to paragraph (1) shall—

(A) review each such complaint to determine whether all legal obligations imposed on the consumer reporting agency under this subchapter (including any obligation imposed by an applicable court or administrative order) have been met with respect to the subject matter of the complaint;

(B) provide reports on a regular basis to the Commission regarding the determinations of and actions taken by the consumer reporting agency, if any, in connection with its review of such complaints; and

(C) maintain, for a reasonable time period, records regarding the disposition of each such complaint that is sufficient to demonstrate compliance with this subsection.

(4) Rulemaking authority

The Commission may prescribe regulations, as appropriate to implement this subsection.

(5) Annual report

The Commission shall submit to the Committee on Banking, Housing, and Urban Affairs of the Senate and the Committee on Financial Services of the House of Representatives an annual report regarding information gathered by the Commission under this subsection.

(f) Reinvestigation requirement applicable to resellers

(1) Exemption from general reinvestigation requirement

Except as provided in paragraph (2), a reseller shall be exempt from the requirements of this section.

(2) Action required upon receiving notice of a dispute

If a reseller receives a notice from a consumer of a dispute concerning the completeness or accuracy of any item of information contained in a consumer report on such consumer produced by the reseller, the reseller shall, within 5 business days of receiving the notice, and free of charge—

(A) determine whether the item of information is incomplete or inaccurate as a result of an act or omission of the reseller; and

(B) if—

(i) the reseller determines that the item of information is incomplete or inaccurate as a result of an act or omission of the reseller, not later than 20 days after receiving the notice, correct the information in the consumer report or delete it; or

(ii) if the reseller determines that the item of information is not incomplete or inaccurate as a result of an act or omission of the reseller, convey the notice of the dispute, together with all relevant information provided by the consumer, to each consumer reporting agency that provided the reseller with the information that is the subject of the dispute, using an address or a notification mechanism specified by the consumer reporting agency for such notices.

(3) Responsibility of consumer reporting agency to notify consumer through reseller

Upon the completion of a reinvestigation under this section of a dispute concerning the completeness or accuracy of any information in the file of a consumer by a consumer reporting agency that received notice of the dispute from a reseller under paragraph (2)—

(A) the notice by the consumer reporting agency under paragraph (6), (7), or (8) of subsection (a) of this section shall be provided to the reseller in lieu of the consumer; and

(B) the reseller shall immediately reconvey such notice to the consumer, including any notice of a deletion by telephone in the manner required under paragraph (8)(A).

(4) Reseller reinvestigations

No provision of this subsection shall be construed as prohibiting a reseller from conducting a reinvestigation of a consumer dispute directly.

15 U.S.C. § 1681j. Charges for certain disclosures

(a) Reasonable charges allowed for certain disclosures

(1) In general. Except as provided in subsections (b), (c), and (d) of this section, a consumer reporting agency may impose a reasonable charge on a consumer—

(A) for making a disclosure to the consumer pursuant to section 1681g of this title, which charge—

(i) shall not exceed $8; and

(ii) shall be indicated to the consumer before making the disclosure; and

(B) for furnishing, pursuant to section 1681i(d) of this title, following a reinvestigation under section 1681i(a) of this title, a statement, codification, or summary to a person designated by the consumer under that section after the 30-day period beginning on the date of

notification of the consumer under paragraph (6) or (8) of section 1681i(a) of this title with respect to the reinvestigation, which charge—

(i) shall not exceed the charge that the agency would impose on each designated recipient for a consumer report; and

(ii) shall be indicated to the consumer before furnishing such information.

(2) Modification of amount. The Federal Trade Commission shall increase the amount referred to in paragraph (1)(A)(i) on January 1 of each year, based proportionally on changes in the Consumer Price Index, with fractional changes rounded to the nearest fifty cents.

(b) Free disclosure after adverse notice to consumer

Each consumer reporting agency that maintains a file on a consumer shall make all disclosures pursuant to section 1681g of this title without charge to the consumer if, not later than 60 days after receipt by such consumer of a notification pursuant to section 1681m of this title, or of a notification from a debt collection agency affiliated with that consumer reporting agency stating that the consumer's credit rating may be or has been adversely affected, the consumer makes a request under section 1681g of this title.

(c) Free disclosure under certain other circumstances

Upon the request of the consumer, a consumer reporting agency shall make all disclosures pursuant to section 1681g of this title once during any 12-month period without charge to that consumer if the consumer certifies in writing that the consumer—

(1) is unemployed and intends to apply for employment in the 60-day period beginning on the date on which the certification is made;

(2) is a recipient of public welfare assistance; or

(3) has reason to believe that the file on the consumer at the agency contains inaccurate information due to fraud.

(d) Other charges prohibited

A consumer reporting agency shall not impose any charge on a consumer for providing any notification required by this subchapter or making any disclosure required by this subchapter, except as authorized by subsection (a) of this section.

15 U.S.C. § 1681k. Public record information for employment purposes

(a) In general

A consumer reporting agency which furnishes a consumer report for employment purposes and which for that purpose compiles and reports items of information on consumers which are matters of public record and are likely to have an adverse effect upon a consumer's ability to obtain employment shall—

(1) at the time such public record information is reported to the user of such consumer report, notify

the consumer of the fact that public record information is being reported by the consumer reporting agency, together with the name and address of the person to whom such information is being reported; or

(2) maintain strict procedures designed to insure that whenever public record information which is likely to have an adverse effect on a consumer's ability to obtain employment is reported it is complete and up to date. For purposes of this paragraph, items of public record relating to arrests, indictments, convictions, suits, tax liens, and outstanding judgments shall be considered up to date if the current public record status of the item at the time of the report is reported.

(b) Exemption for National security investigations

Subsection (a) of this section does not apply in the case of an agency or department of the United States Government that seeks to obtain and use a consumer report for employment purposes, if the head of the agency or department makes a written finding as prescribed under section 1681b(b)(4)(A) of this title.

15 U.S.C. § 1681l. Restrictions on investigative consumer reports

Whenever a consumer reporting agency prepares an investigative consumer report, no adverse information in the consumer report (other than information which is a matter of public record) may be included in a subsequent consumer report unless such adverse information has been verified in the process of making such subsequent consumer report, or the adverse information was received within the three-month period preceding the date the subsequent report is furnished.

15 U.S.C. § 1681m. Requirements on users of consumer reports

(a) Duties of users taking adverse actions on basis of information contained in consumer reports

If any person takes any adverse action with respect to any consumer that is based in whole or in part on any information contained in a consumer report, the person shall—

(1) provide oral, written, or electronic notice of the adverse action to the consumer;

(2) provide to the consumer orally, in writing, or electronically—

(A) the name, address, and telephone number of the consumer reporting agency (including a toll-free telephone number established by the agency if the agency compiles and maintains files on consumers on a nationwide basis) that furnished the report to the person; and

(B) a statement that the consumer reporting agency did not make the decision to take the adverse action and is unable to provide the consumer the specific reasons why the adverse action was taken; and

(3) provide to the consumer an oral, written, or electronic notice of the consumer's right—

(A) to obtain, under section 1681j of this title, a free copy of a consumer report on the consumer from the consumer reporting agency referred to in paragraph (2), which notice shall include an indication of the 60-day period under that section for obtaining such a copy; and

(B) to dispute, under section 1681i of this title, with a consumer reporting agency the accuracy or completeness of any information in a consumer report furnished by the agency.

(b) Adverse action based on information obtained from third parties other than consumer reporting agencies

(1) In general. Whenever credit for personal, family, or household purposes involving a consumer is denied or the charge for such credit is increased either wholly or partly because of information obtained from a person other than a consumer reporting agency bearing upon the consumer's credit worthiness, credit standing, credit capacity, character, general reputation, personal characteristics, or mode of living, the user of such information shall, within a reasonable period of time, upon the consumer's written request for the reasons for such

adverse action received within sixty days after learning of such adverse action, disclose the nature of the information to the consumer. The user of such information shall clearly and accurately disclose to the consumer his right to make such written request at the time such adverse action is communicated to the consumer.

(2) Duties of person taking certain actions based on information provided by affiliate.—

  (A) Duties, generally. If a person takes an action described in subparagraph (B) with respect to a consumer, based in whole or in part on information described in subparagraph (C), the person shall—

   (i) notify the consumer of the action, including a statement that the consumer may obtain the information in accordance with clause (ii); and

   (ii) upon a written request from the consumer received within 60 days after transmittal of the notice required by clause (i), disclose to the consumer the nature of the information upon which the action is based by not later than 30 days after receipt of the request.

  (B) Action described. An action referred to in subparagraph (A) is an adverse action described in section 1681a(k)(1)(A) of this title, taken in connection with

a transaction initiated by the consumer, or any adverse action described in clause (i) or (ii) of section 1681a(k)(1)(B) of this title.

  (C) Information described. Information referred to in subparagraph (A)—

   (i) except as provided in clause (ii), is information that—

    (I) is furnished to the person taking the action by a person related by common ownership or affiliated by common corporate control to the person taking the action; and

    (II) bears on the credit worthiness, credit standing, credit capacity, character, general reputation, personal characteristics, or mode of living of the consumer; and

   (ii) does not include—

    (I) information solely as to transactions or experiences between the consumer and the person furnishing the information; or

    (II) information in a consumer report.

(c) Reasonable procedures to assure compliance

No person shall be held liable for any violation of this section if he shows by a preponderance of the evidence that at the time of the alleged violation he maintained reasonable procedures to assure compliance with the provisions of this section.

(d) Duties of users making written credit or insurance solicitations on the basis of information contained in consumer files

(1) In general. Any person who uses a consumer report on any consumer in connection with any credit or insurance transaction that is not initiated by the consumer, that is provided to that person under section 1681b(c)(1)(B) of this title, shall provide with each written solicitation made to the consumer regarding the transaction a clear and conspicuous statement that—

(A) information contained in the consumer's consumer report was used in connection with the transaction;

(B) the consumer received the offer of credit or insurance because the consumer satisfied the criteria for credit worthiness or insurability under which the consumer was selected for the offer;

(C) if applicable, the credit or insurance may not be extended if, after the consumer responds to the offer, the consumer does not meet the criteria used to select the consumer for the offer or any applicable criteria bearing on credit worthiness or insurability or does not furnish any required collateral;

(D) the consumer has a right to prohibit information contained in the consumer's file with any consumer reporting agency from being used in connection with any credit or insurance transaction that is not initiated by the consumer; and

(E) the consumer may exercise the right referred to in subparagraph (D) by notifying a notification system established under section 1681b(e) of this title.

(2) Disclosure of address and telephone number; format
A statement under paragraph (1) shall—

(A) include the address and toll-free telephone number of the appropriate notification system established under section 1681b(e) of this title; and

(B) be presented in such format and in such type size and manner as to be simple and easy to understand, as established by the Commission, by rule, in consultation with the Federal banking agencies and the National Credit Union Administration.

(3) Maintaining criteria on file. A person who makes an offer of credit or insurance to a consumer under a credit or insurance transaction described in paragraph (1) shall maintain on file the criteria used to select the consumer to receive the offer, all criteria bearing on

credit worthiness or insurability, as applicable, that are the basis for determining whether or not to extend credit or insurance pursuant to the offer, and any requirement for the furnishing of collateral as a condition of the extension of credit or insurance, until the expiration of the 3-year period beginning on the date on which the offer is made to the consumer.

(4) Authority of Federal agencies regarding unfair or deceptive acts or practices not affected. This section is not intended to affect the authority of any Federal or State agency to enforce a prohibition against unfair or deceptive acts or practices, including the making of false or misleading statements in connection with a credit or insurance transaction that is not initiated by the consumer.

(e) Red flag guidelines and regulations required

(1) Guidelines

The Federal banking agencies, the National Credit Union Administration, and the Commission shall jointly, with respect to the entities that are subject to their respective enforcement authority under section 1681s of this title—

(A) establish and maintain guidelines for use by each financial institution and each creditor regarding identity theft with respect to account holders at, or customers of, such entities, and update such guidelines as often as necessary;

(B) prescribe regulations requiring each financial institution and each creditor to establish reasonable policies and procedures for implementing the guidelines established pursuant to subparagraph (A), to identify possible risks to account holders or customers or to the safety and soundness of the institution or customers; and

(C) prescribe regulations applicable to card issuers to ensure that, if a card issuer receives notification of a change of address for an existing account, and within a short period of time (during at least the first 30 days after such notification is received) receives a request for an additional or replacement card for the same account, the card issuer may not issue the additional or replacement card, unless the card issuer, in accordance with reasonable policies and procedures—

(i) notifies the cardholder of the request at the former address of the cardholder and provides to the cardholder a means of promptly reporting incorrect address changes;

(ii) notifies the cardholder of the request by such other means of communication as the

cardholder and the card issuer previously agreed to; or

(iii) uses other means of assessing the validity of the change
of address, in accordance
with reasonable policies and
procedures established by the
card issuer in accordance with
the regulations prescribed under subparagraph (B).

(2) Criteria

(A) In general

In developing the guidelines
required by paragraph (1)(A), the
agencies described in paragraph
(1) shall identify patterns,
practices, and specific forms of
activity that indicate the possible
existence of identity theft.

(B) Inactive accounts

In developing the guidelines
required by paragraph (1)(A), the
agencies described in paragraph
(1) shall consider including
reasonable guidelines providing
that when a transaction occurs
with respect to a credit or deposit
account that has been inactive
for more than 2 years, the
creditor or financial institution
shall follow reasonable policies
and procedures that provide for
notice to be given to a consumer
in a manner reasonably designed
to reduce the likelihood of
identity theft with respect to such
account.

(3) Consistency with verification
requirements

Guidelines established pursuant
to paragraph (1) shall not be
inconsistent with the policies and
procedures required under section
5318(l) of Title 31.

(f) Prohibition on sale or transfer of debt
caused by identity theft

(1) In general

No person shall sell, transfer for
consideration, or place for collection
a debt that such person has been
notified under section 1681c-2 of this
title has resulted from identity theft.

(2) Applicability

The prohibitions of this subsection
shall apply to all persons collecting
a debt described in paragraph (1)
after the date of a notification under
paragraph (1).

(3) Rule of construction

Nothing in this subsection shall be
construed to prohibit—

(A) the repurchase of a debt in any
case in which the assignee of the
debt requires such repurchase
because the debt has resulted
from identity theft;

(B) the securitization of a debt or
the pledging of a portfolio of
debt as collateral in connection
with a borrowing; or

(C) the transfer of debt as a result of
a merger, acquisition, purchase
and assumption transaction, or
transfer of substantially all of the
assets of an entity.

(g) Debt collector communications concerning identity theft

If a person acting as a debt collector

(as that term is defined in subchapter V of this chapter) on behalf of a third party that is a creditor or other user of a consumer report is notified that any information relating to a debt that the person is attempting to collect may be fraudulent or may be the result of identity theft, that person shall—

(1) notify the third party that the information may be fraudulent or may be the result of identity theft; and

(2) upon request of the consumer to whom the debt purportedly relates, provide to the consumer all information to which the consumer would otherwise be entitled if the consumer were not a victim of identity theft, but wished to dispute the debt under provisions of law applicable to that person.

(h) Duties of users in certain credit transactions

(1) In general

Subject to rules prescribed as provided in paragraph (6), if any person uses a consumer report in connection with an application for, or a grant, extension, or other provision of, credit on material terms that are materially less favorable than the most favorable terms available to a substantial proportion of consumers from or through that person, based in whole or in part on a consumer report, the person shall provide an oral, written, or electronic notice to the consumer in the form and manner required by regulations prescribed in accordance with this subsection.

(2) Timing

The notice required under paragraph (1) may be provided at the time of an application for, or a grant, extension, or other provision of, credit or the time of communication of an approval of an application for, or grant, extension, or other provision of, credit, except as provided in the regulations prescribed under paragraph (6).

(3) Exceptions

No notice shall be required from a person under this subsection if—

(A) the consumer applied for specific material terms and was granted those terms, unless those terms were initially specified by the person after the transaction was initiated by the consumer and after the person obtained a consumer report; or

(B) the person has provided or will provide a notice to the consumer under subsection (a) of this section in connection with the transaction.

(4) Other notice not sufficient

A person that is required to provide a notice under subsection (a) of this section cannot meet that requirement by providing a notice under this subsection.

(5) Content and delivery of notice

A notice under this subsection shall, at a minimum—

(A) include a statement informing the consumer that the terms offered to the consumer are set based on information from a consumer report;

(B) identify the consumer reporting agency furnishing the report;

(C) include a statement informing the consumer that the consumer may obtain a copy of a consumer report from that consumer reporting agency without charge; and

(D) include the contact information specified by that consumer reporting agency for obtaining such consumer reports (including a toll-free telephone number established by the agency in the case of a consumer reporting agency described in section 1681a(p) of this title).

(6) Rulemaking

(A) Rules required

The Commission and the Board shall jointly prescribe rules.

(B) Content

Rules required by subparagraph (A) shall address, but are not limited to—

  (i) the form, content, time, and manner of delivery of any notice under this subsection;

  (ii) clarification of the meaning of terms used in this subsection, including what credit terms are material, and when credit terms are materially less favorable;

  (iii) exceptions to the notice requirement under this subsection for classes of persons or transactions regarding which the agencies determine that notice would not significantly benefit consumers;

  (iv) a model notice that may be used to comply with this subsection; and

  (v) the timing of the notice required under paragraph (1), including the circumstances under which the notice must be provided after the terms offered to the consumer were set based on information from a consumer report.

(7) Compliance

A person shall not be liable for failure to perform the duties required by this section if, at the time of the failure, the person maintained reasonable policies and procedures to comply with this section.

(8) Enforcement

(A) No civil actions

Sections 1681n and 1681o of this title shall not apply to any failure by any person to comply with this section.

(B) Administrative enforcement

This section shall be enforced exclusively under section 1681s of this title by the Federal agencies and officials identified in that section.

15 U.S.C. § 1681n. Civil liability for willful noncompliance

(a) In general

Any person who willfully fails to comply with any requirement imposed under this subchapter with respect to any consumer is liable to that consumer in an amount equal to the sum of—

(1)

    (A) any actual damages sustained by the consumer as a result of the failure or damages of not less than $100 and not more than $1,000; or

    (B) in the case of liability of a natural person for obtaining a consumer report under false pretenses or knowingly without a permissible purpose, actual damages sustained by the consumer as a result of the failure or $1,000, whichever is greater;

(2) such amount of punitive damages as the court may allow; and

(3) in the case of any successful action to enforce any liability under this section, the costs of the action together with reasonable attorney's fees as determined by the court.

(b) Civil liability for knowing noncompliance

Any person who obtains a consumer report from a consumer reporting agency under false pretenses or knowingly without a permissible purpose shall be liable to the consumer reporting agency for actual damages sustained by the consumer reporting agency or $1,000, whichever is greater.

(c) Attorney's fees

Upon a finding by the court that an unsuccessful pleading, motion, or other paper filed in connection with an action under this section was filed in bad faith or for purposes of harassment, the court shall award to the prevailing party attorney's fees reasonable in relation to the work expended in responding to the pleading, motion, or other paper.

15 U.S.C. § 1681o. Civil liability for negligent noncompliance

(a) In general

Any person who is negligent in failing to comply with any requirement imposed under this subchapter with respect to any consumer is liable to that consumer in an amount equal to the sum of—

(1) any actual damages sustained by the consumer as a result of the failure; and

(2) in the case of any successful action to enforce any liability under this section, the costs of the action together with reasonable attorney's fees as determined by the court.

(b) Attorney's fees

On a finding by the court that an unsuccessful pleading, motion, or other paper filed in connection with an action under this section was filed in bad faith or for purposes of harassment, the court shall award to the prevailing party attorney's fees reasonable in relation to the work expended in responding to the pleading, motion, or other paper.

15 U.S.C. § 1681p. Jurisdiction of courts; limitation of actions

An action to enforce any liability created under this subchapter may be brought in any appropriate United States district court, without regard to the amount in controversy, or in any other court of competent jurisdiction, not later than the earlier of—

(1) 2 years after the date of discovery by the plaintiff of the violation that is the basis for such liability; or

(2) 5 years after the date on which the violation that is the basis for such liability occurs.

15 U.S.C. § 1681q. Obtaining information under false pretenses

Any person who knowingly and willfully obtains information on a consumer from a consumer reporting agency under false pretenses shall be fined under Title 18, imprisoned for not more than 2 years, or both.

15 U.S.C. § 1681r. Unauthorized disclosures by officers or employees

Any officer or employee of a consumer reporting agency who knowingly and willfully provides information concerning an individual from the agency's files to a person not authorized to receive that information shall be fined under Title 18, imprisoned for not more than 2 years, or both.

15 U.S.C. § 1681s. Administrative enforcement

(a) Enforcement by Federal Trade Commission

(1) Enforcement by Federal Trade Commission. Compliance with the requirements imposed under this subchapter shall be enforced under the Federal Trade Commission Act [15 U.S.C.A. § 41 et seq.] by the Federal Trade Commission with respect to consumer reporting agencies and all other persons subject thereto, except to the extent that enforcement of the requirements imposed under this subchapter is specifically committed to some other government agency under subsection (b) hereof. For the purpose of the exercise by the Federal Trade Commission of its functions and powers under the Federal Trade Commission Act, a violation of any requirement or prohibition imposed under this subchapter shall constitute an unfair or deceptive act or practice in commerce in violation of section 5(a) of the Federal Trade Commission Act [15 U.S.C.A. § 45(a)] and shall be subject to enforcement by the Federal Trade Commission under section 5(b) thereof [15 U.S.C.A. § 45(b)] with respect to any consumer reporting agency or person subject to enforcement by the Federal Trade Commission pursuant to this subsection, irrespective of whether that person is engaged in commerce or meets any other jurisdictional tests in the Federal Trade Commission Act. The Federal Trade Commission shall have such procedural, investigative, and enforcement powers, including the power to issue procedural rules in enforcing compliance with the

requirements imposed under this subchapter and to require the filing of reports, the production of documents, and the appearance of witnesses as though the applicable terms and conditions of the Federal Trade Commission Act were part of this subchapter. Any person violating any of the provisions of this subchapter shall be subject to the penalties and entitled to the privileges and immunities provided in the Federal Trade Commission Act as though the applicable terms and provisions thereof were part of this subchapter.

(2)(A) In the event of a knowing violation, which constitutes a pattern or practice of violations of this subchapter, the Commission may commence a civil action to recover a civil penalty in a district court of the United States against any person that violates this subchapter. In such action, such person shall be liable for a civil penalty of not more than $2,500 per violation.

(B) In determining the amount of a civil penalty under subparagraph (A), the court shall take into account the degree of culpability, any history of prior such conduct, ability to pay, effect on ability to continue to do business, and such other matters as justice may require.

(3) Notwithstanding paragraph (2), a court may not impose any civil penalty on a person for a violation of section 1681s-2(a)(1) of this title unless the person has been enjoined from committing the violation, or ordered not to commit the violation, in an action or proceeding brought by or on behalf of the Federal Trade Commission, and has violated the injunction or order, and the court may not impose any civil penalty for any violation occurring before the date of the violation of the injunction or order.

(b) Enforcement by other agencies

Compliance with the requirements imposed under this subchapter with respect to consumer reporting agencies, persons who use consumer reports from such agencies, persons who furnish information to such agencies, and users of information that are subject to subsection (d) of section 1681m of this title shall be enforced under—

(1) section 8 of the Federal Deposit Insurance Act [12 U.S.C.A. § 1818], in the case of—

(A) national banks, and Federal branches and Federal agencies of foreign banks, by the Office of the Comptroller of the Currency;

(B) member banks of the Federal Reserve System (other than national banks), branches and agencies of foreign banks (other than Federal branches, Federal agencies, and insured State branches of foreign banks), commercial lending companies owned or controlled by foreign banks, and organizations operating under section 25 or 25A of the Federal Reserve Act [12 U.S.C.A. § 601 et seq. or § 611 et seq.], by the Board of Governors of the Federal Reserve System; and

(C) banks insured by the Federal Deposit Insurance Corporation (other than members of the Federal Reserve System) and insured State branches of foreign banks, by the Board of Directors of the Federal Deposit Insurance Corporation;

(2) section 8 of the Federal Deposit Insurance Act [12 U.S.C.A. § 1818], by the Director of the Office of Thrift Supervision, in the case of a savings association the deposits of which are insured by the Federal Deposit Insurance Corporation.

(3) the Federal Credit Union Act [12 U.S.C.A. § 1751 et seq.], by the Administrator of the National Credit Union Administration with respect to any Federal credit union;

(4) subtitle IV of Title 49, by the Secretary of Transportation, with respect to all carriers subject to the jurisdiction of the Surface Transportation Board;

(5) part A of subtitle VII of Title 49, by the Secretary of Transportation with respect to any air carrier or foreign air carrier subject to that part; and

(6) the Packers and Stockyards Act, 1921 [7 U.S.C.A. § 181 et seq.] (except as provided in section 406 of that Act [7 U.S.C.A. §§ 226, 227]), by the Secretary of Agriculture with respect to any activities subject to that Act. The terms used in paragraph (1) that are not defined in this subchapter or otherwise defined in section 3(s) of the Federal Deposit Insurance Act (12 U.S.C. 1813(s)) shall have the meaning given to them in section 1(b) of the International Banking Act of 1978 (12 U.S.C. 3101).

(c) State action for violations

(1) Authority of States. In addition to such other remedies as are provided under State law, if the chief law enforcement officer of a State, or an official or agency designated by a State, has reason to believe that any person has violated or is violating this subchapter, the State—

(A) may bring an action to enjoin such violation in any appropriate United States district court or in any other court of competent jurisdiction;

(B) subject to paragraph (5), may bring an action on behalf of the residents of the State to recover—

(i) damages for which the person is liable to such residents under sections 1681n and 1681o of this title as a result of the violation;

(ii) in the case of a violation described in any of paragraphs

(1) through (3) of section 1681s-2(c) of this title, damages for which the person would, but for section 1681s-2(c) of this title, be liable to such residents as a result of the violation; or

    (iii) damages of not more than $1,000 for each willful or negligent violation; and

(C) in the case of any successful action under subparagraph (A) or (B), shall be awarded the costs of the action and reasonable attorney fees as determined by the court.

(2) Rights of Federal regulators. The State shall serve prior written notice of any action under paragraph (1) upon the Federal Trade Commission or the appropriate Federal regulator determined under subsection (b) of this section and provide the Commission or appropriate Federal regulator with a copy of its complaint, except in any case in which such prior notice is not feasible, in which case the State shall serve such notice immediately upon instituting such action. The Federal Trade Commission or appropriate Federal regulator shall have the right—

(A) to intervene in the action;

(B) upon so intervening, to be heard on all matters arising therein;

(C) to remove the action to the appropriate United States district court; and

(D) to file petitions for appeal.

(3) Investigatory powers. For purposes of bringing any action under this subsection, nothing in this subsection shall prevent the chief law enforcement officer, or an official or agency designated by a State, from exercising the powers conferred on the chief law enforcement officer or such official by the laws of such State to conduct investigations or to administer oaths or affirmations or to compel the attendance of witnesses or the production of documentary and other evidence.

(4) Limitation on State action while Federal action pending. If the Federal Trade Commission or the appropriate Federal regulator has instituted a civil action or an administrative action under section 8 of the Federal Deposit Insurance Act [12 U.S.C.A. § 1818] for a violation of this subchapter, no State may, during the pendency of such action, bring an action under this section against any defendant named in the complaint of the Commission or the appropriate Federal regulator for any violation of this subchapter that is alleged in that complaint.

(5) Limitations on State actions for certain violations

(A) Violation of injunction required. A State may not bring an action against a person under paragraph (1)(B) for a violation described in any of paragraphs

(1) through (3) of section 1681s-2(c) of this title, unless—

   (i) the person has been enjoined from committing the violation, in an action brought by the State under paragraph (1)(A); and

   (ii) the person has violated the injunction.

   (B) Limitation on damages recoverable. In an action against a person under paragraph (1)(B) for a violation described in any of paragraphs (1) through (3) of section 1681s-2(c) of this title, a State may not recover any damages incurred before the date of the violation of an injunction on which the action is based.

(d) Enforcement under other authority

   For the purpose of the exercise by any agency referred to in subsection (b) of this section of its powers under any Act referred to in that subsection, a violation of any requirement imposed under this subchapter shall be deemed to be a violation of a requirement imposed under that Act. In addition to its powers under any provision of law specifically referred to in subsection (b) of this section, each of the agencies referred to in that subsection may exercise, for the purpose of enforcing compliance with any requirement imposed under this subchapter any other authority conferred on it by law.

(e) Regulatory authority

   (1) The Federal banking agencies referred to in paragraphs (1) and (2) of subsection (b) shall jointly prescribe such regulations as necessary to carry out the purposes of this subchapter with respect to any persons identified under paragraphs (1) and (2) of subsection (b) of this section, and the Board of Governors of the Federal Reserve System shall have authority to prescribe regulations consistent with such joint regulations with respect to bank holding companies and affiliates (other than depository institutions and consumer reporting agencies) of such holding companies.

   (2) The Board of the National Credit Union Administration shall prescribe such regulations as necessary to carry out the purposes of this subchapter with respect to any persons identified under paragraph (3) of subsection (b) of this section.

(f) Coordination of consumer complaint investigations

   (1) In general

   Each consumer reporting agency described in section 1681a(p) of this title shall develop and maintain procedures for the referral to each other such agency of any consumer complaint received by the agency alleging identity theft, or requesting a fraud alert under section 1681c-1 of this title or a block under section 1681c-2 of this title.

   (2) Model form and procedure for reporting identity theft

The Commission, in consultation with the Federal banking agencies and the National Credit Union Administration, shall develop a model form and model procedures to be used by consumers who are victims of identity theft for contacting and informing creditors and consumer reporting agencies of the fraud.

(3) Annual summary reports

Each consumer reporting agency described in section 1681a(p) of this title shall submit an annual summary report to the Commission on consumer complaints received by the agency on identity theft or fraud alerts.

(g) FTC regulation of coding of trade names

If the Commission determines that a person described in paragraph (9) of section 1681s-c(a) of this title has not met the requirements of such paragraph, the Commission shall take action to ensure the person's compliance with such paragraph, which may include issuing model guidance or prescribing reasonable policies and procedures, as necessary to ensure that such person complies with such paragraph.

15 U.S.C. § 1681s-1. Information on overdue child support obligations

Notwithstanding any other provision of this subchapter, a consumer reporting agency shall include in any consumer report furnished by the agency in accordance with section 1681b of this title, any information on the failure of the consumer to pay overdue support which—

(1) is provided—

   (A) to the consumer reporting agency by a State or local child support enforcement agency; or

   (B) to the consumer reporting agency and verified by any local, State, or Federal Government agency; and

(2) antedates the report by 7 years or less.

15 U.S.C. § 1681s-2. Responsibilities of furnishers of information to consumer reporting agencies

(a) Duty of furnishers of information to provide accurate information

(1) Prohibition

   (A) Reporting information with actual knowledge of errors

   A person shall not furnish any information relating to a consumer to any consumer reporting agency if the person knows or has reasonable cause to believe that the information is inaccurate.

   (B) Reporting information after notice and confirmation of errors

   A person shall not furnish information relating to a consumer to any consumer reporting agency if—

     (i) the person has been notified by the consumer, at the address specified by the person for such notices, that specific information is inaccurate; and

(ii) the information is, in fact, inaccurate.

(C) No address requirement

A person who clearly and conspicuously specifies to the consumer an address for notices referred to in subparagraph (B) shall not be subject to subparagraph (A); however, nothing in subparagraph (B) shall require a person to specify such an address.

(D) Definition

For purposes of subparagraph (A), the term "reasonable cause to believe that the information is inaccurate" means having specific knowledge, other than solely allegations by the consumer, that would cause a reasonable person to have substantial doubts about the accuracy of the information.

(2) Duty to correct and update information

A person who—

(A) regularly and in the ordinary course of business furnishes information to one or more consumer reporting agencies about the person's transactions or experiences with any consumer; and

(B) has furnished to a consumer reporting agency information that the person determines is not complete or accurate, shall promptly notify the consumer reporting agency of that

determination and provide to the agency any corrections to that information, or any additional information, that is necessary to make the information provided by the person to the agency complete and accurate, and shall not thereafter furnish to the agency any of the information that remains not complete or accurate.

(3) Duty to provide notice of dispute

If the completeness or accuracy of any information furnished by any person to any consumer reporting agency is disputed to such person by a consumer, the person may not furnish the information to any consumer reporting agency without notice that such information is disputed by the consumer.

(4) Duty to provide notice of closed accounts

A person who regularly and in the ordinary course of business furnishes information to a consumer reporting agency regarding a consumer who has a credit account with that person shall notify the agency of the voluntary closure of the account by the consumer, in information regularly furnished for the period in which the account is closed.

(5) Duty to provide notice of delinquency of accounts

(A) In general

A person who furnishes information to a consumer reporting agency regarding a delinquent account being placed for collection, charged to profit or loss, or subjected to any similar action shall, not later than 90 days after furnishing the information, notify the agency of the date of delinquency on the account, which shall be the month and year of the commencement of the delinquency on the account that immediately preceded the action.

(B) Rule of construction

For purposes of this paragraph only, and provided that the consumer does not dispute the information, a person that furnishes information on a delinquent account that is placed for collection, charged for profit or loss, or subjected to any similar action, complies with this paragraph, if—

(i) the person reports the same date of delinquency as that provided by the creditor to which the account was owed at the time at which the commencement of the delinquency occurred, if the creditor previously reported that date of delinquency to a consumer reporting agency;

(ii) the creditor did not previously report the date of delinquency to a consumer reporting agency, and the person establishes and fol-

lows reasonable procedures to obtain the date of delinquency from the creditor or another reliable source and reports that date to a consumer reporting agency as the date of delinquency; or

(iii) the creditor did not previously report the date of delinquency to a consumer reporting agency and the date of delinquency cannot be reasonably obtained as provided in clause (ii), the person establishes and follows reasonable procedures to ensure the date reported as the date of delinquency precedes the date on which the account is placed for collection, charged to profit or loss, or subjected to any similar action, and reports such date to the credit reporting agency.

(6) Duties of furnishers upon notice of identity theft-related information

(A) Reasonable procedures

A person that furnishes information to any consumer reporting agency shall have in place reasonable procedures to respond to any notification that it receives from a consumer reporting agency under section 1681c-2 of this title relating to information resulting from identity theft, to prevent that person from refurnishing such blocked information.

(B) Information alleged to result from identity theft
If a consumer submits an identity theft report to a person who furnishes information to a consumer reporting agency at the address specified by that person for receiving such reports stating that information maintained by such person that purports to relate to the consumer resulted from identity theft, the person may not furnish such information that purports to relate to the consumer to any consumer reporting agency, unless the person subsequently knows or is informed by the consumer that the information is correct.

(7) Negative information

(A) Notice to consumer required

(i) In general
If any financial institution that extends credit and regularly and in the ordinary course of business furnishes information to a consumer reporting agency described in section 1681a(p) of this title furnishes negative information to such an agency regarding credit extended to a customer, the financial institution shall provide a notice of such furnishing of negative information, in writing, to the customer.

(ii) Notice effective for subsequent submissions
After providing such notice, the financial institution may submit additional negative information to a consumer reporting agency described in section 1681a(p) of this title with respect to the same transaction, extension of credit, account, or customer without providing additional notice to the customer.

(B) Time of notice

(i) In general
The notice required under subparagraph (A) shall be provided to the customer prior to, or no later than 30 days after, furnishing the negative information to a consumer reporting agency described in section 1681a(p) of this title.

(ii) Coordination with new account disclosures
If the notice is provided to the customer prior to furnishing the negative information to a consumer reporting agency, the notice may not be included in the initial disclosures provided under section 1637(a) of this title.

(C) Coordination with other disclosures
The notice required under subparagraph (A)—

(i) may be included on or with any notice of default, any billing statement, or any other materials provided to the customer; and

(ii) must be clear and conspicuous.

(D) Model disclosure

(i) Duty of board to prepare
The Board shall prescribe a brief model disclosure a financial institution may use to comply with subparagraph (A), which shall not exceed 30 words.

(ii) Use of model not required
No provision of this paragraph shall be construed as requiring a financial institution to use any such model form prescribed by the Board.

(iii) Compliance using model
A financial institution shall be deemed to be in compliance with subparagraph (A) if the financial institution uses any such model form prescribed by the Board, or the financial institution uses any such model form and rearranges its format.

(E) Use of notice without submitting negative information
No provision of this paragraph shall be construed as requiring a financial institution that has provided a customer with a notice described in subparagraph (A) to furnish negative information about the customer to a consumer reporting agency.

(F) Safe harbor
A financial institution shall not be liable for failure to perform the duties required by this paragraph if, at the time of the failure, the financial institution maintained reasonable policies and procedures to comply with this paragraph or the financial institution reasonably believed that the institution is prohibited, by law, from contacting the consumer.

(G) Definitions
For purposes of this paragraph, the following definitions shall apply:

(i) Negative information
The term "negative information" means information concerning a customer's delinquencies, late payments, insolvency, or any form of default.

(ii) Customer; financial institution
The terms "customer" and "financial institution" have the same meanings as in section 6809 of this title.

(8) Ability of consumer to dispute information directly with furnisher

(A) In general
The Federal banking agencies, the National Credit Union Administration, and the

Commission shall jointly prescribe regulations that shall identify the circumstances under which a furnisher shall be required to reinvestigate a dispute concerning the accuracy of information contained in a consumer report on the consumer, based on a direct request of a consumer.

(B) Considerations

In prescribing regulations under subparagraph (A), the agencies shall weigh—

   (i) the benefits to consumers with the costs on furnishers and the credit reporting system;

   (ii) the impact on the overall accuracy and integrity of consumer reports of any such requirements;

   (iii) whether direct contact by the consumer with the furnisher would likely result in the most expeditious resolution of any such dispute; and

   (iv) the potential impact on the credit reporting process if credit repair organizations, as defined in section 1679a(3) of this title, including entities that would be a credit repair organization, but for section 1679a(3)(B)(i) of this title, are able to circumvent the prohibition in subparagraph (G).

(C) Applicability

Subparagraphs (D) through (G) shall apply in any circumstance identified under the regulations promulgated under subparagraph (A).

(D) Submitting a notice of dispute

A consumer who seeks to dispute the accuracy of information shall provide a dispute notice directly to such person at the address specified by the person for such notices that—

   (i) identifies the specific information that is being disputed;

   (ii) explains the basis for the dispute; and

   (iii) includes all supporting documentation required by the furnisher to substantiate the basis of the dispute.

(E) Duty of person after receiving notice of dispute

After receiving a notice of dispute from a consumer pursuant to subparagraph (D), the person that provided the information in dispute to a consumer reporting agency shall—

   (i) conduct an investigation with respect to the disputed information;

   (ii) review all relevant information provided by the consumer with the notice;

   (iii) complete such person's investigation of the dispute and report the results of the investigation to the consumer before the expiration of the period under section 1681i(a)(1) of this title within which a consumer reporting agency would be required to complete its action if the consumer had elected to dispute the information under that section; and

(iv) if the investigation finds that the information reported was inaccurate, promptly notify each consumer reporting agency to which the person furnished the inaccurate information of that determination and provide to the agency any correction to that information that is necessary to make the information provided by the person accurate.

(F) Frivolous or irrelevant dispute

  (i) In general

    This paragraph shall not apply if the person receiving a notice of a dispute from a consumer reasonably determines that the dispute is frivolous or irrelevant, including—

    (I) by reason of the failure of a consumer to provide sufficient information to investigate the disputed information; or

    (II) the submission by a consumer of a dispute that is substantially the same as a dispute previously submitted by or for the consumer, either directly to the person or through a consumer reporting agency under subsection (b) of this section, with respect to which the person has already performed the person's duties under this paragraph or subsection (b), as applicable.

  (ii) Notice of determination

    Upon making any determination under clause (i) that a dispute is frivolous or irrelevant, the person shall notify the consumer of such determination not later than 5 business days after making such determination, by mail or, if authorized by the consumer for that purpose, by any other means available to the person.

  (iii) Contents of notice

    A notice under clause (ii) shall include—

    (I) the reasons for the determination under clause (i); and

    (II) identification of any information required to investigate the disputed information, which may consist of a standardized form describing the general nature of such information.

(G) Exclusion of credit repair organizations

This paragraph shall not apply if the notice of the dispute is submitted by, is prepared on behalf of the consumer by, or is submitted on a form supplied to the consumer by, a credit repair organization, as defined in section 1679a(3) of this title, or an entity that would be a credit repair organization, but for section 1679a(3)(B)(i) of this title.

(9) Duty to provide notice of status as medical information furnisher

A person whose primary business is providing medical services, products, or devices, or the person's agent or assignee, who furnishes information to a consumer reporting agency on a consumer shall be considered a medical information furnisher for purposes of this subchapter, and shall notify the agency of such status.

(b) Duties of furnishers of information upon notice of dispute

(1) In general

After receiving notice pursuant to section 1681i(a)(2) of this title of a dispute with regard to the completeness or accuracy of any information provided by a person to a consumer reporting agency, the person shall—

(A) conduct an investigation with respect to the disputed information;

(B) review all relevant information provided by the consumer reporting agency pursuant to section 1681i(a)(2) of this title;

(C) report the results of the investigation to the consumer reporting agency;

(D) if the investigation finds that the information is incomplete or inaccurate, report those results to all other consumer reporting agencies to which the person furnished the information and that compile and maintain files on consumers on a nationwide basis; and

(E) if an item of information disputed by a consumer is found to be inaccurate or incomplete or cannot be verified after any reinvestigation under paragraph (1), for purposes of reporting to a consumer reporting agency only, as appropriate, based on the results of the reinvestigation promptly—

(i) modify that item of information;

(ii) delete that item of information; or

(iii) permanently block the reporting of that item of information.

(2) Deadline

A person shall complete all investigations, reviews, and reports required under paragraph (1) regarding information provided by the person to a consumer reporting agency, before the expiration of the period under section 1681i(a)(1) of this title within which the consumer reporting agency is required to complete actions required by that section regarding that information.

(c) Limitation on liability

Except as provided in section 1681s(c)(1)(B) of this title, sections 1681n and 1681o of this title do not apply to any violation of—

  (1) subsection (a) of this section, including any regulations issued thereunder;

  (2) subsection (e) of this section, except that nothing in this paragraph shall limit, expand, or otherwise affect liability under section 1681n or 1681o of this title, as applicable, for violations of subsection (b) of this section; or

  (3) subsection (e) of section 1681m of this title.

(d) Limitation on enforcement

The provisions of law described in paragraphs (1) through (3) of subsection (c) of this section (other than with respect to the exception described in paragraph (2) of subsection (c) of this section) shall be enforced exclusively as provided under section 1681s of this title by the Federal agencies and officials and the State officials identified in section 1681s of this title.

(e) Accuracy guidelines and regulations required

  (1) Guidelines

  The Federal banking agencies, the National Credit Union Administration, and the Commission shall, with respect to the entities that are subject to their respective enforcement authority under section 1681m of this title, and in coordination as described in paragraph (2)—

    (A) establish and maintain guidelines for use by each person that furnishes information to a consumer reporting agency regarding the accuracy and integrity of the information relating to consumers that such entities furnish to consumer reporting agencies, and update such guidelines as often as necessary; and

    (B) prescribe regulations requiring each person that furnishes information to a consumer reporting agency to establish reasonable policies and procedures for implementing the guidelines established pursuant to subparagraph (A).

  (2) Coordination

  Each agency required to prescribe regulations under paragraph (1) shall consult and coordinate with each other such agency so that, to the extent possible, the regulations prescribed by each such entity are consistent and comparable with the regulations prescribed by each other such agency.

  (3) Criteria

  In developing the guidelines required by paragraph (1)(A), the agencies described in paragraph (1) shall—

(A) identify patterns, practices, and specific forms of activity that can compromise the accuracy and integrity of information furnished to consumer reporting agencies;

(B) review the methods (including technological means) used to furnish information relating to consumers to consumer reporting agencies;

(C) determine whether persons that furnish information to consumer reporting agencies maintain and enforce policies to assure the accuracy and integrity of information furnished to consumer reporting agencies; and

(D) examine the policies and processes that persons that furnish information to consumer reporting agencies employ to conduct reinvestigations and correct inaccurate information relating to consumers that has been furnished to consumer reporting agencies.

15 U.S.C. § 1681s-3. Affiliate sharing

(a) Special rule for solicitation for purposes of marketing

(1) Notice

Any person that receives from another person related to it by common ownership or affiliated by corporate control a communication of information that would be a consumer report, but for clauses (i), (ii), and (iii) of section 1681a(d)(2)(A) of this title, may not use the information to make a solicitation for marketing purposes to a consumer about its products or services, unless—

(A) it is clearly and conspicuously disclosed to the consumer that the information may be communicated among such persons for purposes of making such solicitations to the consumer; and

(B) the consumer is provided an opportunity and a simple method to prohibit the making of such solicitations to the consumer by such person.

(2) Consumer choice

(A) In general

The notice required under paragraph (1) shall allow the consumer the opportunity to prohibit all solicitations referred to in such paragraph, and may allow the consumer to choose from different options when electing to prohibit the sending of such solicitations, including options regarding the types of entities and information covered, and which methods of delivering solicitations the consumer elects to prohibit.

(B) Format

Notwithstanding subparagraph (A), the notice required under paragraph (1) shall be clear, conspicuous, and concise, and any method provided under paragraph (1)(B) shall be simple. The regulations prescribed to implement this section shall provide specific guidance regarding how to comply with such standards.

(3) Duration

  (A) In general

    The election of a consumer pursuant to paragraph (1)(B) to prohibit the making of solicitations shall be effective for at least 5 years, beginning on the date on which the person receives the election of the consumer, unless the consumer requests that such election be revoked.

  (B) Notice upon expiration of effective period

    At such time as the election of a consumer pursuant to paragraph (1)(B) is no longer effective, a person may not use information that the person receives in the manner described in paragraph (1) to make any solicitation for marketing purposes to the consumer, unless the consumer receives a notice and an opportunity, using a simple method, to extend the opt-out for another period of at least 5 years, pursuant to the procedures described in paragraph (1).

(4) Scope

  This section shall not apply to a person—

  (A) using information to make a solicitation for marketing purposes to a consumer with whom the person has a pre-existing business relationship;

  (B) using information to facilitate communications to an individual for whose benefit the person provides employee benefit or other services pursuant to a contract with an employer related to and arising out of the current employment relationship or status of the individual as a participant or beneficiary of an employee benefit plan;

  (C) using information to perform services on behalf of another person related by common ownership or affiliated by corporate control, except that this subparagraph shall not be construed as permitting a person to send solicitations on behalf of another person, if such other person would not be permitted to send the solicitation on its own behalf as a result of the election of the consumer to prohibit solicitations under paragraph (1)(B);

  (D) using information in response to a communication initiated by the consumer;

(E) using information in response to solicitations authorized or requested by the consumer; or

(F) if compliance with this section by that person would prevent compliance by that person with any provision of State insurance laws pertaining to unfair discrimination in any State in which the person is lawfully doing business.

(5) No retroactivity

This subsection shall not prohibit the use of information to send a solicitation to a consumer if such information was received prior to the date on which persons are required to comply with regulations implementing this subsection.

(b) Notice for other purposes permissible

A notice or other disclosure under this section may be coordinated and consolidated with any other notice required to be issued under any other provision of law by a person that is subject to this section, and a notice or other disclosure that is equivalent to the notice required by subsection (a) of this section, and that is provided by a person described in subsection (a) of this section to a consumer together with disclosures required by any other provision of law, shall satisfy the requirements of subsection (a) of this section.

(c) User requirements

Requirements with respect to the use by a person of information received from another person related to it by common ownership or affiliated by corporate control, such as the requirements of this section, constitute requirements with respect to the exchange of information among persons affiliated by common ownership or common corporate control, within the meaning of section 1681t(b)(2) of this title.

(d) Definitions

For purposes of this section, the following definitions shall apply:

(1) Pre-existing business relationship

The term "pre-existing business relationship" means a relationship between a person, or a person's licensed agent, and a consumer, based on—

(A) a financial contract between a person and a consumer which is in force;

(B) the purchase, rental, or lease by the consumer of that person's goods or services, or a financial transaction (including holding an active account or a policy in force or having another continuing relationship) between the consumer and that person during the 18-month period immediately preceding the date on which the consumer is sent a solicitation covered by this section;

(C) an inquiry or application by the consumer regarding a product or service offered by that person, during the 3-month period immediately preceding the date on which the consumer is sent a solicitation covered by this section; or

(D) any other pre-existing customer relationship defined in the regulations implementing this section.

(2) Solicitation

The term "solicitation" means the marketing of a product or service initiated by a person to a particular consumer that is based on an exchange of information described in subsection (a) of this section, and is intended to encourage the consumer to purchase such product or service, but does not include communications that are directed at the general public or determined not to be a solicitation by the regulations prescribed under this section.

15 U.S.C. § 1681t. Relation to State laws

(a) In general

Except as provided in subsections (b) and (c) of this section, this subchapter does not annul, alter, affect, or exempt any person subject to the provisions of this subchapter from complying with the laws of any State with respect to the collection, distribution, or use of any information on consumers, or for the prevention or mitigation of identity theft, except to the extent that those laws are inconsistent with any provision of this subchapter, and then only to the extent of the inconsistency.

(b) General exceptions

No requirement or prohibition may be imposed under the laws of any State—

(1) with respect to any subject matter regulated under—

(A) subsection (c) or (e) of section 1681b of this title, relating to the prescreening of consumer reports;

(B) section 1681i of this title, relating to the time by which a consumer reporting agency must take any action, including the provision of notification to a consumer or other person, in any procedure related to the disputed accuracy of information in a consumer's file, except that this subparagraph shall not apply to any State law in effect on September 30, 1996;

(C) subsections (a) and (b) of section 1681m of this title, relating to the duties of a person who takes any adverse action with respect to a consumer;

(D) section 1681m(d) of this title, relating to the duties of persons who use a consumer report of a consumer in connection with any credit or insurance transaction that is not initiated by the consumer and that consists of a firm offer of credit or insurance;

(E) section 1681c of this title, relating to information contained in consumer reports, except that this subparagraph shall not apply to any State law in effect on September 30, 1996;

(F) section 1681s-2 of this title, relating to the responsibilities of persons who furnish information to consumer reporting agencies, except that this paragraph shall not apply—

    (i) with respect to section 54A(a) of chapter 93 of the Massachusetts Annotated Laws (as in effect on September 30, 1996); or

    (ii) with respect to section 1785.25(a) of the California Civil Code (as in effect on September 30, 1996);

(G) section 1681g(e) of this title, relating to information available to victims under section 1681g(e) of this title;

(H) section 1681s-3 of this title, relating to the exchange and use of information to make a solicitation for marketing purposes; or

(I) section 1681m(h) of this title, relating to the duties of users of consumer reports to provide notice with respect to terms in certain credit transactions;

(2) with respect to the exchange of information among persons affiliated by common ownership or common corporate control, except that this paragraph shall not apply with respect to subsection (a) or (c)(1) of section 2480e of title 9, Vermont Statutes Annotated (as in effect on September 30, 1996);

(3) with respect to the disclosures required to be made under subsection (c), (d), (e), or (g) of section 1681g of this title, or subsection (f) of section 1681g of this title relating to the disclosure of credit scores for credit granting purposes, except that this paragraph—

(A) shall not apply with respect to sections 1785.10, 1785.16, and 1785.20.2 of the California Civil Code (as in effect on December 4, 2003) and section 1785.15 through section 1785.15.2 of such Code (as in effect on such date);

(B) shall not apply with respect to sections 5-3-106(2) and 212-14.3- 104.3 of the Colorado Revised Statutes (as in effect on December 4, 2003); and

(C) shall not be construed as limiting, annulling, affecting, or superseding any provision of the laws of any State regulating the use in an insurance activity, or regulating disclosures concerning such use, of a credit-based insurance score of a consumer by any person engaged in the business of insurance;

(4) with respect to the frequency of any disclosure under section 1681j(a) of this title, except that this paragraph shall not apply—

(A) with respect to section 12-14.3-105(1)(d) of the Colorado

Revised Statutes (as in effect on December 4, 2003);

(B) with respect to section 10-1-393(29)(C) of the Georgia Code (as in effect on December 4, 2003);

(C) with respect to section 1316.2 of title 10 of the Maine Revised Statutes (as in effect on December 4, 2003);

(D) with respect to sections 14-1209(a)(1) and 14-1209(b)(1)(i) of the Commercial Law Article of the Code of Maryland (as in effect on December 4, 2003);

(E) with respect to section 59(d) and section 59(e) of chapter 93 of the General Laws of Massachusetts (as in effect December 4, 2003);

(F) with respect to section 56:11-37.10(a)(1) of the New Jersey Revised Statutes (as in effect on December 4, 2003); or

(G) with respect to section 2480c(a)(1) of title 9 of the Vermont Statutes Annotated (as in effect on December 4, 2003); or

(5) with respect to the conduct required by the specific provisions of—

(A) section 1681c(g) of this title;

(B) section 1681c-1 of this title;

(C) section 1681c-2 of this title;

(D) section 1681g(a)(1)(A) of this title;

(E) section 1681j(a) of this title;

(F) subsections (e), (f), and (g) of section 1681m of this title;

(G) section 1681s(f) of this title;

(H) section 1681s-2(a)(6) of this title; or

(I) section 1681w of this title.

(c) "Firm offer of credit or insurance" defined

Notwithstanding any definition of the term "firm offer of credit or insurance" (or any equivalent term) under the laws of any State, the definition of that term contained in section 1681a(l) of this title shall be construed to apply in the enforcement and interpretation of the laws of any State governing consumer reports.

(d) Limitations

Subsections (b) and (c) of this section do not affect any settlement, agreement, or consent judgment between any State Attorney General and any consumer reporting agency in effect on September 30, 1996.

15 U.S.C. § 1681u. Disclosures to FBI for counterintelligence purposes

(a) Identity of financial institutions

Notwithstanding section 1681b of this title or any other provision of this subchapter, a consumer reporting agency shall furnish to the Federal Bureau of Investigation the names and addresses of all financial institutions (as that term is defined in section 3401 of Title 12) at which a consumer maintains or has maintained an account, to the extent that information is in the files of the agency, when presented with a written request for that information, signed by the Director of the Federal Bureau of Investigation, or the Director's designee in a position not lower than Deputy Assistant Director at Bureau headquarters or a Special Agent in Charge of a Bureau field office designated by the Director, which certifies compliance with this section. The Director or the Director's designee may make such a certification only if the Director or the Director's designee has determined in writing, that such information is sought for the conduct of an authorized investigation to protect against international terrorism or clandestine intelligence activities, provided that such an investigation of a United States person is not conducted solely upon the basis of activities protected by the first amendment to the Constitution of the United States.

(b) Identifying information

Notwithstanding the provisions of section 1681b of this title or any other provision of this subchapter, a consumer reporting agency shall furnish identifying information respecting a consumer, limited to name, address, former addresses, places of employment, or former places of employment, to the Federal Bureau of Investigation when presented with a written request, signed by the Director or the Director's designee in a position not lower than Deputy Assistant Director at Bureau headquarters or a Special Agent in Charge of a Bureau field office designated by the Director, which certifies compliance with this subsection. The Director or the Director's designee may make such a certification only if the Director or the Director's designee

has determined in writing that such information is sought for the conduct of an authorized investigation to protect against international terrorism or clandestine intelligence activities, provided that such an investigation of a United States person is not conducted solely upon the basis of activities protected by the first amendment to the Constitution of the United States.

(c) Court order for disclosure of consumer reports

Notwithstanding section 1681b of this title or any other provision of this subchapter, if requested in writing by the Director of the Federal Bureau of Investigation, or a designee of the Director in a position not lower than Deputy Assistant Director at Bureau headquarters or a Special Agent in Charge in a Bureau field office designated by the Director, a court may issue an order ex parte directing a consumer reporting agency to furnish a consumer report to the Federal Bureau of Investigation, upon a showing in camera that the consumer report is sought for the conduct of an authorized investigation to protect against international terrorism or clandestine intelligence activities, provided that such an investigation of a United States person is not conducted solely upon the basis of activities protected by the first amendment to the Constitution of the United States.

The terms of an order issued under this subsection shall not disclose that the order is issued for purposes of a counterintelligence investigation.

(d) Confidentiality

(1) If the Director of the Federal Bureau of Investigation, or his designee in a position not lower than Deputy Assistant Director at Bureau headquarters or a Special Agent in Charge in a Bureau field office designated by the Director, certifies that otherwise there may result a danger to the national security of the United States, interference with a criminal, counterterrorism, or counterintelligence investigation, interference with diplomatic relations, or danger to the life or physical safety of any person, no consumer reporting agency or officer, employee, or agent of a consumer reporting agency shall disclose to any person (other than those to whom such disclosure is necessary to comply with the request or an attorney to obtain legal advice or legal assistance with respect to the request) that the Federal Bureau of Investigation has sought or obtained the identity of financial institutions or a consumer report respecting any consumer under subsection (a), (b), or (c) of this section, and no consumer reporting agency or officer, employee, or agent of a consumer reporting agency shall include in any consumer report any information that would indicate that the Federal Bureau of Investigation

has sought or obtained such information on a consumer report.

(2) The request shall notify the person or entity to whom the request is directed of the nondisclosure requirement under paragraph (1).

(3) Any recipient disclosing to those persons necessary to comply with the request or to an attorney to obtain legal advice or legal assistance with respect to the request shall inform such persons of any applicable nondisclosure requirement. Any person who receives a disclosure under this subsection shall be subject to the same prohibitions on disclosure under paragraph (1).

(4) At the request of the Director of the Federal Bureau of Investigation or the designee of the Director, any person making or intending to make a disclosure under this section shall identify to the Director or such designee the person to whom such disclosure will be made or to whom such disclosure was made prior to the request, except that nothing in this section shall require a person to inform the Director or such designee of the identity of an attorney to whom disclosure was made or will be made to obtain legal advice or legal assistance with respect to the request for the identity of financial institutions or a consumer report respecting any consumer under this section.

(e) Payment of fees

The Federal Bureau of Investigation shall, subject to the availability of appropriations, pay to the consumer reporting agency assembling or providing report or information in accordance with procedures established under this section a fee for reimbursement for such costs as are reasonably necessary and which have been directly incurred in searching, reproducing, or transporting books, papers, records, or other data required or requested to be produced under this section.

(f) Limit on dissemination

The Federal Bureau of Investigation may not disseminate information obtained pursuant to this section outside of the Federal Bureau of Investigation, except to other Federal agencies as may be necessary for the approval or conduct of a foreign counterintelligence investigation, or, where the information concerns a person subject to the Uniform Code of Military Justice, to appropriate investigative authorities within the military department concerned as may be necessary for the conduct of a joint foreign counterintelligence investigation.

(g) Rules of construction

Nothing in this section shall be construed to prohibit information from being furnished by the Federal Bureau of Investigation pursuant to a subpoena or court order, in connection with a judicial or administrative proceeding to enforce the provisions of this subchapter. Nothing in this section shall be construed to authorize or permit the withholding of information from the Congress.

(h) Reports to Congress

(1) On a semiannual basis, the Attorney General shall fully inform the Permanent Select Committee on Intelligence and the Committee on Banking, Finance, and Urban Affairs of the House of Representatives, and the Select Committee on Intelligence and the Committee on Banking, Housing, and Urban Affairs of the Senate concerning all requests made pursuant to subsections (a), (b), and (c) of this section.

(2) In the case of the semiannual reports required to be submitted under paragraph (1) to the Permanent Select Committee on Intelligence of the House of Representatives and the Select Committee on Intelligence of the Senate, the submittal dates for such reports shall be as provided in section 415b of Title 50.

(i) Damages

Any agency or department of the United States obtaining or disclosing any consumer reports, records, or information contained therein in violation of this section is liable to the consumer to whom such consumer reports, records, or information relate in an amount equal to the sum of—

(1) $100, without regard to the volume of consumer reports, records, or information involved;

(2) any actual damages sustained by the consumer as a result of the disclosure;

(3) if the violation is found to have been willful or intentional, such punitive damages as a court may allow; and

(4) in the case of any successful action to enforce liability under this subsection, the costs of the action, together with reasonable attorney fees, as determined by the court.

(j) Disciplinary actions for violations

If a court determines that any agency or department of the United States has violated any provision of this section and the court finds that the circumstances surrounding the violation raise questions of whether or not an officer or employee of the agency or department acted willfully or intentionally with respect to the violation, the agency or department shall promptly initiate a proceeding to determine whether or not disciplinary action is warranted against the officer or employee who was responsible for the violation.

(k) Good-faith exception

Notwithstanding any other provision of this subchapter, any consumer reporting agency or agent or employee thereof making disclosure of consumer reports or identifying information pursuant to this subsection in good-faith reliance upon a certification of the Federal Bureau of Investigation pursuant to provisions of this section shall not be liable to any person for such disclosure under this subchapter, the constitution of any State, or any law or regulation of any State or any political subdivision of any State.

(l) Limitation of remedies

Notwithstanding any other provision of this subchapter, the remedies and sanctions set forth in this section shall be the only judicial remedies and sanctions for violation of this section.

(m) Injunctive relief

In addition to any other remedy contained in this section, injunctive relief shall be available to require compliance with the procedures of this section. In the event of any successful action under this subsection, costs together with reasonable attorney fees, as determined by the court, may be recovered.

15 U.S.C. § 1681v. Disclosures to governmental agencies for counterterrorism purposes

(a) Disclosure

Notwithstanding section 1681b of this title or any other provision of this subchapter, a consumer reporting agency shall furnish a consumer report of a consumer and all other information in a consumer's file to a government agency authorized to conduct investigations of, or intelligence or counterintelligence activities or analysis related to, international terrorism when presented with a written certification by such government agency that such information is necessary for the agency's conduct or such investigation, activity, or analysis.

(b) Form of certification

The certification described in subsection

(a) of this section shall be signed by a supervisory official designated by the head of a Federal agency or an officer of a Federal agency whose appointment to office is required to be made by the President, by and with the advice and consent of the Senate.

(c) Confidentiality

(1) If the head of a government agency authorized to conduct investigations of intelligence or counterintelligence activities or analysis related to international terrorism, or his designee, certifies that otherwise there may result a danger to the national security of the United States, interference with a criminal, counterterrorism, or counterintelligence investigation, interference with diplomatic relations, or danger to the life or physical safety of any person, no consumer reporting agency or officer, employee, or agent of such consumer reporting agency, shall disclose to any person (other than those to whom such disclosure is necessary to comply with the request or an attorney to obtain legal advice or legal assistance with respect to the request), or specify in any consumer report, that a government agency has sought or obtained access to information under subsection (a) of this section.

(2) The request shall notify the person or entity to whom the request is directed of the nondisclosure requirement under paragraph (1).

(3) Any recipient disclosing to those persons necessary to comply with the request or to any attorney to obtain legal advice or legal assistance with respect to the request shall inform such persons of any applicable nondisclosure requirement. Any person who receives a disclosure under this subsection shall be subject to the same prohibitions on disclosure under paragraph (1).

(4) At the request of the authorized government agency, any person making or intending to make a disclosure under this section shall identify to the requesting official of the authorized government agency the person to whom such disclosure will be made or to whom such disclosure was made prior to the request, except that nothing in this section shall require a person to inform the requesting official of the identity of an attorney to whom disclosure was made or will be made to obtain legal advice or legal assistance with respect to the request for information under subsection (a) of this section.

(d) Rule of construction

Nothing in section 1681u of this title shall be construed to limit the authority of the Director of the Federal Bureau of Investigation under this section.

(e) Safe harbor

Notwithstanding any other provision of this subchapter, any consumer reporting agency or agent or employee thereof making disclosure of consumer reports or other information pursuant to this section in good-faith reliance upon a certification of a government agency pursuant to the provisions of this section shall not be liable to any person for such disclosure under this subchapter, the constitution of any State, or any law or regulation of any State or any political subdivision of any State.

15 U.S.C. § 1681w. Disposal of records

(a) Regulations

    (1) In general

Not later than 1 year after December 4, 2003, the Federal banking agencies, the National Credit Union Administration, and the Commission with respect to the entities that are subject to their respective enforcement authority under section 1681s of this title, and the Securities and Exchange Commission, and in coordination as described in paragraph (2), shall issue final regulations requiring any person that maintains or otherwise possesses consumer information, or any compilation of consumer information, derived from consumer reports for a business purpose to properly dispose of any such information or compilation.

    (2) Coordination

Each agency required to prescribe regulations under paragraph (1) shall—

      (A) consult and coordinate with each other such agency so that, to the extent possible, the regulations prescribed by each such agency are consistent and comparable with the regulations by each such other agency; and

      (B) ensure that such regulations are consistent with the requirements and regulations issued pursuant to Public Law 106-102 and other provisions of Federal law.

    (3) Exemption authority

In issuing regulations under this section, the Federal banking agencies, the National Credit Union Administration, the Commission, and the Securities and Exchange Commission may exempt any person or class of persons from application of those regulations, as such agency deems appropriate to carry out the purpose of this section.

(b) Rule of construction

Nothing in this section shall be construed—

    (1) to require a person to maintain or destroy any record pertaining to a consumer that is not imposed under other law; or

    (2) to alter or affect any requirement imposed under any other provision of law to maintain or destroy such a record.

15 U.S.C. § 1681x. Corporate and technological circumvention prohibited

The Commission shall prescribe regulations, to become effective not later than 90 days after December 4, 2003, to prevent a consumer reporting agency from circumventing or evading treatment as a consumer reporting agency described in section 1681a(p) of this title for purposes of this subchapter, including—

(1) by means of a corporate reorganization or restructuring, including a merger, acquisition, dissolution, divestiture, or asset sale of a consumer reporting agency; or

(2) by maintaining or merging public record and credit account information in a manner that is substantially equivalent to that described in paragraphs (1) and (2) of section 1681a(p) of this title, in the manner described in section 1681a(p) of this title.

Text of the Federal Credit Repair Organizations Act

15 U.S.C. § 1679. Findings and purposes

(a) Findings

The Congress makes the following findings:

(1) Consumers have a vital interest in establishing and maintaining their credit worthiness and credit standing in order to obtain and use credit. As a result, consumers who have experienced credit problems may seek assistance from credit repair organizations which offer to improve the credit standing of such consumers.

(2) Certain advertising and business practices of some companies engaged in the business of credit repair services have worked a financial hardship upon consumers, particularly those of limited economic means and who are inexperienced in credit matters.

(b) Purposes

The purposes of this subchapter are—

(1) to ensure that prospective buyers of the services of credit repair organizations are provided with the information necessary to make an informed decision regarding the purchase of such services; and

(2) to protect the public from unfair or deceptive advertising and business practices by credit repair organizations.

15 U.S.C. § 1679a. Definitions

For purposes of this subchapter, the following definitions apply:

(1) Consumer

The term "consumer" means an individual.

(2) Consumer credit transaction

The term "consumer credit transaction" means any transaction in which credit is offered or extended to an individual for personal, family, or household purposes.

(3) Credit repair organization

The term "credit repair organization"—

(A) means any person who uses any instrumentality of interstate commerce or the mails to sell, provide, or perform (or represent that such person can or will sell, provide, or perform) any service, in return for the payment of money or other valuable consideration, for the express or implied purpose of—

    (i) improving any consumer's credit record, credit history, or credit rating; or

    (ii) providing advice or assistance to any consumer with regard to any activity or service described in clause (i); and

(B) does not include—

    (i) any nonprofit organization which is exempt from taxation under section 501(c)(3) of Title 26;

    (ii) any creditor (as defined in section 1602 of this title), with respect to any consumer, to the extent the creditor is assisting the consumer to restructure any debt owed by the consumer to the creditor; or

    (iii) any depository institution (as that term is defined in section 1813 of Title 12) or any Federal or State credit union (as those terms are defined in section 1752 of Title 12), or any affiliate or subsidiary of such a depository institution or credit union.

(4) Credit

The term "credit" has the meaning given to such term in section 1602(e) of this title.

15 U.S.C. § 1679b. Prohibited practices

(a) In general

No person may—

(1) make any statement, or counsel or advise any consumer to make any statement, which is untrue or misleading (or which, upon the exercise of reasonable care, should be known by the credit repair organization, officer, employee, agent, or other person to be untrue or misleading) with respect to any consumer's credit worthiness, credit standing, or credit capacity to—

    (A) any consumer reporting agency (as defined in section 1681a(f) of this title); or

    (B) any person—

        (i) who has extended credit to the consumer; or

        (ii) to whom the consumer has applied or is applying for an extension of credit;

(2) make any statement, or counsel or advise any consumer to make any statement, the intended effect of which is to alter the consumer's identification to prevent the display of the consumer's credit record, history, or rating for the purpose of concealing adverse information that is accurate and not obsolete to—

    (A) any consumer reporting agency;

    (B) any person—

        (i) who has extended credit to the consumer; or

        (ii) to whom the consumer has applied or is applying for an extension of credit;

(3) make or use any untrue or misleading representation of the services of the credit repair organization; or

(4) engage, directly or indirectly, in any act, practice, or course of business that constitutes or results in the commission of, or an attempt to commit, a fraud or deception on any person in connection with the offer or sale of the services of the credit repair organization.

(b) Payment in advance

No credit repair organization may charge or receive any money or other valuable consideration for the performance of any service which the credit repair organization has agreed to perform for any consumer before such service is fully performed.

15 U.S.C. § 1679c. Disclosures

(a) Disclosure required

Any credit repair organization shall provide any consumer with the following written statement before any contract or agreement between the consumer and the credit repair organization is executed:

"Consumer Credit File Rights Under State and Federal Law

"You have a right to dispute inaccurate information in your credit report by contacting the credit bureau directly. However, neither you nor any 'credit repair' company or credit repair organization has the right to have accurate, current, and verifiable information removed from your credit report. The credit bureau must remove accurate, negative information from your report only if it is over 7 years old. Bankruptcy information can be reported for 10 years.

"You have a right to obtain a copy of your credit report from a credit bureau. You may be charged a reasonable fee. There is no fee, however, if you have been turned down for credit, employment, insurance, or a rental dwelling because of information in your credit report within the preceding 60 days. The credit bureau must provide someone to help you interpret the information in your credit file. You are entitled to receive a free copy of your credit report if you are unemployed and intend to apply for employment in the next 60 days, if you are a recipient of public welfare assistance, or if you have reason to believe that there is inaccurate information in your credit report due to fraud.

"You have a right to sue a credit repair organization that violates the Credit Repair Organization Act. This law prohibits deceptive practices by credit repair organizations.

"You have the right to cancel your contract with any credit repair organization for any reason within 3 business days from the date you signed it.

"Credit bureaus are required to follow reasonable procedures to ensure that the information they report is accurate. However, mistakes may occur.

"You may, on your own, notify a credit bureau in writing that you dispute the accuracy of information in your credit file. The credit bureau must then reinvestigate and modify or remove inaccurate or incomplete information. The credit bureau may not charge any fee for this service. Any pertinent information and copies of all documents you have concerning an error should be given to the credit bureau.

"If the credit bureau's reinvestigation does not resolve the dispute to your satisfaction, you may send a brief statement to the credit bureau, to be kept in your file, explaining why you think the record is inaccurate. The credit bureau must include a summary of your statement about disputed information with any report it issues about you.

"The Federal Trade Commission regulates credit bureaus and credit repair organizations. For more information contact:

"The Public Reference Branch
"Federal Trade Commission
"Washington, D.C. 20580."

(b) Separate statement requirement

The written statement required under this section shall be provided as a document which is separate from any written contract or other agreement between the credit repair organization and the consumer or any other written material provided to the consumer.

(c) Retention of compliance records

(1) In general

The credit repair organization shall maintain a copy of the statement signed by the consumer acknowledging receipt of the statement.

(2) Maintenance for 2 years

The copy of any consumer's statement shall be maintained in the organization's files for 2 years after the date on which the statement is signed by the consumer.

15 U.S.C. § 1679d. Credit repair organizations contracts

(a) Written contracts required

No services may be provided by any credit repair organization for any consumer—

(1) unless a written and dated contract (for the purchase of such services) which meets the requirements of subsection (b) of this section has been signed by the consumer; or

(2) before the end of the 3-business-day period beginning on the date the contract is signed.

(b) Terms and conditions of contract

No contract referred to in subsection (a) of this section meets the requirements of this subsection unless such contract includes (in writing)—

(1) the terms and conditions of payment, including the total amount of all payments to be made by the consumer to the credit repair organization or to any other person;

(2) a full and detailed description of the services to be performed by the credit repair organization for the consumer, including—

(A) all guarantees of performance; and

(B) an estimate of—

(i) the date by which the performance of the services (to

be performed by the credit repair organization or any other person) will be complete; or

   (ii) the length of the period necessary to perform such services;

(3) the credit repair organization's name and principal business address; and

(4) a conspicuous statement in bold face type, in immediate proximity to the space reserved for the consumer's signature on the contract, which reads as follows: "You may cancel this contract without penalty or obligation at any time before midnight of the 3rd business day after the date on which you signed the contract. See the attached notice of cancellation form for an explanation of this right.".

15 U.S.C. § 1679e. Right to cancel contract

(a) In general

Any consumer may cancel any contract with any credit repair organization without penalty or obligation by notifying the credit repair organization of the consumer's intention to do so at any time before midnight of the 3rd business day which begins after the date on which the contract or agreement between the consumer and the credit repair organization is executed or would, but for this subsection, become enforceable against the parties.

(b) Cancellation form and other information

Each contract shall be accompanied by a form, in duplicate, which has the heading "Notice of Cancellation" and contains in bold face type the following statement:

"You may cancel this contract, without any penalty or obligation, at any time before midnight of the 3rd day which begins after the date the contract is signed by you.

"To cancel this contract, mail or deliver a signed, dated copy of this cancellation notice, or any other written notice to [name of credit repair organization] at [address of credit repair organization] before midnight on [date]

"I hereby cancel this transaction, [date]

[purchaser's signature]."

(c) Consumer copy of contract required

Any consumer who enters into any contract with any credit repair organization shall be given, by the organization—

(1) a copy of the completed contract and the disclosure statement required under section 1679c of this title; and

(2) a copy of any other document the credit repair organization requires the consumer to sign, at the time the contract or the other document is signed.

15 U.S.C. § 1679f. Noncompliance with this subchapter

(a) Consumer waivers invalid

Any waiver by any consumer of any protection provided by or any right of the consumer under this subchapter—

(1) shall be treated as void; and

(2) may not be enforced by any Federal or State court or any other person.

(b) Attempt to obtain waiver

Any attempt by any person to obtain a waiver from any consumer of any protection provided by or any right of the consumer under this subchapter shall be treated as a violation of this subchapter.

(c) Contracts not in compliance

Any contract for services which does not comply with the applicable provisions of this subchapter—

(1) shall be treated as void; and

(2) may not be enforced by any Federal or State court or any other person.

15 U.S.C. § 1679g. Civil liability

(a) Liability established

Any person who fails to comply with any provision of this subchapter with respect to any other person shall be liable to such person in an amount equal to the sum of the amounts determined under each of the following paragraphs:

(1) Actual damages

The greater of—

(A) the amount of any actual damage sustained by such person as a result of such failure; or

(B) any amount paid by the person to the credit repair organization.

(2) Punitive damages

(A) Individual actions

In the case of any action by an individual, such additional amount as the court may allow.

(B) Class actions

In the case of a class action, the sum of—

(i) the aggregate of the amount which the court may allow for each named plaintiff; and

(ii) the aggregate of the amount which the court may allow for each other class member, without regard to any minimum individual recovery.

(3) Attorneys' fees

In the case of any successful action to enforce any liability under paragraph (1) or (2), the costs of the action, together with reasonable attorneys' fees.

(b) Factors to be considered in awarding punitive damages

In determining the amount of any liability of any credit repair organization under subsection (a)(2) of this section, the court shall consider, among other relevant factors—

(1) the frequency and persistence of noncompliance by the credit repair organization;

(2) the nature of the noncompliance;

(3) the extent to which such noncompliance was intentional; and

(4) in the case of any class action, the number of consumers adversely affected.

15 U.S.C. § 1679h. Administrative enforcement

(a) In general

Compliance with the requirements imposed under this subchapter with respect to credit repair organizations shall be enforced under the Federal Trade Commission Act [15 U.S.C.A. § 41 et seq.] by the Federal Trade Commission.

(b) Violations of this subchapter treated as violations of Federal Trade Commission Act

(1) In general

For the purpose of the exercise by the Federal Trade Commission of the Commission's functions and powers under the Federal Trade Commission Act [15 U.S.C.A. § 41 et seq.], any violation of any requirement or prohibition imposed under this subchapter with respect to credit repair organizations shall constitute an unfair or deceptive act or practice in commerce in violation of section 5(a) of the Federal Trade Commission Act [15 U.S.C.A. § 45(a)].

(2) Enforcement authority under other law

All functions and powers of the Federal Trade Commission under the Federal Trade Commission Act [15 U.S.C.A. § 41 et seq.] shall be available to the Commission to enforce compliance with this subchapter by any person subject to enforcement by the Federal Trade Commission pursuant to this subsection, including the power to enforce the provisions of this subchapter in the same manner as if the violation had been a violation of any Federal Trade Commission trade regulation rule, without regard to whether the credit repair organization—

(A) is engaged in commerce; or

(B) meets any other jurisdictional tests in the Federal Trade Commission Act [15 U.S.C.A. § 41 et seq.].

(c) State action for violations

(1) Authority of States

In addition to such other remedies as are provided under State law, whenever the chief law enforcement officer of a State, or an official or agency designated by a State, has reason to believe that any person has violated or is violating this subchapter, the State—

(A) may bring an action to enjoin such violation;

(B) may bring an action on behalf of its residents to recover damages for which the person is liable to such residents under section 1679g of this title as a result of the violation; and

(C) in the case of any successful action under subparagraph (A) or (B), shall be awarded the costs of the action and reasonable attorney fees as determined by the court.

(2) Rights of Commission

(A) Notice to Commission

The State shall serve prior written notice of any civil action under paragraph (1) upon the Federal Trade Commission and provide the Commission with a copy of its complaint, except in any case where such prior notice is not feasible, in which case the State shall serve such notice immediately upon instituting such action.

(B) Intervention

The Commission shall have the right—

   (i) to intervene in any action referred to in subparagraph (A);

   (ii) upon so intervening, to be heard on all matters arising in the action; and

   (iii) to file petitions for appeal.

(3) Investigatory powers

For purposes of bringing any action under this subsection, nothing in this subsection shall prevent the chief law enforcement officer, or an official or agency designated by a State, from exercising the powers conferred on the chief law enforcement officer or such official by the laws of such State to conduct investigations or to administer oaths or affirmations or to compel the attendance of witnesses or the production of documentary and other evidence.

(4) Limitation

Whenever the Federal Trade Commission has instituted a civil action for violation of this subchapter, no State may, during the pendency of such action, bring an action under this section against any defendant named in the complaint of the Commission for any violation of this subchapter that is alleged in that complaint.

15 U.S.C. § 1679i. Statute of limitations

Any action to enforce any liability under this subchapter may be brought before the later of—

(1) the end of the 5-year period beginning on the date of the occurrence of the violation involved; or

(2) in any case in which any credit repair organization has materially and willfully misrepresented any information which—

   (A) the credit repair organization is required, by any provision of this subchapter, to disclose to any consumer; and

   (B) is material to the establishment of the credit repair organization's liability to the consumer under this subchapter, the end of the 5-year period beginning on the date of the discovery by the consumer of the misrepresentation.

15 U.S.C. § 1679j. Relation to State law

This subchapter shall not annul, alter, affect, or exempt any person subject to the provisions of this subchapter from complying with any law of any State except to the extent that such law is inconsistent with any provision of this subchapter, and then only to the extent of the inconsistency. ■

Forms and Letters

File Name	Form
F01.rtf	F-1: Outstanding Debts
F02.rtf	F-2: Daily Expenditures
F03.rtf	F-3: Monthly Income From All Sources
F04.rtf	F-4: Monthly Budget
F05.rtf	F-5: Dispute Credit Card Bill
F06.rtf	F-6: Error on Credit Card Bill
F07.rtf	F-7: Make Payment If Negative Information Removed or Account Re-aged
F08.rtf	F-8: Request Short-Term Small Payments
F09.rtf	F-9: Request Long-Term Small Payments
F10.rtf	F-10: Request Short-Term Pay Nothing
F11.rtf	F-11: Request Long-Term Pay Nothing
F12.rtf	F-12: Request Rewrite of Loan Terms
F13.rtf	F-13: Offer to Give Secured Property Back
F14.rtf	F-14: Cashing Check Constitutes Payment in Full (Outside of California)
F15.rtf	F-15: Cashing Check Constitutes Payment in Full-First Letter (California)
F16.rtf	F-16: Cashing Check Constitutes Payment in Full-Second Letter (California)
F17.rtf	F-17: Inform Creditor of Judgment Proof Status
F18.rtf	F-18: Inform Creditor of Plan To File for Bankruptcy
F19.rtf	F-19: Request Direct Negotiation With Creditor
F20.rtf	F-20: Dispute Amount of Bill or Quality of Goods or Services Received
F21.rtf	F-21: Collection Agency: Cease All Contact
F22.rtf	F-22: Complaint About Collection Agency Harassment
F23.rtf	F-23: Request Credit File
F24.rtf	F-24: Request Reinvestigation
F25.rtf	F-25: Request Follow-Up After Reinvestigation
F26.rtf	F-26: Request Removal of Incorrect Information by Creditor
F27.rtf	F-27: Creditor Verification
F28.rtf	F-28: Request Addition of Account Histories
F29.rtf	F-29: Request Addition of Information Showing Stability
affidavit.pdf	ID Theft Affidavit and Instructions
	Annual Credit Report Request Form

Outstanding Debts

Outstanding Debts	Monthly Payment	Amount Behind

Rent or mortgage (include second mortgage, home equity loans)

Utilities and telephone

Transportation expenses

car loans/lease payments

maintenance payments

auto insurance

Child care

Alimony or child support

Education expenses

student loans

tuition expenses

Personal and other loans

bank loans

loan consolidator

Lawyer or accountant bills

Outstanding Debts	Monthly Payment	Amount Behind

Medical (doctor and hospital) bills

Insurance

homeowners or renters
disability
medical or dental
life

Credit and charge cards

Department store charges

Back taxes

Federal
State
Other (such as property)

Other unpaid bills

TOTALS $ _____ $ _____

Daily Expenditures for Week of _____

Sunday's Expenditures	Cost	Monday's Expenditures	Cost	Tuesday's Expenditures	Cost	Wednesday's Expenditures	Cost
Daily Total:		**Daily Total:**		**Daily Total:**		**Daily Total:**	

Thursday's Expenditures	Cost	Friday's Expenditures	Cost	Saturday's Expenditures	Cost	Other Expenditures	Cost
Daily Total:		**Daily Total:**		**Daily Total:**		**Weekly Total:**	

Monthly Income From All Sources

1 Source of income		2 Amount of each payment	3 Period covered by each payment	4 Amount per month
A. Wages or Salary				
Job 1: _____ _____	Gross pay, including overtime::	$ _____	_____	
	Subtract:	_____		
	Federal taxes	_____		
	State taxes	_____		
	Social Security (FICA)	_____		
	Union dues	_____		
	Insurance payments	_____		
	Child support wage withholding	_____		
	Other mandatory deductions (specify): _____ _____			
	Subtotal:	$ _____	_____	_____
Job 2: _____ _____	Gross pay, including overtime::	$ _____	_____	
	Subtract:	_____		
	Federal taxes	_____		
	State taxes	_____		
	Social Security (FICA)	_____		
	Union dues	_____		
	Insurance payments	_____		
	Child support wage withholding	_____		
	Other mandatory deductions (specify): _____ _____			
	Subtotal:	$ _____	_____	_____
Job 3: _____ _____	Gross pay, including overtime::	$ _____	_____	
	Subtract:	_____		
	Federal taxes	_____		
	State taxes	_____		
	Social Security (FICA)	_____		
	Union dues	_____		
	Insurance payments	_____		
	Child support wage withholding	_____		
	Other mandatory deductions (specify): _____ _____			
	Subtotal:	$ _____	_____	_____

Monthly Income From All Sources (cont'd)

1 Source of income		2 Amount of each payment	3 Period covered by each payment	4 Amount per month
B. Self-Employment Income				
Job 1: _____ _____	Gross pay, including overtime::	$ _____	_____	
	Subtract:			
	Federal taxes	_____		
	State taxes	_____		
	Self-employment taxes	_____		
	Other mandatory deductions (specify): _____ _____	_____		
	Subtotal:	$ _____	_____	_____
Job 2: _____ _____	Gross pay, including overtime::	$ _____	_____	
	Subtract:			
	Federal taxes	_____		
	State taxes	_____		
	Self-employment taxes	_____		
	Other mandatory deductions (specify): _____ _____	_____		
	Subtotal:	$ _____	_____	_____
C. Other Sources				
Bonuses _____		_____		_____
Commissions _____		_____		_____
Dividends and interest _____		_____		_____
Rent, lease, or license income _____		_____		_____
Royalties _____		_____		_____
Note or trust income _____		_____		_____
Alimony or child support you receive _____		_____		_____
Pension or retirement income _____		_____		_____
Social Security _____		_____		_____
Other public assistance _____		_____		_____
Other (specify): _____		_____		_____
_____		_____		_____
_____		_____		_____
_____		_____		_____
_____		_____		_____
_____		_____		_____
	Total monthly income			$ _____

Monthly Budget

Expense Category	Projected												
Home													
Rent/mortgage													
Property tax													
Insurance													
Homeowners assn. dues													
Telephone													
Gas/electric													
Water/sewer													
Cable													
Garbage/recycling													
Household supplies													
Housewares													
Furniture/appliances													
Cleaning													
Yard/pool care													
Repairs/maintenance													
Food													
Groceries													
Breakfast out													
Lunch out													
Dinner out													
Coffee/tea													
Snacks													
Clothing													
Clothes, shoes/ accessories													
Laundry, dry cleaning													
Mending													

Self Care													
Toiletries/cosmetics													
Haircuts													
Massage													
Gym membership													
Donations													
Health Care													
Insurance													
Medications													
Vitamins													
Doctor													
Dentist													
Eye care													
Therapy													
Transportation													
Car payments (buy or lease)													
Insurance													
Registration													
Gas													
Maintenance/repairs													
Parking													
Tolls													
Public transit													
Parking tickets													
Road service (such as AAA)													
Entertainment													
Music													
Movies/rentals													
Concerts, theater, ballet, etc.													
Museums													

Sporting events												
Hobbies /lessons												
Club dues or membership												
Film/developing costs												
Books, magazines/ newspapers												
Software/games												
Dependent Care												
Child care												
Clothing												
Allowance												
School expenses												
Toys/entertainment												
Pets												
Food/supplies												
Veterinarian												
Grooming												
Education												
Tuition												
Loan payments												
Books/supplies												
Travel												
Gifts/Cards												
Personal Business												
Supplies												
Copying												
Postage												
Bank/credit card fees												
Legal fees												
Accountant												

Taxes													
Insurance													
Savings/ investments													
Total expenses													
Projected monthly income													
Difference													

Date: _____

_____

_____

_____

Attn: Customer Service

Name(s) on account: _____

Account number: _____

To Whom It May Concern:

I am writing to dispute the following charge that appears on my billing statement dated

_____, 20_____.

Merchant's name: _____

Amount in dispute: _____

I am withholding payment of $ _____ , which represents the unpaid balance on the disputed item.

I am disputing this amount for the following reason(s):

_____

_____

_____

_____

_____

As required by law, I have tried in good faith to resolve this dispute with the merchant. [*Describe your efforts*] _____ .

Furthermore, I wish to point out that this purchase was for more than $50 and was made [*cross out one*] in the state in which I live/within 100 miles of my home.

Please verify this dispute with the merchant and remove this item, and all late and interest charges attributed to this item, from my billing statement.

Sincerely,

_____

[*your signature*]

Name: _____

Address: _____

_____

Home phone: _____

Email address: _____

Date: _____

_____

_____

_____

Attn: Customer Service

Name(s) on account: _____

Account number: _____

To Whom It May Concern:

I am writing to point out an error that appears on my billing statement dated

_____, 20_____.

Merchant's name: _____

Amount in error: _____

I am withholding this amount.

The problem is as follows:

_____

_____

_____

_____

_____

I understand that the law requires you to acknowledge receipt of this letter within 30 days unless you correct this billing error before then. Furthermore, I understand that within two billing cycles (but in no event more than 90 days), you must correct the error or explain why you believe the amount to be correct.

Sincerely,

_____
[your signature]

Name: _____

Address: _____

_____

Home phone: _____

Email address: _____

Date: _____

_____

_____

_____

Attn: Customer Service

Name(s) on account: _____

Account number: _____

To Whom It May Concern:

I received a copy of my credit report from _____.
It lists my payments to you as delinquent.

My past financial problems are behind me and I am now in a position to resolve this matter. I can pay
a lump sum amount of $_____ [*or* I can pay installments in the amount of
$_____ per month for _____ months] if you will agree to do the following:

☐ [*if the amount of the debt is not disputed*] If I make a lump-sum payment of $_____
by _____, 20 ____, you will release all claims against me arising from this account and will
submit a Universal Data Form to Experian, Equifax, and TransUnion deleting the account/trade
line.

☐ [*if the amount of the debt is disputed*] I dispute the amount of the debt. If I make a lump-sum
payment of $_____ by _____, 20 ____, you will acknowledge that the balance owed
on the account is $[*the amount of the lump-sum payment*], you will release all claims against me
arising from this account, and you will submit a Universal Data Form to Experian, Equifax, and
TransUnion deleting the account/trade line.

☐ [*if you propose to make installment payments*] If I agree to pay off the debt in installments, you
agree to re-age my account—that is, make the current month the first repayment month and
show no late payments as long as I make the agreed-upon monthly payments.

If my offer is acceptable to you, please initial the accepted proposal, sign the acceptance below, and return this letter to me in the enclosed envelope.

Sincerely,

_____
                    [your signature]

Name: _____

Address: _____

_____

Home phone: _____

Email address: _____

Agreed to and accepted on this _____ day of _____, 20_____.

By: _____

Name (print): _____

Title: _____

Date: _____

_____

_____

_____

Attn: Customer Service

Name(s) on account: _____

Account number: _____

To Whom It May Concern:

At the present, I cannot pay the monthly amount required under the agreement for the following reason(s):

_____

_____

_____

_____

_____

_____

I can pay $_____ per month right now and expect to resume making the full monthly payment when the following occurs:

_____

_____

_____

Please accept the reduced payments until then. If necessary, add the unpaid amount to the end of the loan or account period and extend it by a few months.

Thank you for your understanding and help. Please write within 20 days to let me know if this is acceptable.

Sincerely,

_____

[your signature]

Name: _____

Address: _____

_____

Home phone: _____

Email address: _____

Date: _____

_____

_____

_____

Attn: Customer Service

Name(s) on account: _____

Account number: _____

To Whom It May Concern:

At the present, I cannot pay the monthly amount required under the agreement for the following reason(s):

_____

_____

_____

_____

_____

_____

I can pay you only $_____ per month for the indefinite future. Please accept the reduced payments. I promise to inform you immediately if my financial condition improves and I am able to resume making normal payments.

Thank you for your understanding and help. Please write within 20 days to let me know if this is acceptable.

Sincerely,

_____
[*your signature*]

Name: _____

Address: _____

_____

Home phone: _____

Email address: _____

Date: _____

_____

_____

_____

Attn: Customer Service

Name(s) on account: _____

Account number: _____

To Whom It May Concern:

At the present, I cannot pay the monthly amount required under the agreement for the following reason(s):

_____

_____

_____

_____

_____

I expect to resume making the full monthly payment when the following occurs:

_____

_____

_____

If necessary, add the unpaid amount to the end of the loan or account period and extend it by a few months.

Thank you for your understanding and help. Please write within 20 days if this is unacceptable.

Sincerely,

_____
　　　　　　　[your signature]

Name: _____

Address: _____

_____

Home phone: _____

Email address: _____

Date: _____

_____

_____

_____

Attn: Customer Service

Name(s) on account: _____

Account number: _____

To Whom It May Concern:

At the present, I cannot pay the monthly amount required under the agreement for the following reason(s):

_____

_____

_____

_____

_____

Due to my desperate financial situation, I cannot make any payments for the indefinite future. [*Describe hardship*] _____ .

I promise to inform you immediately if my financial condition improves and I am able to resume making normal payments.

Thank you for your understanding and help. Please write within 20 days if this is unacceptable.

Sincerely,

_____
[*your signature*]

Name: _____

Address: _____

_____

Home phone: _____

Email address: _____

Date: _____

_____

_____

_____

Attn: Customer Service

Name(s) on account: _____

Account number: _____

To Whom It May Concern:

At the present, I cannot pay the monthly amount required under the agreement for the following reason(s):

_____

_____

_____

_____

_____

_____

_____

I would like the terms of the loan rewritten in order to reduce the amount of the monthly payments.

Thank you for your understanding and help. Please call me as soon as possible in order that we may discuss new loan terms.

Sincerely,

_____
                    [your signature]

Name: _____

Address: _____

_____

Home phone: _____

Email address: _____

Date: _____

_____

_____

_____

Attn: Customer Service

Name(s) on account: _____

Account number: _____

To Whom It May Concern:

I cannot pay the monthly amount required under my agreement with you. I invite you to come pick up the collateral. Or I will return it to you, if you can assure me in writing that the entire debt will be canceled when the property is returned, and that I will not be liable for any deficiency judgment. Please let me know where to return the collateral.

Thank you for your attention to this matter. Please send me a written confirmation within 20 days if this is acceptable.

Sincerely,

_____
[your signature]

Name: _____

Address: _____

_____

Home phone: _____

Email address: _____

Date: _____

_____

_____

_____

Attn: Customer Service

Name(s) on account: _____

Account number: _____

To Whom It May Concern:

Enclosed is a check for $_____ to cover the balance of the account. Cashing this check constitutes payment in full.

Sincerely,

_____
[your signature]

Name: _____

Address: _____

_____

Home phone: _____

[Send this letter to the person, office, or place designated by the creditor for communications regarding disputed debts—or to the proper collection agent if you are no longer dealing with the creditor company itself.]

Date: _____

_____

_____

_____

Attn: Customer Service

Name(s) on account: _____

Account number: _____

To Whom It May Concern:

Regarding the above-referenced account, I dispute the amount you claim that I owe you for the following reason(s):

_____

_____

_____

_____

_____

_____

_____

I believe that I owe you no more than $_____. It is obvious that there is a good-faith dispute over the amount of this bill.

In a good-faith effort to satisfy this debt, I will send you a check for $_____ with a restrictive endorsement; if you cash that check, it will constitute an accord and satisfaction. In other words, you will receive from me a check that states, "Cashing this check constitutes payment in full." If you cash that check, it will fully satisfy my obligation to you.

Sincerely,

_____
                [your signature]

Name: _____

Address: _____

_____

Home phone: _____

[Send this letter to the person, office, or place designated by the creditor for communications regarding disputed debts—or to the proper collection agent if you are no longer dealing with the creditor company itself.]

Date: _____

_____

_____

_____

Attn: Customer Service

Name(s) on account: _____

Account number: _____

To Whom It May Concern:

[Wait a reasonable time before sending this letter, and indicate that amount of time here. Two weeks is probably reasonable, but more or less time may be reasonable in your particular situation.]

[Two weeks] have passed since I sent you a letter dated _____, 20_____ stating my intention to send you a check with a restrictive endorsement.

Enclosed is a check for $_____ to cover the balance of my account. This check is tendered in accordance with my earlier letter. If you cash this check, you agree that my debt is satisfied in full.

Sincerely,

_____
[your signature]

Name: _____

Address: _____

_____

Home phone: _____

Enclosed: Check stating on front: "This check is tendered in accordance with my letter of _____, 20_____. Cashing this check constitutes payment in full."

Date: _____

_____

_____

_____

Attn: Collections Department

Name(s) on account: _____

Account number: _____

To Whom It May Concern:

This letter is to advise you that I am not able to make payments on my account due to the following conditions:

_____

_____

_____

_____

_____

I cannot work sufficient hours to meet my current expenses. My only sources of income are:

_____

_____

I am familiar with the law and know that I am "judgment proof." If I file for bankruptcy, I will claim all my property as exempt, and if you sue me and obtain a judgment, you could not collect any of my property to satisfy the judgment.

Please cease all collection activities you have taken or are considering taking. While I will provide you with reasonable financial or medical information, I must avoid stress. This includes high-pressure collection activity and lawsuits.

If my current situation improves and I am able to resume payments, I will notify you at once.

Thank you for your understanding and help.

Sincerely,

_____
[your signature]

Name: _____

Address: _____

_____

Home phone: _____

Date: _____

_____

_____

_____

Attn: Collections Department

Name(s) on account: _____

Account number: _____

To Whom It May Concern:

Please cease all collection activities you have taken or are considering taking against me. I am planning to file a petition in bankruptcy court in the coming months.

Sincerely,

_____
                  [your signature]

Name: _____

Address: _____

_____

Home phone: _____

©nolo

Date: _____

_____

_____

_____

Name(s) on account: _____

Account number: _____

Creditor: _____

To: _____

I have been contacted several times by you regarding my past due account with the credit grantor referenced above. I do not, however, wish to discuss this matter with you. I would like to talk directly with the creditor's collections department.

Please contact the collections department of the credit grantor and indicate my desire to be in touch with them.

Thank you for your help.

Sincerely,

_____
                    [your signature]

Name: _____

Address: _____

_____

Home phone: _____

Date: _____

_____

_____

_____

To: _____

I am writing to dispute the following bill you are attempting to collect.

Name(s) on account: _____

Account number: _____

Creditor: _____

Amount in dispute: _____

I am disputing this bill for the following reason(s):

_____

_____

_____

_____

_____

_____

Please return this bill to the creditor immediately and remove any "sent to collection agency" notation that may be in my credit file.

Thank you for your attention to this matter.

Sincerely,

_____
[your signature]

Name: _____

Address: _____

_____

Home phone: _____

cc: Credit grantor, _____

Date: _____

_____

_____

_____

Name(s) on account: _____

Account number: _____

Creditor: _____

To: _____

Since approximately _____, 20_____, I have received several phone calls and letters from you concerning my overdue account with the above-named creditor.

Accordingly, under 15 U.S.C. § 1692c, this is my formal notice to you to cease all further communications with me.

Sincerely,

_____
[*your signature*]

Name: _____

Address: _____

_____

Home phone: _____

Date: _____

_____

_____

_____

Name(s) on account: _____

Account number: _____

Date loan/debt incurred: _____

Original loan/debt amount: _____

Amount past due: _____

Re: Collection agency: _____

To Whom It May Concern:

I have been unable to pay the full amount of the loan/debt noted above for the following reason(s):

_____

_____

_____

I have the right to be treated by a collection agency with dignity and respect. The collection agency you hired (as noted above), however, has engaged in the following practices, which violate the federal Fair Debt Collection Practices Act:

_____

_____

_____

I am willing to forgo the legal remedies I have available, including a lawsuit in small claims court seeking punitive damages against you and the agency, in exchange for your written promise to permanently cease all efforts to collect this debt and remove all negative entries regarding this debt from my credit file. I expect to hear from you immediately.

Sincerely,

_____
                    [your signature]

Name: _____

Address: _____

_____

Home phone: _____

cc: Federal Trade Commission
     State Collection Agency Licensing Board
     Collection Agency: _____

Date: _____

_____

_____

_____

To Whom It May Concern:

Please send me a copy of my credit report.

Full name: _____

Date of birth: _____

Social Security number _____

Spouse's name: _____

Telephone number: _____

Current address: _____

_____

(Check one:)

☐ I was denied credit on _____ by _____

_____. Enclosed is a copy of the rejection letter.

☐ I hereby certify that I am unemployed and intend to apply for a job within the next 60 days.

☐ I hereby certify that I receive public assistance/welfare.

☐ I hereby certify that I believe there is erroneous information in my file due to fraud.

☐ I have not been denied credit within the preceding 60 days. Enclosed is a copy of a

document identifying me by my name and address and payment in the amount of $

_____.

Thank you for your attention to this matter.

Sincerely,

_____

[your signature]

Date: _____

_____

_____

_____

Report or confirmation number: _____

This is a request for you to reinvestigate the following items which appear on my credit report:

☐ The following personal information about me is incorrect:

Erroneous Information   *Correct Information*

_____

_____

_____

☐ The following accounts are not mine:

Creditor's Name   *Account Number*   *Explanation*

_____

_____

_____

☐ The account status is incorrect for the following accounts:

Creditor's Name   *Account Number*   *Correct Status*

_____

_____

_____

☐ The following information is too old to be included in my report:

Creditor's Name   *Account Number*   *Date of Last Activity*

_____

_____

_____

☐ The following inquiries are older than two years:

Creditor's Name   *Date of Inquiry*

_____

_____

_____

☐ The following inquiries were not authorized:

Creditor's Name   Date of Inquiry   Explanation

_____

_____

_____

☐ The following accounts were closed by me and should say so:

Creditor's Name   Account Number

_____

_____

_____

☐ Other incorrect information:

Explanation

_____

_____

_____

I understand that you will check each specified item, above, with the credit grantor reporting the information, remove any information the credit grantor cannot verify, or modify information that is incorrect or incomeplete. I further understand that under 15 U.S.C. §1681i(a), you must complete your reinvestigation within 30 days of receipt of this letter. Thank you for your attention to this matter.

Sincerely,

_____
                    [your signature]

Name: _____

Address: _____

_____

Home phone: _____

Social Security number _____

Date of birth: _____

Enclosures: [list, if any:]   _____

_____

_____

_____

Date: _____

_____

_____

_____

Report or confirmation number: _____

To Whom It May Concern:

On _____, 20_____, I sent you a request to reinvestigate several items on my credit report. I have enclosed a photocopy of my original request. The federal Fair Credit Reporting Act requires that you complete your reinvestigation of my request within 30 days. It has been more than 30 days.

I assume that I have not received a reply because you have been unable to verify the information. Therefore, please remove the incorrect items from my credit report at once and send a corrected credit report to me and to anyone who has requested a copy of my credit report within the previous six months, or within the previous two years if requested for employment purposes.

Thank you for your immediate attention to this matter. I have sent a copy of this letter to the Federal Trade Commission.

Sincerely,

_____
                 [your signature]

Name: _____

Address: _____

_____

Home phone: _____

Social Security number _____

cc: Federal Trade Commission

Date: _____

_____

_____

_____

To Whom It May Concern:

On _____, 20_____ , I received a copy of my credit report from

_____

credit bureau. Included in that report was the following incorrect information reported by you:

_____

_____

_____

I requested that the credit bureau remove that information from my file. The bureau has refused, however, informing me that your company claims the information is accurate as reported.

This is not true. The following is the correct information:

_____

_____

_____

_____

I have enclosed copies of the following documentation supporting my claim that the information you reported is incorrect:

_____

_____

This negative mark is damaging my credit. Please contact Experian, TransUnion, and Equifax immediately and remove this information from my credit file. I expect to receive confirmation from you within 20 days that you have directed the credit bureaus to remove this information.

Thank you for your immediate attention to this matter.

Sincerely,

_____
                    [your signature]

Name: _____

Address: _____

_____

Home phone: _____

Social Security number _____

Date: _____

_____

_____

_____

Attn: Customer Service

Name(s) on account: _____

Account number: _____

To Whom It May Concern:

On _____, 20_____, I received a copy
of my credit report from you. It included erroneous information reported by
_____.

I just received a letter from that creditor indicating that the information in my credit report is not
accurate and should not be in my credit file. I have enclosed a copy of the letter.

[OR]

On _____, 20_____, I met with _____
_____ from the above-named creditor. This person
agreed with me that the information in my credit
report is not accurate and should not be in my credit file. You can reach this person at
(_____) _____.

This negative mark is damaging my credit. Please remove the information at once and send a
corrected credit report to me and to anyone who has requested a copy of my credit report within
the previous six months, or within the previous two years if requested for employment purposes.

Sincerely,

_____
[your signature]

Name: _____

Address: _____

_____

Home phone: _____

Social Security number _____

Date of birth _____

Date: _____

_____

_____

_____

Re: [name] _____

Current address: _____

_____

Telephone number: _____

Date of birth _____

Social Security number _____

Spouse's name _____

To Whom It May Concern:

I received a copy of my credit report from your company on _____ and found accounts missing. Please add the following account histories to my credit file. I have enclosed photocopies of my most recent account statement and photocopies of canceled checks showing my payment history.

Creditor's Name	Creditor's Billing Address	Account Number	Date Opened	Credit Limit or Amount of Loan	Outstanding Balance

Once you have processed this request, please send me an updated credit report. If there is a fee of any kind, please let me know the amount so that I can send you a check or give you my credit card number. If you are unable to add these accounts to my credit report, please send me an explanation.

Thank you for your prompt attention to this matter.

Sincerely,

_____

[your signature]

Date: _____

_____

_____

_____

Re: [name] _____

Current address _____

_____

Telephone number _____

Date of birth _____

Social Security number _____

Spouse's name _____

To Whom It May Concern:

I received a copy of my credit report from your company on _____
and found that important information is missing. Please add the following information to my credit
file. I have enclosed photocopies of verifying documentation.

_____

_____

_____

_____

_____

_____

_____

Once you have processed this request, please send me an updated credit report. If there is a fee of any
kind, please let me know the amount so that I can send you a check or give you my credit card number.
If you are unable to add this information to my credit report, please send me an explanation.

Thank you for your prompt attention to this matter.

Sincerely,

_____

[your signature]

Instructions for
Completing the ID Theft Affidavit

To make certain that you do not become responsible for any debts incurred by an identity thief, you must prove to each of the companies where accounts were opened or used in your name that you didn't create the debt.

A group of credit grantors, consumer advocates, and attorneys at the Federal Trade Commission (FTC) developed an ID Theft Affidavit to make it easier for fraud victims to report information. While many companies accept this affidavit, others require that you submit more or different forms. Before you send the affidavit, contact each company to find out if they accept it.

It will be necessary to provide the information in this affidavit anywhere a **new** account was opened in your name. The information will enable the companies to investigate the fraud and decide the outcome of your claim. If someone made unauthorized charges to an **existing** account, call the company for instructions.

This affidavit has two parts:

- **Part One** — the ID Theft Affidavit — is where you report general information about yourself and the theft.
- **Part Two** — the Fraudulent Account Statement — is where you describe the fraudulent account(s) opened in your name. Use a separate Fraudulent Account Statement for each company you need to write to.

When you send the affidavit to the companies, attach copies (NOT originals) of any supporting documents (for example, driver's license or police report). Before submitting your affidavit, review the disputed account(s) with family members or friends who may have information about the account(s) or access to them.

Complete this affidavit as soon as possible. Many creditors ask that you send it within two weeks. Delays on your part could slow the investigation.

Be as accurate and complete as possible. You may choose not to provide some of the information requested. However, incorrect or incomplete information will slow the process of investigating your claim and absolving the debt. Print clearly.

When you have finished completing the affidavit, mail a copy to each creditor, bank, or company that provided the thief with the unauthorized credit, goods, or services you describe. Attach a copy of the Fraudulent Account Statement with information only on accounts opened at the institution to which you are sending the packet, as well as any other supporting documentation you are able to provide.

Send the appropriate documents to each company by certified mail, return receipt requested, so you can prove that it was received. The companies will review your claim and send you a written response telling you the outcome of their investigation. Keep a copy of everything you submit.

If you are unable to complete the affidavit, a legal guardian or someone with power of attorney may complete it for you. Except as noted, the information you provide will be used only by the company to process your affidavit, investigate the events you report, and help stop further fraud. If this affidavit is requested in a lawsuit, the company might have to provide it to the requesting party. Completing this affidavit does not guarantee that the identity thief will be prosecuted or that the debt will be cleared.

DO NOT SEND AFFIDAVIT TO THE FTC OR ANY OTHER GOVERNMENT AGENCY

If you haven't already done so, report the fraud to the following organizations:

1. Any one of the nationwide consumer reporting companies to place a fraud alert on your credit report. Fraud alerts can help prevent an identity thief from opening any more accounts in your name. The company you call is required to contact the other two, which will place an alert on their versions of your report, too.

   - **Equifax:** 1-800-525-6285; www.equifax.com

   - **Experian:** 1-888-EXPERIAN (397-3742); www.experian.com

   - **TransUnion:** 1-800-680-7289; www.transunion.com

   In addition to placing the fraud alert, the three consumer reporting companies will send you free copies of your credit reports, and, if you ask, they will display only the last four digits of your Social Security number on your credit reports.

2. The security or fraud department of each company where you know, or believe, accounts have been tampered with or opened fraudulently. Close the accounts. Follow up in writing, and include copies (NOT originals) of supporting documents. *It's important to notify credit card companies and banks in writing.* Send your letters by certified mail, return receipt requested, so you can document what the company received and when. Keep a file of your correspondence and enclosures.

   When you open new accounts, use new Personal Identification Numbers (PINs) and passwords. Avoid using easily available information like your mother's maiden name, your birth date, the last four digits of your Social Security number or your phone number, or a series of consecutive numbers.

3. Your local police or the police in the community where the identity theft took place to file a report. Get a copy of the police report or, at the very least, the number of the report. It can help you deal with creditors who need proof of the crime. If the police are reluctant to take your report, ask to file a "Miscellaneous Incidents" report, or try another jurisdiction, like your state police. You also can check with your state Attorney General's office to find out if state law requires the police to take reports for identity theft. Check the Blue Pages of your telephone directory for the phone number or check www.naag.org for a list of state Attorneys General.

4. The Federal Trade Commission. By sharing your identity theft complaint with the FTC, you will provide important information that can help law enforcement officials across the nation track down identity thieves and stop them. The FTC also can refer victims' complaints to other government agencies and companies for further action, as well as investigate companies for violations of laws that the FTC enforces.

   You can file a complaint online at **www.consumer.gov/idtheft**. If you don't have Internet access, call the FTC's Identity Theft Hotline, toll-free: 1-877-IDTHEFT (438-4338); TTY: 1-866-653-4261; or write: Identity Theft Clearinghouse, Federal Trade Commission, 600 Pennsylvania Avenue, NW, Washington, DC 20580.

DO NOT SEND AFFIDAVIT TO THE FTC OR ANY OTHER GOVERNMENT AGENCY

ID Theft Affidavit

Victim Information

(1) My full legal name is _____

(First)   (Middle)   (Last)   (Jr., Sr., III)

(2) (If different from above) When the events described in this affidavit took place, I was known as

_____

(First)   (Middle)   (Last)   (Jr., Sr., III)

(3) My date of birth is _____

(day/month/year)

(4) My Social Security number is_____

(5) My driver's license or identification card state and number are_____

(6) My current address is _____

City _____ State _____ Zip Code _____

(7) I have lived at this address since _____

(month/year)

(8) (If different from above) When the events described in this affidavit took place, my address was

_____

City _____ State _____ Zip Code _____

(9) I lived at the address in Item 8 from _____ until _____

(month/year)   (month/year)

(10) My daytime telephone number is (____)_____

My evening telephone number is (____)_____

DO NOT SEND AFFIDAVIT TO THE FTC OR ANY OTHER GOVERNMENT AGENCY

How the Fraud Occurred

Check all that apply for items 11 - 17:

(11) ❏ I did not authorize anyone to use my name or personal information to seek the money, credit, loans, goods or services described in this report.

(12) ❏ I did not receive any benefit, money, goods or services as a result of the events described in this report.

(13) ❏ My identification documents (for example, credit cards; birth certificate; driver's license; Social Security card; etc.) were ❏ stolen ❏ lost on or about _____.
(day/month/year)

(14) ❏ To the best of my knowledge and belief, the following person(s) used my information (for example, my name, address, date of birth, existing account numbers, Social Security number, mother's maiden name, etc.) or identification documents to get money, credit, loans, goods or services without my knowledge or authorization:

_____   _____
Name (if known)   Name (if known)

_____   _____
Address (if known)   Address (if known)

_____   _____
Phone number(s) (if known)   Phone number(s) (if known)

_____   _____
Additional information (if known)   Additional information (if known)

(15) ❏ I do NOT know who used my information or identification documents to get money, credit, loans, goods or services without my knowledge or authorization.

(16) ❏ Additional comments: (For example, description of the fraud, which documents or information were used or how the identity thief gained access to your information.)

_____

_____

_____

_____

_____

(Attach additional pages as necessary.)

DO NOT SEND AFFIDAVIT TO THE FTC OR ANY OTHER GOVERNMENT AGENCY

Victim's Law Enforcement Actions

(17) (check one) I ❑ am ❑ am not willing to assist in the prosecution of the person(s) who committed this fraud.

(18) (check one) I ❑ am ❑ am not authorizing the release of this information to law enforcement for the purpose of assisting them in the investigation and prosecution of the person(s) who committed this fraud.

(19) (check all that apply) I ❑ have ❑ have not reported the events described in this affidavit to the police or other law enforcement agency. The police ❑ did ❑ did not write a report. *In the event you have contacted the police or other law enforcement agency, please complete the following:*

(Agency #1) _____ (Officer/Agency personnel taking report)

(Date of report) _____ (Report number, if any)

(Phone number) _____ (email address, if any)

(Agency #2) _____ (Officer/Agency personnel taking report)

(Date of report) _____ (Report number, if any)

(Phone number) _____ (email address, if any)

Documentation Checklist

Please indicate the supporting documentation you are able to provide to the companies you plan to notify. Attach copies (NOT originals) to the affidavit before sending it to the companies.

(20) ❑ A copy of a valid government-issued photo-identification card (for example, your driver's license, state-issued ID card or your passport). If you are under 16 and don't have a photo-ID, you may submit a copy of your birth certificate or a copy of your official school records showing your enrollment and place of residence.

(21) ❑ Proof of residency during the time the disputed bill occurred, the loan was made or the other event took place (for example, a rental/lease agreement in your name, a copy of a utility bill or a copy of an insurance bill).

DO NOT SEND AFFIDAVIT TO THE FTC OR ANY OTHER GOVERNMENT AGENCY

(22) ❑ A copy of the report you filed with the police or sheriff's department. If you are unable to obtain a report or report number from the police, please indicate that in Item 19. Some companies only need the report number, not a copy of the report. You may want to check with each company.

Signature

I certify that, to the best of my knowledge and belief, all the information on and attached to this affidavit is true, correct, and complete and made in good faith. I also understand that is affidavit or the information it contains may be made available to federal, state, and/or local law enforcement agencies for such action within their jurisdiction as they deem appropriate. I understand that knowingly making any false or fraudulent statement or representation to the government may constitute a violation of 18 U.S.C. §1001 or other federal, state, or local criminal statutes, and may result in imposition of a fine or imprisonment or both.

_____   _____
(signature)   (date signed)

_____
(Notary)

[Check with each company. Creditors sometimes require notarization. If they do not, please have one witness (non-relative) sign below that you completed and signed this affidavit.]

Witness:

_____   _____
(signature)   (printed name)

_____   _____
(date)   (telephone number)

DO NOT SEND AFFIDAVIT TO THE FTC OR ANY OTHER GOVERNMENT AGENCY

Fraudulent Account Statement

<table>
<tr><td align="center">**Completing this Statement**</td></tr>
<tr><td>

- Make as many copies of this page as you need. **Complete a separate page for each company you're notifying and only send it to that company.** Include a copy of your signed affidavit.
- List only the account(s) you're disputing with the company receiving this form. **See the example below.**
- If a collection agency sent you a statement, letter or notice about the fraudulent account, attach a copy of that document (**NOT** the original).

</td></tr>
</table>

I declare (check all that apply):

❑ As a result of the event(s) described in the ID Theft Affidavit, the following account(s) was/were opened at your company in my name without my knowledge, permission or authorization using my personal information or identifying documents:

Creditor Name/Address *(the company that opened the account or provided the goods or services)*	Account Number	Type of unauthorized credit/goods/services provided by creditor *(if known)*	Date issued or opened *(if known)*	Amount/Value provided *(the amount charged or the cost of the goods/services)*
Example Example National Bank 22 Main Street Columbus, Ohio 22722	01234567-89	auto loan	01/05/2002	$25,500.00

❑ During the time of the accounts described above, I had the following account open with your company:

Billing name _____

Billing address _____

Account number _____

DO NOT SEND AFFIDAVIT TO THE FTC OR ANY OTHER GOVERNMENT AGENCY

EQUIFAX®   experían®   TransUnion®

Annual Credit Report Request Form

You have the right to get a free copy of your credit file disclosure, commonly called a credit report, once every 12 months, from each of the nationwide consumer credit reporting companies - Equifax, Experian and TransUnion.
For instant access to your free credit report, visit www.annualcreditreport.com.

For more information on obtaining your free credit report, visit www.annualcreditreport.com or call 877-322-8228.

Use this form if you prefer to write to request your credit report from any, or all, of the nationwide consumer credit reporting companies. The following information is required to process your request. **Omission of any information may delay your request.**

Once complete, fold (do not staple or tape), place into a #10 envelope, affix required postage and mail to:
Annual Credit Report Request Service P.O. Box 105281 Atlanta, GA 30348-5281.

Please use a Black or Blue Pen and write your responses in PRINTED CAPITAL LETTERS without touching the sides of the boxes like the examples listed below:

A B C D E F G H I J K L M N O P Q R S T U V W X Y Z   0 1 2 3 4 5 6 7 8 9

Social Security Number:

☐☐☐ - ☐☐ - ☐☐☐☐

Date of Birth:

☐☐ / ☐☐ / ☐☐☐☐
Month   Day   Year

Fold Here   Fold Here

First Name   M.I.

Last Name   JR, SR, III, etc.

Current Mailing Address:

House Number   **Street Name**

Apartment Number / Private Mailbox   **For Puerto Rico Only: Print Urbanization Name**

City   **State**   **ZipCode**

Previous Mailing Address (complete only if at current mailing address for less than two years):

House Number   **Street Name**

Fold Here   Fold Here

Apartment Number / Private Mailbox   **For Puerto Rico Only: Print Urbanization Name**

City   **State**   **ZipCode**

Shade Circle Like This → ●

Not Like This → ⊗ ⊘

I want a credit report from (shade each that you would like to receive):
○ Equifax
○ Experian
○ TransUnion

○ **Shade here if, for security reasons, you want your credit report to include no more than the last four digits of your Social Security Number.**

31238

If additional information is needed to process your request, the consumer credit reporting company will contact you by mail.

Your request will be processed within 15 days of receipt and then mailed to you.

Copyright 2004, Central Source LLC

How to Use the Forms CD-ROM

The tear-out forms in Appendix 3 are included on a CD-ROM in the back of the book. This CD-ROM, which can be used with Windows computers, installs files that you use with software programs that are already installed on your computer. It is not a stand-alone software program. Please read this Appendix and the README.TXT file included on the CD-ROM for instructions on using the Forms CD.

Note to Mac users: This CD-ROM and its files should also work on Macintosh computers. Please note, however, that Nolo cannot provide technical support for non-Windows users.

How to View the README File

If you do not know how to view the file README.TXT, insert the Forms CD-ROM into your computer's CD-ROM drive and follow these instructions:

- Windows 2000, XP, and Vista: (1) On your PC's desktop, double click the My Computer icon; (2) double click the icon for the CD-ROM drive into which the Forms CD-ROM was inserted; (3) double click the file README.TXT.
- Macintosh: (1) On your Mac desktop, double click the icon for the CD-ROM that you inserted; (2) double click on the file README.TXT.

While the README file is open, print it out by using the Print command in the File menu.

Installing the Form Files Onto Your Computer

Word processing forms that you can open, complete, print, and save with your word processing program (see Using the Word Processing Files to Create Documents, below) are contained on the CD-ROM. Before you can do anything with the files on the CD-ROM, you need to install them onto your hard disk. In accordance with U.S. copyright laws, remember that copies of the CD-ROM and its files are for your personal use only.

Insert the Forms CD and do the following:

Windows 2000, XP, and Vista Users

Follow the instructions that appear on the screen. (If nothing happens when you insert the Forms CD-ROM, then (1) double click the My Computer icon; (2) double click the icon for the CD-ROM drive into which the Forms CD-ROM was inserted; and (3) double click the file WELCOME.EXE.)

By default, all the files are installed to the \Credit Repair Forms folder in the \Program Files folder of your computer. A folder called "Credit Repair Forms" is added to the "Programs" folder of the Start menu.

Macintosh Users

Step 1: If the "Credit Repair Forms CD" window is not open, open it by double clicking the "Credit Repair Forms CD" icon.

Step 2: Select the "Credit Repair Forms" folder icon.

Step 3: Drag and drop the folder icon onto the icon of your hard disk.

Using the Word Processing Files to Create Documents

This section concerns the files for forms that can be opened and edited with your word processing program.

All word processing forms come in rich text format. These files have the extension "RTF." For example, the Monthly Budget form discussed in Chapter 2 (Form F-4) in Appendix 3, is on the file F04.rtf. All forms, their file names, and file formats are listed in Appendix 3.

RTF files can be read by most recent word processing programs including all versions of MS Word for Windows and Macintosh, WordPad for Windows, and recent versions of WordPerfect for Windows and Macintosh.

To use a form from the CD to create your documents you must: (1) open a file in your word processor or text editor; (2) edit the form by filling in the required information; (3) print it out; and (4) rename and save your revised file.

The following are general instructions. However, each word processor uses different commands to open, format, save, and print documents. Please read your word processor's manual for specific instructions on performing these tasks.

Do not call Nolo's technical support if you have questions on how to use your word processor or your computer.

Step 1: Opening a File

There are three ways to open the word processing files included on the CD-ROM after you have installed them onto your computer.

- Windows users can open a file by selecting its "shortcut" as follows: (1) Click the Windows "Start" button; (2) open the "Programs" folder; (3) open the "Credit Repair Forms" subfolder; and (4) click on the shortcut to the form you want to work with.

- Both Windows and Macintosh users can open a file directly by double clicking on it. Use My Computer or Windows Explorer (Windows 2000, XP, and Vista) or the Finder (Macintosh) to go to the folder you installed or copied the CD-ROM's files to. Then, double click on the specific file you want to open.

- You can also open a file from within your word processor. To do this, you must first start your word processor. Then, go to the File menu and choose the Open command. This opens a dialog box where you will tell the program (1) the type of file you want to open (*.rtf*); and (2) the location and name of the file (you will need to navigate through the directory tree to get to the folder on your hard disk where the CD's files have been installed).

Where Are the Files Installed?

Windows Users: RTF files are installed by default to a folder named \Credit Repair Forms in the \Program Files folder of your computer.

Macintosh Users: RTF files are located in the "Credit Repair Forms" folder.

Step 2: Editing Your Document

Fill in the appropriate information according to the instructions and sample agreements in the book. Underlines are used to indicate where you need to enter your information, frequently followed by instructions in brackets. *Be sure to delete the underlines and instructions from your edited document.* You will also want to make sure that any signature lines in your completed documents appear on a page with at least some text from the document itself.

Editing Forms That Have Optional or Alternative Text

Some of the forms have check boxes before text. The check boxes indicate:

- Optional text, where you choose whether to include or exclude the given text.
- Alternative text, where you select one alternative to include and exclude the other alternatives.

If you are using the tear-out forms in Appendix C, you simply mark the appropriate box to make your choice.

If you are using the Forms CD, however, we recommend that instead of marking the check boxes, you do the following:

Optional text

If you don't want to include optional text, just delete it from your document.

If you **do want** to include optional text, just leave it in your document.

In either case, delete the check box itself as well as the italicized instructions that the text is optional.

Alternative text

First delete all the alternatives that you do not want to include.

Then delete the remaining check boxes, as well as the italicized instructions that you need to select one of the alternatives provided.

Step 3: Printing Out the Document

Use your word processor's or text editor's "Print" command to print out your document.

Step 4: Saving Your Document

After filling in the form, use the "Save As" command to save and rename the file. Because all the files are "read-only," you will not be able to use the "Save" command. This is for your protection. *If you save the file without renaming it, the underlines that indicate where you need to enter your information will be lost, and you will not be able to create a new document with this file without recopying the original file from the CD-ROM.* ■

Index

Get the Latest in the Law

 Nolo's Legal Updater
We'll send you an email whenever a new edition of your book is published!
Sign up at **www.nolo.com/legalupdater**.

 Updates at Nolo.com
Check **www.nolo.com/update** to find recent changes in the law that
affect the current edition of your book.

 Nolo Customer Service
To make sure that this edition of the book is the most recent one, call us at
800-728-3555 and ask one of our friendly customer service representatives
(7:00 am to 6:00 pm PST, weekdays only). Or find out at **www.nolo.com**.

 Complete the Registration & Comment Card ...
... and we'll do the work for you! Just indicate your preferences below:

- -

Registration & Comment Card

NAME _____ DATE _____

ADDRESS _____

CITY _____ STATE _____ ZIP _____

PHONE _____ EMAIL _____

COMMENTS _____

WAS THIS BOOK EASY TO USE?   (VERY EASY)   5   4   3   2   1   (VERY DIFFICULT)

☐ Yes, you can quote me in future Nolo promotional materials. *Please include phone number above.*

☐ Yes, send me **Nolo's Legal Updater** via email when a new edition of this book is available.

Yes, I want to sign up for the following email newsletters:

   ☐ **NoloBriefs** (monthly)
   ☐ **Nolo's Special Offer** (monthly)
   ☐ **Nolo's BizBriefs** (monthly)
   ☐ **Every Landlord's Quarterly** (four times a year)

☐ Yes, you can give my contact info to carefully selected
partners whose products may be of interest to me.

NOLO

CREP 8.0

Nolo
950 Parker Street
Berkeley, CA 94710-9867
www.nolo.com

collate CD

Melrose Public Library
Melrose, MA

YOUR LEGAL COMPANION